Epworth C

Genera
Ivor H

The Book o

Epworth Commentaries

Already published

The Book of Job
C. S. Rodd
Isaiah 1–39
David Stacey
The Book of Jeremiah
Henry McKeating
The Books of Amos and Hosea
Harry Mowvley
The Gospel of Matthew
Ivor H. Jones
The Gospel of Luke
Judith Lieu
The Gospel of John
Kenneth Grayston
The Acts of the Apostles
James D. G. Dunn
The Epistle to the Romans
Kenneth Grayston
The First Epistle to the Corinthians
Nigel Watson
The Second Epistle to the Corinthians
Nigel Watson
The Epistle to the Galatians
John Ziesler
The Epistle to the Ephesians
Larry J. Kreitzer
The Epistle to the Philippians
Howard Marshall
The Epistle to the Colossians
Roy Yates
The Epistle to the Hebrews
Paul Ellingworth
The Epistle of James
Michael J. Townsend
The Epistles of Peter and Jude
David G. Horrell
The Johannine Epistles
William Loader
Revelation
Christopher Rowland

The Book of
JEREMIAH

Henry McKeating

EPWORTH PRESS

0 7162 0526 2

First Published 1999
by Epworth Press
20 Ivatt Way
Peterborough, PE3 7PG

Typeset by Regent Typesetting, London
Printed and bound in Great Britain by
Biddles Ltd, Guildford and King's Lynn

CONTENTS

General Introduction   vii

About this Commentary   1

Introduction   5
Why the book of Jeremiah is important   5
The structure of the book of Jeremiah   6
The major public events of Jeremiah's lifetime   8
Outline of the book of Jeremiah   9
Materials of which the book is composed   10
The two books of Jeremiah   11
The composition of the book of Jeremiah   12
Scepticism and credulity   13

Commentary   17

Chapters 1–25 Sayings attributed to Jeremiah   17
1.1–3   Introduction to the book   17
1.4–19   Jeremiah's call and first visions   21
2.1–4.4   God's appeal to Israel and Judah   26
4.5–6.30   Threats of imminent destruction   42
7.1–8.3   Jeremiah's temple speech and associated
               prophecies   53
8.4–10.25   Miscellaneous short oracles   63
11.1–20.18   Judgment; rejection and persecution; the
               prophet's complaints   75
    11.1–17   Judah's covenant-breaking   76
    11.18 – 12.6   The first two 'confessions'   80
    12.7 – 13.27   Prophecies of doom   85
    14.1 – 15.9   Laments on the people's behalf   90
    15.10 – 21   Two more 'confessions'   96
    16.1 – 17.27   Judgment on Judah – leading to
                    'confession' number five   98

18.1 – 23	Of potters – leading to 'confession' number six	105
19.1 – 20.6	Of pots and persecution	109
20.7 – 18	Jeremiah's lament – 'confession' number seven	110
21.1 – 24.10	Warnings to kings and people	112
21.1 – 10	Zedekiah formally consults the prophet	112
21.11 – 22.30	Condemnations of kings	114
23.1 – 8	Bad and good shepherds	119
23.9 – 40	Condemnations of prophets	121
24.1 – 10	Vision of the good and the bad figs	125
25.1 – 14	Summary of the book so far	128
25.15 – 38	Judgment on foreign nations	129

Chapters 26 – 45 Reports of the Prophet's Activities   132

26.1 – 24	Again the temple speech: the trial of Jeremiah	132
27.1 – 29.32	Jeremiah opposes false prophets	137
30.1 – 33.26	Promises of restoration for the people	145
34.1 – 39.18	Events under Jehoiakim and Zedekiah	163
34.1 – 22	Address to Zedekiah: release of slaves	163
35.1 – 19	The Rechabites	167
36.1 – 32	The writing of the scroll	169
37.1 – 38.28	During the final siege of Jerusalem: consultations between king and prophet	174
39.1 – 18	The fall of the city	180
40.1 – 45.5	After the capture of Jerusalem	183

Chapters 46 – 51 Prophecies against Foreign Nations   196

46.2 – 28	Oracles against the Egyptians	197
47.1–7	Oracles against the Philistines	200
48.1 – 47	Oracles against the Moabites	202
49.1 – 6	An oracle against the Ammonites	208
49.7 – 22	Oracles against the Edomites	209
49.23 – 27	An oracle against Damascus	211
49.28 – 33	An oracle against Kedar	212
49.34 – 39	An oracle against Elam	213
50.1 – 51.64	Against Babylon	213

Chapter 52 Appendix – The Fall of Jerusalem   226

For Further Reading   230

GENERAL INTRODUCTION

The *Epworth Preachers' Commentaries* that Greville P. Lewis edited so successfully in the 1950s and 1960s having now served their turn, the Epworth Press has commissioned a team of distinguished academics who are also preachers and teachers to create a new series of commentaries that will serve the 1990s and beyond. We have seized the opportunity offered by the publication in 1989 of the Revised English Bible to use this very readable and scholarly version as the basis of our commentaries, and we are grateful to the Oxford and Cambridge University Presses for the requisite licence. Our authors will nevertheless be free to cite and discuss other translations wherever they think that these will illuminate the original text.

Just as the books that make up the Bible differ in their provenance and purpose, so our authors will necessarily differ in the structure and bearing of their commentaries. But they will all strive to get as close as possible to the intention of the original writers, expounding their texts in the light of the place, time, circumstances, and culture that gave them birth, and showing why each work was received by Jews and Christians into their respective Canons of Holy Scripture. They will seek to make full use of the dramatic advance in biblical scholarship world-wide but at the same time to explain technical terms in the language of the common reader, and to suggest ways in which scripture can help towards the living of a Christian life today. They will endeavour to produce commentaries that can be used with confidence in ecumenical, multi-racial, and multi-faith situations, and not by scholars only but by preachers, teachers, students, church members, and anyone who wants to improve his or her understanding of the Bible.

Ivor H. Jones

ABOUT THIS COMMENTARY

There is an abundance of commentaries available on the book of Jeremiah, of great variety. There are the large and detailed, the brief and basic, the technical, which only a Hebraist can really get the most out of, and those that assume that the reader knows very little. They vary in approach from commentators who take almost everything in the text at its face value to those who appear to take nothing at its face value. There are those who read the book from an avowedly Christian standpoint (the great majority) and those who think of themselves as offering a detached interpretation that presupposes no religious convictions.

With such a range of commentaries on offer it seemed to me most useful to stick closely to the original aim of the Epworth Commentary series and design this commentary very specifically for preachers. I take it for granted that readers are interested in scripture and informed about scripture. The commentary is not written for people who know little or nothing about the Bible to begin with. I assume that if I refer in passing to other books of the Bible, or characters in other parts of the Bible, the reader knows what I am talking about. But I also assume that not all preachers know every last word about the Bible; that most of them (like me) are still learning, and that many are not familiar with the technical vocabulary that scholars sometimes use. (I also assume that most readers are not used to counting backwards, and may need reminding that the year 586 is later than 597, and that 538 is later still.)

What is a preacher most likely to want to know about the book of Jeremiah? Having consulted several preachers, who all said very similar things, I have worked out the following checklist and have tried to be guided by it in the writing of this commentary.

1.   The preacher needs to have obvious difficulties explained, and information offered on matters with which he/she may be unfamiliar.

2.   The preacher needs background information about the events and circumstances of the period, and about the society in which the prophet was operating.

3.   The preacher is likely to need help in seeing the book of Jeremiah as a whole; i.e., in perceiving its structure and in picking out the broad issues with which the prophet deals. A particular problem is that the book of Jeremiah is not organized chronologically. Most readers appreciate assistance in establishing the order in which things happen.

4.   The preacher may appreciate help in seeing connections, both within the book, and between the book and other parts of scripture. Such connections often spark off thoughts which lead to new insights.

5.   The preacher is likely to appreciate other 'leads' which will provoke thought.

6.   In all this the preacher is likely to be asking, in relation to any particular passage in the book: What is this passage about? To whom is it addressed? And what is it trying to say to this people and that situation? (These questions are in many cases deceptively simple, as we shall see.)

7.   But having looked at all that, the preacher will want to know, What do I make of it? What am I to tell my congregation about it? How do I explore it with them? How, if it all, does the text relate to me, to them, and to our own situation here and now?

This commentary will not provide knock-down answers to these last questions. Even if it could, it would not try, because any attempt to offer ready made answers to such questions would deny the prophetic role which is the preacher's own. What it will try to offer is leads, indications of directions in which significance may be found.

Perhaps it would be useful to say a little more at this point about what this commentary is not trying to do. Most readers will not be Hebraists, and purely linguistic comment will therefore rarely be in order; though it is often necessary to point out where questions of interpretation spring from linguistic ambiguities and problems.

Most preachers will not wish for excessively technical critical arguments. For example, questions about exactly how the book was composed, the order in which passages were put together or built up, are fascinating to scholars, but preachers are unlikely to want to devote too much time to them. Critical questions, of course, do sometimes affect interpretation, and in such cases we at least need to register that these questions exist, but this commentary will try to limit discussion of critical matters to those which have a direct bearing on how we understand the text's meaning.

Most readers will not have at the top of their agenda questions which are of purely antiquarian relevance: they will be primarily concerned with the message Jeremiah has for us today. Nevertheless, a warning is in order here. What looks as if it is of purely antiquarian interest may, on examination, turn out not to be so. More broadly, our whole understanding of Jeremiah's significance for today must be based firmly on our estimate of what he meant for his own time. We should try to understand him as well we can in his own context before we rush to relate him to our own.

INTRODUCTION

ɓ

Why the book of Jeremiah is important

Jeremiah is an important thinker in his own right. His contribution to the theology of the Old Testament is a unique one. Spiritually he is presented to us as one of the great saints among the people of God. His understanding of God, and his relationship with God, have therefore much to teach us.

But prophets do not prophesy in a vacuum. Jeremiah's thinking was worked out in a particular place at a particular time, and in response to particular circumstances. The events through which he lived were some of the most momentous in Israel's history. How Jeremiah faced them, and how he tried to help his people face them, and how he interpreted them, are therefore of the very greatest interest. How or where do we see God at work in the world? If we are people of faith we are bound to ask this question, because if God is real, and if he is the sort of God of whom the Bible speaks, he must be at work in the world. Jeremiah asks himself this question during times of great upheaval. To the question: 'Where is God at work in all this; and what is he doing?' there were many voices giving conflicting answers. Jeremiah's words have been preserved and handed down to us because, with hindsight, it could be seen that his answers were better than most other people's. But Jeremiah himself did not have the benefit of hindsight, and at the time had no guarantee of his own rightness. The book has a good deal to say about his doubts and uncertainties. The book is important because it appears to give us insights into those doubts and uncertainties, to a degree that makes it unique in biblical literature. It contains not only the prophet's public utterances, but some of what seem to be his private thoughts and prayers.

A not insignificant reason for the book's importance is that, alone

5

among the Old Testament literature, it offers us an account of how at least some of its contents came to be written down. Up to this point prophecy had been an almost exclusively oral phenomenon. Jeremiah was operating at precisely that stage in history at which it was just beginning to assume written form, and some of the first steps in that process are actually described in the book.

The structure of the book of Jeremiah

When we read a modern book we expect it to 'hang together'. Each chapter connects logically with the one before it and leads into the next. We expect there to be a readily discernible pattern, of one sort or another. If it is a book about the life and work of a particular person, for instance, the commonest sort of pattern would be a chronological one; i. e., the author would probably take us stage by stage through the subject's career.

The book of Jeremiah does not at first sight hang together in any very obvious way. It is mostly about Jeremiah, certainly (though in 40.7–41.18 we have a narrative in which he does not appear at all), but it does not follow his career in any orderly fashion. And though it contains a great many oracles said to be spoken by him, we are often not told of the context in which he uttered them or the circumstances which called them forth.

There is some structure to the book, however, if we look carefully, and though it is not a structure which to the mind of the modern reader is a very satisfactory one, to be aware of what order there is, does help us in understanding the book. Jer. 36 is unique in prophetic literature in giving us what appears to be an account of how some of the prophet's oracles came to be written down. The story in this chapter is clearly not describing the writing of our existing book of Jeremiah. For one thing, the story implies that the scroll contained oracles, and oracles only, and there is a great deal in our book of Jeremiah which is not oracle. For another, we are told that the writing of the scroll by Baruch happened 'in the fourth year of Jehoiakim' (36.1), i.e. 604 BCE. At this stage Jeremiah still had half his career ahead of him and was to have a lot more to say. So Baruch's scroll could only have contained a collection of the prophet's output of oracles up to that date.

Some scholars have spent much time in debating which particular parts of the book were included in Baruch's original scroll, and which may have been added when he wrote out the second edition (King Zedekiah having burnt the first one). I shall make no attempt to discuss these questions. In my opinion we simply do not have the kind of information available that would enable us to answer them. The most we could do would be to identify some oracles which seem to belong sufficiently early in Jeremiah's career for it to be possible that they were included in the scroll. Even this is not a specially useful exercise.

Jer. 36, therefore, describes the writing down of a collection of oracles which most readers assume must eventually have found their way into our present book. Were other collections made, at other points in the prophet's career, and perhaps for other purposes? 25.13 looks as if it might be a reference to one. And certainly the book as we have it does look as if it might be made up of sub-collections of material, some of them organized around particular themes and maybe reflecting specific periods of the prophet's life. 2.1–4.4, for example, has a strong thematic unity and is often supposed (though there is no hard evidence for this) to represent Jeremiah's preaching during the early period of his ministry in the reign of Josiah. Chapters 30–33 make up a well-defined collection of hopeful prophecies traditionally called 'The Book of Consolation'. Chapters 46–51 consist exclusively of oracles against foreign nations. It is evident from this that whoever put the book of Jeremiah together was much more interested in arranging the material according to subject matter than in arranging it in chronological order, though the arranger has been very far from consistent in applying even this principle. That the book has been compiled from sub-collections, and that these sub-collections have not been rigorously edited into a coherent whole, is demonstrated by the very considerable number of oracles which are repeated, or partially repeated, in different contexts.

Although the editors of the book have not made it easy for us, most readers do find it helpful to look for some sort of chronological perspective in the material; i.e., to arrive at some sort of outline of Jeremiah's career and to appreciate as far as possible at what points in that career he did and said particular things. Commentators normally spend a good deal of effort attempting to clarify things in this way.

How do we go about this? Faced with a prophetic oracle or an account of an incident in the prophet's life, how do we find whereabouts in his career it fits? Sometimes the text actually gives us a date, though it is often not a very precise one; e.g., Jer. 3.6, 'In the reign of King Josiah the Lord said to me ...'. 25.1 is more exact: 'In the fourth year of Jehoiakim'. 26.1 has 'At the beginning of the reign of Jehoiakim ...' cf. 27.1. 28.1 is unusual in dating an oracle to the exact month.

Sometimes no actual date is given, but the passage refers to events or circumstances which allow us to place it. E.g., Jer. 21.1–3 makes it clear that the events that follow took place not merely in the reign of Zedekiah, but after hostilities between Judah and the invading Babylonians had begun.

Or the content of an oracle itself may in other ways give us an indication of its setting; e.g. Jer. 22.10–11, which is evidently uttered shortly after King Jehoiakin's deportation in 597.

All in all these indicators help us to fix the chronological context of a good deal of the material in the book, but they do not by any means allow us to date all of it. Often we have no such definite evidence to guide us, and if we are to date the material at all, we must rely on intelligent guesswork. Occasionally we have to admit that there is not much evidence on which we can even base a guess.

The major public events of Jeremiah's lifetime

This summary table may be found useful in establishing a chronological framework for the period of Jeremiah's life. The reader may find it helpful to refer back to this when chronological questions are discussed.

640	King Josiah comes to the throne. According to Jer. 1.2 the prophet's call took place in 626.
621	The finding of 'The Book of the Law' in the temple. According to II Chron. 34.3 Josiah's reform had already begun in 627.
609	The death of Josiah at Megiddo. Josiah is succeeded briefly by Jehoahaz but then by Jehoiakim.
605	The Battle of Carchemish (between Babylon, on the one hand, and Egypt and Assyria on the other) marks the definitive end of the Assyrian empire and seriously weakens Egypt. Babylon is now the only 'superpower' to be seriously reckoned with.
598	Jehoiakim, having rebelled against Babylon, dies. Jehoiakin his son takes over.

597 Jerusalem capitulates, Jehoiakin is removed to Babylon and replaced by Zedekiah. This is the first deportation.

587/6 Zedekiah's rebellion against Babylon is punished by the second deportation. Jerusalem's walls and its temple are destroyed, and Zedekiah is replaced by a governor, Gedaliah.

582? Gedaliah is assassinated. The Jewish leaders flee to Egypt, taking Jeremiah with them.

Outline of the book of Jeremiah

For reasons that have already been sufficiently indicated, it is not possible to produce a clear and coherent outline of the book's structure, and not all scholars would offer identical schemes. It may nevertheless be helpful, even in a rough and ready way, to pick out what shape there is. As we have already noted, there are some sections which readily identify themselves, and between them we must set out as best we can those materials whose structure is less well defined.

We may observe that the book falls into four major divisions, or three major divisions and an appendix, though each of the major divisions is very diverse. Chapters 1–25 consists mainly, though not exclusively, of sayings attributed to Jeremiah. 26–45 principally comprises reports of the prophet's activities. 46–51, the most homogeneous of these large divisions, is the collection of oracles against foreign nations. Chapter 52 is a brief historical appendix.

Analysing the major divisions further reveals the first two as rather untidy.

1.1–3   is an introduction to the book.

1.4–19   gives us an account of the prophet's call, together with some associated visions.

2.1–4.4   identifies itself by its thematic unity. It is an appeal, though an appeal of a somewhat threatening kind. There is little indication that the fulfilment of the threats is imminent.

4.5–6.30   continues the threats, but in this collection the fulfilment of the threats does appear to be regarded as imminent.

7.1–8.3   is an account of Jeremiah's temple speech and some associated prophecies.

8.4–10.25   is much more disparate and consists of miscellaneous short oracles.

11.1–20.18 is held together by a repeated structure in which deuteronomic prose is dominant.

Chapters 21–24 make up another of the fairly well defined sections, consisting of oracles principally against the nation's leaders. The whole of chapters 1–24 is rounded off in 25.1–14, and 25.15–38 introduces the theme of judgment on foreign nations, though in the Hebrew form of the book the rest of the oracles on the nations are postponed until chapters 46–51.

The second of the major divisions begins by reverting to the subject of the important temple speech, (ch. 26); then focusses on conflicts with false prophets (chs 27–29) before being interrupted by the Book of Consolation (chs 30–33). From chapter 34 to the end of this major division in chapter 45 we have what is basically a narrative account of things that happened to Jeremiah from the beginning of the Babylonian assault through to his final journey into Egypt. This account is not, however, all in chronological order.

The third major division, the collection of oracles against the nations, needs no further analysis at this point, and neither does the short historical appendix of chapter 52.

Materials of which the book is composed

The book of Jeremiah, like most prophetic books, contains several different kinds of material. Most obviously, it contains records of what the prophet said. This is usually in the form of oracles. Prophetic oracles are sometimes in the form of poetry, sometimes of prose. In translation the distinction is usually not very obvious, but modern editions of the Bible normally print the text in a way that makes it quite clear which is prose and which is poetry. Merely by flicking over the pages of a Bible one may establish that the book of Isaiah is composed mainly of poetry with some prose passages interspersed. Ezekiel, by contrast, is primarily prose, with occasional, and usually brief, poetic sections. Jeremiah is roughly half and half. Jeremiah chapter 2, for example, consists almost entirely of poetic oracles. Chapter 16 is mostly of teaching in prose form.

Not all the prose material is oracular; much of it is narrative. If the oracles tell us what the prophet said, the narrative material gives us an account of what he did, or of events in which he was involved. Jer. 36, for instance, tells us the story of his dictation of the scroll, and its subsequent destruction by the king and later re-affirmation by the prophet. Another example is the long narrative in chapters 40–43 about what happened to Jeremiah when Jerusalem fell to the Babylonians, and how he was later taken to Egypt.

The distinction between passages setting out what the prophet did and those telling us what he said is not a sharp one. We sometimes have stories about what the prophet did, but the purpose of the story is to explain how certain oracles came to be delivered. E.g., 18.1–12 tells how Jeremiah paid a visit to a pottery, but the reason for telling us this is that the prophet turned the experience into a kind of parable. Chapters 27–28 give us an account of some of Jeremiah's actions, and are therefore a piece of narrative, but the actions are really enacted oracles; cf. 32.6–15. Chapter 26 is an account of how Jeremiah was put on trial, and is therefore a narrative, but it does include a summary of the speech which he made which led to his arrest, so it has oracular material embedded in it. While we are on the subject of narrative there is another important distinction to be drawn between passages which are presented as if the prophet himself is speaking, i.e., in the first person, such as the account of his call in chapter 1, where we have such expressions as: 'The word of the Lord came to me' (1.4, 1.11); 'I said ...' (1.6); and other passages which are presented in the third person; i.e., someone else is telling us about the prophet, and what he said or did. We have many examples of the latter: chapters 7, 25, 27, 30, 32, 33, 34, 40, 44 all begin, not with the words 'The word of the Lord came to me', but 'The word ... came to Jeremiah'. Someone other than Jeremiah is addressing us.

It is always salutary, when reading a prophetic text, to keep asking ourselves, 'Who is saying these words? And to whom?' The answers often make a difference to the way we understand the passage.

The two books of Jeremiah

It is a significant fact that the book of Jeremiah exists in two quite distinct forms. There is the Hebrew Jeremiah, which is the one translated in our usual English versions, and the Greek Jeremiah (which is, incidentally, the book of Jeremiah as it would have been familiar to the Greek-speaking first Christians, such as St Paul). They represent two distinct versions of the book. The Greek Jeremiah is substantially shorter. It is shorter not in the sense that it contains fewer chapters and verses, but shorter in that it omits numerous formulae, words and titles, and so on, which have the effect of reducing its length by about an eighth. It also differs in its arrangement. Some sections, specifically the oracles against foreign nations, appear in different positions in the two versions of the book. It is not wise to assume that the Hebrew version appearing in our modern Bibles is necessarily the original, or more 'correct' of the two. Many scholars have concluded that the Greek Jeremiah actually reflects an older edition of the book than the one that has come down to us in Hebrew. Where there are differences of substance between the two versions, the witness of the Greek Jeremiah deserves to be taken very seriously.

In fact, the differences rarely are differences of substance, and it may seem to the reader that they are therefore unimportant, but the very existence of two such distinct editions is significant in itself. It proves that the shape of the book of Jeremiah was not seen as fixed and final until quite a late stage in the biblical period. The Jeremiah tradition was still in a flexible state as much as two and a half centuries after the prophet's lifetime.

The composition of the book of Jeremiah

The question of how the book of Jeremiah was put together, and by whom, has been much debated, and there is still no unanimity about it. Two issues in particular have excited discussion. One is the part played in the production of the book by the people we call the Deuteronomic School. That they played some part is hardly to be disputed; at many points in the book their ideas and their language are very evident. We cannot always be sure, however, how far these ideas and this language have been introduced by editors or those who have handed on the material, and to what extent the ideas and language of the deuteronomists (who were, after all, the prophet's contemporaries) had already been appropriated by Jeremiah himself.

However large or small a hand the deuteronomists had in shaping the book of Jeremiah, there can be little doubt that at a later stage people of deuteronomic persuasion edited all the prophetic books, together with the books of Joshua, Judges, Samuel and Kings, to make a single corpus, and that what we might call these 'general editors' may at that stage have modified the substance of the books still further.

The question of how far the deuteronomists are likely to have imposed their own views on the book of Jeremiah I have taken up at what seem to me to be relevant points in the commentary on the text (1.2, 8.8, 11.1–14).

The other question that arises in connection with the book's composition is the part played by Baruch. Earlier commentators and other biblical scholars were very interested in this question, and some were inclined to be very precise in their indications of which parts of the book were owed directly to him. He was widely credited with having preserved and passed on much of the third person narrative material, and was by many held responsible for the incorporation of the more intimate and personal passages, such as the so-called 'confessions'. These are natural enough suggestions to make. The evidence of the book indicates that Baruch was a close confederate of the prophet, and chapter 36 tells us explicitly that it was he who actually took down the prophet's oracles in writing in Jehoiakim's reign, and he who in person publicly read them. We are also told that after the scroll's destruction by the king, Baruch himself, on the prophet's instructions, rewrote the scroll and added to it (36.32). What more natural, then, than that at a further stage he should have expanded the scroll yet more, incorporating later oracles, conceivably incorporating his own memoirs of Jeremiah, and incorporating, perhaps, more personal utterances of the prophet which were not originally intended as public statements?

All this, indeed, is possible; some might even say likely. But all that we know, or all that we are actually told, about Baruch's involvement in the preservation of Jeremiah's words, is that he wrote, and then re-wrote, with expansions, the scroll of 604 BCE. The rest is guesswork. And even if we judge it very likely, on the basis of what we are told, that Baruch did have a larger hand in the matter, we have no way of knowing how extensive his activities were, or which particular parts of the material we owe to him. For this reason, though I freely acknowledge the possibility that Baruch has been instrumental, and perhaps largely intrumental, in preserving and handing on, and maybe ordering, some of the material of the book of Jeremiah, I have not in the commentary spent any time trying to identify more precisely the extent of his work. There are limits to the usefulness of discussing questions which are purely matters of speculation. (See also the commentary on 45.1.)

Scepticism and credulity

In recent years some commentators have taken a very sceptical attitude to the book of Jeremiah, seeing it as having been largely shaped, or even fabricated, by later editors who used it to represent their own views. They have concluded that the book can tell us little about any real, historical prophet called Jeremiah. Such approaches have to be taken seriously. What they point to are real doubts, real ambiguities in the evidence, real possibilities that the book is not, after all, what it appears to be. My own perspective, having looked carefully at the reasons for scepticism, is that there almost certainly was a real person called Jeremiah, and that we can know something about him. But it has to be recognized that not all that is said about him in the book is necessarily true, and that not all the words ascribed to him are necessarily ones he uttered. It has to be recognized too that those who passed on to us his words and the accounts of his deeds, had axes of their own to grind in doing so, and are likely to have presented their material in ways which suited their own purposes, perhaps at the cost of distorting the material itself.

In reading the book of Jeremiah we have to face the fact that for much of the time an agnosticism is being imposed on us. We would dearly like to know whether the words we read are the words which Jeremiah actually spoke, and whether they genuinely reflect his mind. We would like to be sure what allowances to make for the perspectives of his editors, and of the collectors of the materials of the book. But we cannot. The acceptance of this uncertainty is a precondition of our reading.

In the commentary we shall have much to say about the prophet's preoccupation with *sheqer*, 'falsehood', 'illusion'. For Jeremiah *sheqer* is the great enemy. His opponents, prophets and kings especially, are misled by *sheqer*. His greatest fear is that he himself is infected by the disease he seeks to combat; that he too is a victim of *sheqer* and a purveyor of false messages. To read the book is to share the problem. Anyone who reads, or attempts to interpret, the book of Jeremiah, must acknowledge when he begins, and when he has ended, the possibility that he has got it wrong. The reader, like the prophet himself in his lifetime, has to face the truth that in the last resort he does not know, for certain, what is genuine and what is not. One of the few things we can learn from the book with certainty, is that certainty is a luxury God does not allow us.

Those who preserved and passed on the materials of the book of Jeremiah were convinced that on the questions that mattered most, Jeremiah had not been a victim of falsehood. He had been proved right by events. The reader's natural instinct is to agree. But here we must be careful. The political thrust of the prophet's message was that the rise of Babylon to world domination was inevitable and irresistible, and that for a small nation in Judah's position the sensible course of action was to accept the realities and not incite Babylonian hostility. This judgment does seem to be justified by events. The ethical dimension to the message, as with all the canonical prophets, is the primary requirement of social justice, and the religious one is that God demands faithfulness in worship of himself, and the rejection of other deities. The priority given to social justice the Christian reader will approve, and likewise the rejection of heathen worship, which certainly involved practices no Christian would countenance. But Jeremiah's thesis, and that of his editors, is that Judah's failure on the ethical and religious fronts was what ultimately led to disaster by provoking divine punishment. Can we conclude that this interpretation, too, was justified by events? Many readers of the book will doubtless answer unequivocally 'Yes' to this question. But others of us are less satisfied. The prophet's thesis implies a very simplistic understanding of history. The idea that God punishes with disaster nations which do not meet his moral standards and religious requirements is one not well borne out by the study of history in general. The conviction that in the exile Judah was suffering for her sins was an important one at the time. It enabled her people to make sense of what was happening to them, and therefore helped them to cope with those traumatic events, and to maintain hope that there was still a future for them. It was a life-saving and morale-saving conviction. It was vital that the prophet believed it; that the creators of the book believed it. But whether a present-day reader should believe it is another matter entirely.

COMMENTARY

Sayings attributed to Jeremiah
1–25

Introduction to the book
1.1–3

1.1 *The words of Jeremiah.* 'Words' in biblical Hebrew does not necessarily refer only to speech. Words are not just things said. They may include things done. The book that follows does not, in fact, contain only *the words of Jeremiah*, in our normal understanding of that phrase. A considerable part of the book consists of stories about Jeremiah, i.e. his deeds. It also offers us a good deal of information about the context in which he is said to have prophesied and the situations and events to which he was responding.

Of the priests at Anathoth. Though Jeremiah is a priest, he does not belong to the powerful Jerusalem priesthood, as Ezekiel did. Anathoth is listed in Josh. 21.18 as one of the levitical cities. It was therefore one of those provincial religious centres which were suppressed by Josiah's reform.

I Kings 1–2 tells how when David became very old his sons Adonijah and Solomon were rivals to succeed him. Adonijah was backed by the priest Abiathar (among others); Solomon by the priest Zadok. After Solomon won the struggle he dealt with his rival's supporters. In I Kings 2.26–27 Abiathar is banished from court to his family home, Anathoth. It appears, therefore, that Jeremiah belonged to this old priesthood, whose history stretched at least as far back as Eli, Samuel's mentor, which had lost the power struggle away back near the beginning of the monarchy.

By contrast with Ezekiel, there is little or nothing in Jeremiah to suggest that priestly and cultic interests have much influenced his thinking or his language.

Anathoth, the modern Anata, is about three miles (five kilometres) north-east of Jerusalem; near, but not on, the main road north from the capital. Anata has easy access to the capital city, and is yet on the edge of the wilderness. Around Anata are little fields of tolerable soil, but immediately to the east of the village, stony and rock-scabbed countryside stretches away until after a very few miles it dips into the rain shadow and becomes desert as it descends steeply towards the Jordan valley.

Anathoth in Benjamin. At the time of the conquest under Joshua Benjamin appears to have been an important tribe, but by Jeremiah's day was probably numerically small. The territory of Benjamin lay on the border between the Northern and Southern kingdoms. In the patriarchal stories Benjamin is described as Joseph's younger brother, which links the tribe most closely with the larger Joseph tribes, Ephraim and Manasseh, of the north. But at the time of the division of the kingdom, at the end of Solomon's reign, Benjamin seems to have sided with Judah and remained loyal to the dynasty of David (I Kings 12.21–24). The ambivalence of Benjamin, having sympathies both north and south, may explain Jeremiah's lack of any strong Judahite nationalistic feelings.

To an Englishman and to many other people of the West, tribe or clan mean little or nothing. But to many people in the world they mean a very great deal. Tribe and clan certainly meant a great deal in the world in which Jeremiah lived. What would it mean to be a Benjaminite, specifically? What stories would children of Benjamin be told, and what ghosts would live alongside them in that homeland? Benjamin had a reputation for violence. The Blessing of Jacob says (Gen. 49.27), 'Benjamin is a ravening wolf: in the morning he devours the prey, in the evening he snatches a share of the spoil'. If we think of the Benjaminite traditions on which Jeremiah would have been reared, the stories of the heroes and anti-heroes of his tribe, we shall understand how that reputation was gained. There is the ambiguous Ehud (Judg. 3.15ff.) the left-handed judge; resourceful, certainly; courageous, no doubt; a deliverer of his people. But Ehud delivers his people not by winning battles, but by political assassination. There is the story of the levite and his concubine in Judg. 19–21, and of what they suffered at the hands of Benjaminites; where our horror at the behaviour of the men of Gibeah is matched only by our horror at the behaviour of the victim himself, and by our horror at the response of the rest of Israel, whose only solution to the compounding problem is to pile deception upon deception and atrocity upon atrocity.

And then there is Saul, the Benjaminite king: Saul, breathing out fire and slaughter against David, whom he had once befriended; to whom he had given his daughter in marriage, and then taken her away; Saul, who was possessed by the spirit of prophecy, but then by the spirits of evil; Saul, who, in the days of his loyalty, had driven the witches and necromancers out of the land, but who in his extremity resorted to just such a one, but who came, nevertheless, at the last to meet the archers at Gilboa. Jeremiah offers us words which would make his perfect epitaph: 'A heart deceitful above all things, and desperately sick'. It is worth bearing all this background in mind as we read the book of Jeremiah. It is a very violent book.

1.2 *The word of the Lord came to him*. This is what characterizes a prophet. A prophet is someone who receives the word and is controlled by the word.

In the thirteenth year of the reign of Josiah. This would make the year 626 BCE. According to II Kings 22 the finding of the Book of the Law, which was so influential in shaping Josiah's reform, took place in the king's eighteenth year, i.e. 621. But according to II Chron. 34 the reform itself actually began some years earlier, in Josiah's twelfth year, viz. 627. If the Chronicler's information is correct, then the reform was already in progress at the time of Jeremiah's call, and the early years of his ministry were ones during which momentous events were taking place. Even if the Chronicler is mistaken, and the impression given in Kings that the reform began with the discovery of the Law Book is a correct one, the reform would still have been happening within five years of Jeremiah's call to prophesy. This being so, it is remarkable that the book seems to be virtually silent on the subject of the reform. There are one or two sayings in it that might be allusions to the reform, but no unambiguous references to this most important happening in the history of the nation. This silence is very hard to explain.

One possibility is that the date given in 1.2 is wrong, and that Jeremiah was not active as a prophet as early as this. The date in 1.3, indicating the end of Jeremiah's prophetic work, is certainly wrong, for it contradicts the evidence of the book itself. It suggests that Jeremiah's prophesying continued only up to the fall of Jerusalem to the Babylonians in 586 BCE. Now the book contains a considerable amount of material relating to Jeremiah's career after 586; e.g. chs

40–55 do so quite explicitly. So whoever was responsible for the dates in 1.2–3 certainly did not accurately indicate the contents of the present book of Jeremiah. If the information about the end of the prophet's ministry is faulty, the information about its beginning may be equally so.

There is not in fact much material in the book which demands a context during the reign of Josiah. There is much, especially in the early chapters, which might come from this period, and which is usually assumed to do so. But not much of it requires such an early date. It is possible, therefore, that Jeremiah left little or nothing on record concerning the reform because he did not become active as a prophet until its main phases were over. He may not have prophesied during Josiah's reign at all. 36.2, however, does repeat the claim that he did.

But other explanations for the prophet's silence are possible. There was much in the reform which a prophet could not but have approved of. On the other hand, it made the Jerusalem temple and its worship very central to the religious life of the nation. Jeremiah seems to have had little love for the temple and to have been unconvinced of the value of sacrificial worship. If the reform thus contained features which he would have been unhappy to support and yet others which he could not have disapproved of, he may have resolved simply to keep his own counsel.

Another possibility is that, since we know that the material of the book passed through the hands of deuteronomic editors, Jeremiah may have expressed unfavourable views of the reform which the deuteronomic editors suppressed. This is perhaps the least likely explanation, for if the deuteronomic editors were so anxious to enlist Jeremiah as a supporter of Josiah's policies, and were prepared to modify the record to this end, one might wonder why they did not credit the prophet with a few spurious oracles to make it look as if he was firmly on their side. The fact that there are no such oracles in favour of the reform suggests that the deuteronomists resisted any temptation to remake Jeremiah in their own image.

There are two indirect pieces of evidence that Jeremiah did lend some support to the reform, even if he stopped short of outright endorsement. In 22.15–16 clear approval is expressed of King Josiah. If these words are genuinely by Jeremiah, they suggest that he can hardly have been strongly opposed to the reform, for Jeremiah could scarcely have spoken so warmly of a king whose principal act of policy he thoroughly condemned.

A stronger argument is that the book makes clear at a number of points that Jeremiah's own family and the people at Anathoth were very bitterly antagonistic to him. This antagonism is never explained. It would, however, make excellent sense if Jeremiah had supported, or at least not wholeheartedly opposed, the reform that closed the religious centre at Anathoth and deprived his family and many of his neighbours of their livelihood.

To return to the question of the dates in 1.2–3, there may be a certain artificiality about them in any case and we should perhaps be well advised not to put too much faith in them. They mark the limits of Jeremiah's ministry as 626 to 586, making it forty years. This is a suspiciously round figure. Is it fortuitous, or is the book's organizer, in crediting him with this conventional number of years, suggesting that Jeremiah is a prophet after the order of Moses, whose ministry was likewise forty years in length, i.e. if we reckon from the exodus until the entry into the promised land?

1.3 *Until the end of the eleventh year of Zedekiah ... in the fifth month ...* This looks like a contradiction. The *fifth month* is hardly *the end of the year*. The answer is that two systems of reckoning were in use simultaneously. The months could be indicated by number, beginning in spring, so that *the fifth month* would be around August; but the regnal years of kings seem to have been reckoned from an autumn New Year. So when the city fell in August it would be nearly the end of Zedekiah's regnal year.

Josiah ... Jehoiakim ... Zedekiah. It is significant that these three kings are named here at the beginning of the book. They were very different men, whose very different policies provided the stepping stones along which Judah stumbled to disaster, and Jeremiah's responses to the three shape his ministry.

Jeremiah's call and first visions
1.4–19

The exposition of scripture can never be a purely detached and objective exercise. Whatever else scripture offers us, it offers a record of the experience of a people who believed they had encountered God, and that God had spoken to them. We shall not fully understand their words unless we have in some sense shared that experience, or are prepared to share it.

The rest of ch. 1 belongs to a recognizable category. It is an account of a divine 'call'. Other prophets describe such calls too, but no two accounts are alike. The preacher's own call will be different again. But unless there is something in the prophet's experience which is recognizable as the preacher's own, then the preacher, and thus the preacher's hearers, will be missing something.

The preacher can only effectively preach by recognizing that he, or she, and the prophet are 'in this together'. They are on the same side, sharing the same job, of communicating what it means to face a divine demand. The prophet's experience of call will help the preacher understand his own call better, and the preacher's own call will illuminate her understanding of the prophet's. This is the 'strange work' of exposition and of preaching, that one may be partner in a task with someone who died two and a half millennia ago.

It is a worthwhile exercise to make a list of all those people in scripture who are said to have received a 'call'. It is a long list. The call is not always a call to prophesy, but sometimes to other kinds of action or response. What, if anything, do all these experiences of 'call' have in common? In what ways do they differ?

1.4   *This word of the Lord came to me.* The prophet can only speak what is given to him. This conviction is powerfully expressed elsewhere in scripture, e.g., I Kings 22.13–14, and see Num. 22–24. Prophets speak of the Lord 'putting a word into their mouths'. The prophet has no choice about what he says. Later in the book this becomes a very serious issue for Jeremiah. There is another aspect to this sense of compulsion which the prophet feels: it does not appear to him that he has any choice about whether he takes on the task.

1.5   expresses the conviction that the prophet was actually born for the task. His designation as a prophet was predetermined before his birth. In a sense, his 'call' took place long ago, before the prophet even knew about it. Something similar is said of the Servant of the Lord in Isa. 49.1.

Perhaps this notion of compulsion was a less startling one to the writer and to ancient readers than it is to us. We, in our age, are obsessed with the notion of choice. In all sorts of spheres of our lives the right to choose is declared, or assumed, to be an entitlement. Until quite modern times few human beings would have thought so. Our ancestors made very few choices. A person's social station, way of making a living, place of residence, would in most cases be pre-determined. Their marriage partners would usually be selected by someone else. Only the rich would have any choices, and even they not very many. Any changes that came would likely be imposed by fate or necessity, not choice. Jeremiah is therefore not different from most of his contemporaries in doing what he is obliged to do.

It might look as if the backbone of the Bible story is about people who nevertheless did make choices; Abraham, who left his home in Ur to go to the land of promise; Moses, who led his people out of Egypt ... The reader can readily enough prolong the series. The interesting thing is that the Bible itself does not represent any of these momentous 'choices' as choices at all. It does not see them as human decisions, but as directives from God.

1.5 *I appointed you a prophet to the nations.* The scale and scope of the prophet's job is enormous. There is nothing domestic about it; cf. 1.10.

1.6 *I am not skilled in speaking.* This sort of objection is found in other accounts of prophetic calls. See, e.g. Ex. 4.10.

I am too young. We do not know how old Jeremiah was. The Hebrew word used here is not a precise one. He was not married, so it is likely that he was at most a young teenager. Age is no barrier to a prophetic call. Samuel, too, appears to have been quite young when first summoned. The combination of Jeremiah's youth and the scope of the task with which he is presented looks a little ludicrous. Is this youngster really expected to address governments and call kings to account? The answer is, yes.

1.7–8 The double theme of the call, prophetic self-doubt answered by divine reassurance, is echoed and re-echoed throughout the book.

1.9 *Then the Lord stretched out his hand, ... touching my mouth.* Compare Isa. 6.7 where the prophet's mouth is touched and purified, and Ezek. 2.8–3.3 where the mouth is also concerned, but in the eating of a book. This probably means in Ezekiel's case that the prophet is called to communicate in writing. But Isaiah and Jeremiah are still primarily speakers.

1.10 *This day I give you authority over nations and kingdoms to uproot and to pull down, to destroy and to demolish, to build and to plant.* This is a very important summary of the prophet's total work. That work is first of all judgmental and destructive. This is the aspect which is perhaps most obvious in the book. It certainly dominates the early part of the prophet's career, up to the fall of the city in 586.

All human institutions, however fine and noble, however well-conceived, however well-administered, are provisional. Even at their best, they are the best we have for the time being. This is as true of religious institutions as of any others. In the view of the Old Testament writers, if such institutions become too important to us, then God may deprive us of them. They have become idols. All human institutions are under judgment, and may at any time need to be renewed or replaced. Judah, during Jeremiah's lifetime, was to lose all that was dearest to her. It is this destruction, and subsequent possibility of rebuilding, that it is Jeremiah's job to interpret.

There is a positive side to the message. The book does contain promises of forgiveness and restoration. These are likely to reflect for the most part developments after 586. The disaster has now happened; God has made his discipline felt, and felt severely. Now there is a place for mercy and salvation. The formula set out in this verse is quoted or alluded to several times in the rest of the book; for example, at the end of ch. 12, in 18.7–10, quite crucially at 31.28 and then again in 42.10 and 45.4.

The prophetic call is often, though not invariably, associated with a vision or visions. Moses, Isaiah, Jeremiah and Ezekiel all report visions. But the label 'vision' masks significant differences. Isaiah's vision is of the Lord enthroned in his temple. Ezekiel likewise sees God enthroned, but in the open, and in a vision which is, if anything, even more spectacular and overpowering than Isaiah's. For Moses, the vision is the mysterious one of a burning bush.

Jeremiah's 'visions' are of twigs bursting into bloom, and of a pot boiling on the fire. Do such commonplace sights really deserve the same name as the extraordinary perceptions of Moses, Isaiah and Ezekiel? 'Visions' such as Jeremiah's are not unparalleled elsewhere in prophecy. See, e.g., Amos 8.1–3. But the crucial thing for a prophet is to perceive the meaning and significance of what he sees, whether it presents itself as ordinary or extraordinary. For Jeremiah, at least at this particular point, to receive a 'vision' is to become aware of the significance of the ordinary. What we call 'vision' is frequently the transformation of the ordinary. (An interesting example of this is in I Kings 22, where Micaiah's vision of the deliberations in the heavenly court is clearly related to what was going on in the earthly court before his bodily eyes.) The prophetic vision is the point at which the worldly and the other-worldly intersect. The prophet becomes aware of the supernatural world which in reality always interpenetrates this one, and he perceives the other-worldly in what is common. An archetypal example (though not in the context of a call) is the incident in II Kings 6.11–17. The young man in this story is terrified to see a besieging army threatening the city. When Elisha prays: 'Open his eyes that he may see', nothing changes, except the young man's perception. The 'horses of fire and chariots of fire' which he becomes aware of were actually there all the time.

Perhaps it ought not to be assumed that these visions recorded here in association with Jeremiah's call necessarily took place at the time of the call. They may have been placed in this context because their content is relevant to the call, rather than because they happened at the same time.

1.12 *I am on the watch.* The transformation and significance of the ordinary are expressed here, as not infrequently in prophecy, through a pun. We do not take puns very seriously, and regard them as a rather crude form of humour, but this was not so in the ancient world. Similarities of names and words were not seen as accidental. They could be deeply significant. Dream analysis confirms that the clue to the meaning of our dream images is often to be found in punning similarities of words. This suggests that the pun appeals to something quite deep in the human mind. Another well known prophetic pun is in Amos 8.1–2.

On the watch. The same Hebrew verb is used in 5.6; on which see the note.

The second 'vision' is of *a cauldron on a fire*. The Hebrew is a little obscure but the implication seems to be that the cauldron is about to boil over. It signifies a disaster which will come upon the country *from the north*. 1.13 briefly describes what is seen. Vv.14–16 offer the interpretation. Jeremiah sees the threat from the north as a threat of military attack. Some older commentators speculated about the identity of the 'enemy from the north' in the book of Jeremiah, and a popular theory identified this enemy with the Scythians, an invading people from the steppes of Asia. But there is no serious evidence that the Scythians were ever a threat to Judah during this period. There is in reality nothing mysterious about the identity of the enemy from the north. Virtually any enemy who invaded Israel, unless it was the Egyptians, had to come from the north. On Israel's west, of course, was the sea, from which threats rarely came. The only significant invaders who in ancient times entered the land from the west were the Philistines. And eastwards Israel is bounded by great tracts of desert. Nomadic tribesmen might invade from there, but not imperial armies. The north was the only avenue of approach for them. The real 'enemy from the north' in Jeremiah's lifetime was the Babylonians, as the rest of the book makes clear. The phrase would not have been an obscure one to his contemporaries. It seems to have been a habit of prophets (and not only the biblical ones, but pagan ones too) to use deliberately indirect language. For example, the book of Amos is focussed very much on the threat to Israel of military attack by the Assyrians; yet the Assyrians are never once mentioned in it by name.

1.14–19   presents us with a single picture, of a city under siege. But the picture is described twice and applied in two different ways. In vv.14–16 the city is Jerusalem, and the picture conveys Jeremiah's characteristic message of judgment: Jerusalem is to be destroyed because of the wickedness of its inhabitants. In vv.17–19 the besieged city is an image of the prophet himself, threatened on all sides. Jerusalem cannot hold out, because the Lord has decreed her destruction. The prophet is being likened to a city which can hold out, because God wills that he should succeed. Both aspects of the image make it appropriate that it should be placed here, at the beginning, in the context of the prophet's call.

1.15   *Their kings will come and each will set his throne in place before the gates of Jerusalem.* This is what happened after a city was captured; the conqueror would hold court, and usually punish the leaders of his defeated foes. The court is held outside the gates because it needs to be public, and in the cramped conditions of an ancient city there was rarely much open space inside where an assembly of any size could meet. Such an assembly had to meet outside the gate or at the threshing floor (which might indeed be the same place. See I Kings 22.10).

God's appeal to Israel and Judah

2.1–4.4

One of the questions which permeates the book of Jeremiah, sometimes directly addressed, but often just a little below the surface, is the question of authentication. How do we know the prophet is right? How does the prophet himself know he is right?

The short answer is, of course, that we don't, or at least that his first hearers didn't; and he himself didn't. He had to trust that he was right, and to ask his hearers to trust him.

But there are some pointers to whether Jeremiah was a true prophet and a number of these pointers are indicated in the book. Most important is the one available to us, but not available to them. We have the benefit of knowing that in very many respects Jeremiah was proved right by events. And as we read the book we need to keep remembering that whoever edited and put the book together, though he may not have lived very long after Jeremiah himself, shared our perspective, not that of the prophet and his first hearers. He already knew that Jeremiah had been vindicated, which is the reason why he produced the book at all. The pointers available during Jeremiah's ministry, or at least during the early part of it, were less conclusive, but were nonetheless important. Several of them are indicated here, at the book's beginning.

Authentication is almost certainly the main reason for including the account of the prophet's call. A true prophet is called by God, and the claim that he was called is best made here, at the start of the book. This is not only an assurance to his hearers, and later his readers, but to the prophet himself. He needs to know he has authority for the words he utters. And the call is confirmed by visions, which bear witness to the prophet's inspiration. Both of these we are assured of in chapter 1. But how do we know, and how does the prophet know, that the experience of a call is not simply the invention of his own brain, the visions products of his imagination, and the word he speaks an expression of his own wishful thinking?

It is not accident that chapter 2 goes straight on with a message that is rooted in the traditions of God's people. The message is not something that the prophet makes up, because it can be checked by, and itself appeals back to, revelation already received, words already spoken by earlier prophets, visions already acknowledged as being from God. Of course, God does sometimes reveal new things through his prophets, but if they are truly of God then they are in character with the 'former things' already known. The message is authenticated partly by the fact that it is grounded in a tradition already respected and approved.

This is one way in which we can distinguish true religion from what is merely a religious cult. The leader of a cult may also be convinced that he has a call, and may sincerely claim that he has experienced visions, and may be certain in his own mind that his message is true. But the message cannot be checked against a tradition; against the common witness of the people of God. (Cf. I John 4.6.)

2.1–4.4   forms a major unit with its connecting theme of the adultery of the nation. There is no sense of imminent disaster in these oracles, and those scholars may be right who claim that the collection relates to an early period in Jeremiah's activities. 3.6 offers us a date 'in the reign of Josiah', though we may not assume that this date is meant to apply to the whole unit. The various oracles in ch.2 relate to the theme of Israel's idyllic beginnings and the incomprehensibility of her subsequent unfaithfulness.

2.1   *The word of the Lord came to me.* All this material is still expressed in the first person. As in ch.1 the prophet himself is addressing us.

There is a strong coherence about the themes and images in this section 2.1–4.4. Much of it relates to accusations of false worship. But what is in mind is clearly Baal worship. This gives us some reason to see these oracles as genuinely emanating from pre-exilic Palestine and as reflecting the interests of the community at that time, since there is no evidence that Baal worship was any longer an issue once the exile had taken place. The post-exilic Israelite community was aware of alternative religions, and their attractions, but Baal worship, specifically, was apparently no longer a live option.

2.2   *These are the words of the Lord.* It is easy to overlook these little formulae with which the text of prophetic books, particularly Jeremiah, is salted. They are useful in that they sometimes help us to see where oracles begin and end, though they are not infallible in this regard. At this particular point we have a little clutch of three of them. Chapter 1 ends with *This is the word of the Lord*, which is the formula rounding off the previous oracle. 2.1 reads *The word of the Lord came to me*; and 2.2a has *These are the words of the Lord*. So chapter 2 begins with a double formula. It is probable that the formula in 2.1 introduces the whole of the next large unit, whereas the formula in 2.2a is meant to introduce simply the next oracle, constituted by vv.2–3.

I remember in your favour the loyalty of your youth, your love during your bridal days. These words refer back to a happy time at the beginning of Israel's relationship with her God, when she was 'in love' with her divine husband, and when she was faithful to him. The prophet Hosea reflects a similar understanding of that early period when in 2.14–15 he talks of the possibility of a 'second honeymoon' in the wilderness, where Israel 'will respond as in her youth, as when she came up from Egypt'. When was this honeymoon period? Whoever wrote the account of Israel in the wilderness which we have in our Pentateuch knows of no such time. According to the Pentateuch Israel from the beginning was ungrateful and rebellious. Ezekiel, recounting the history of his people in ch.20 of his book, says that even before they left Egypt Israel was impenitently attached to Egyptian idols (Ezek. 20.7–8). When he tells the same story in parable form in chs 16 and 23, though in both he employs the image of the marriage, he speaks of no honeymoon.

Clearly there was more than one understanding of the wilderness tradition current in Israel. Hosea and Jeremiah reflect what was probably an older one that Israel's 'marriage' began with a period of harmony and young love. Ezekiel and the editors of the Pentateuch reflect a more pessimistic picture of the wilderness period that probably developed at the time of the exile, when Israel's thinkers looked back on their nation's story and concluded that at no time had her response to God been an adequate and proper one.

The imagery of 2.3 is not self-explanatory. The 'first-fruits' of any crop belonged to God and were sacred (Ex.23.16; 34.32; Lev. 23.10–21; Num. 28.26). They were meant to be offered to him in the sanctuary. Any human being who consumed them was in grave danger of divine retribution. The young Israel was like the first-fruits; God's special possession which he would guard jealously. The implication, which the prophet does not spell out, is that God does not treat Israel like that any more, because she has violated the special relationship that once existed between her and the Lord.

2.4 and 5 offer us what looks like another double introductory formula. There is no concluding formula until the end of v.19 though the initial unit should probably be regarded as ending with v.13, vv.14–19 being a separate oracle.

Although 2.4–13 is a fresh oracle, in subject matter it follows closely and logically from the preceding one. The prophet is pursuing the question: 'What went wrong?' The prophet seems genuinely puzzled. God did nothing to call the relationship into question. It looks like sheer perversity on Israel's part. The prophet can only conclude that perversity it is, and many of the succeeding images express this view. The tone of the whole chapter is one of incredulity. Israel's behaviour does not make sense.

Of course, human behaviour quite often does not make sense. Relationships can become soured and embittered, and eventually self-destructive, and sometimes for reasons that are very hard to perceive, even by the people involved – perhaps especially by the people involved. Individuals can behave in ways that suggest that they are determined to destroy themselves and many of those around them. Communities may do the same. And to the outsider it may all look quite inexplicable. Such an observer's natural response is to say, 'But why don't they just stop?' But they don't. It is just such an intractable situation that Jeremiah perceives his people, and their relationship to their God, to be in.

2.5 … *pursuing worthless idols, and becoming worthless like them.* The word translated *worthless idols* is the one used in Ecclesiastes, where it is traditionally rendered 'vanity'. It signifies something inconsequential, vapid, without substance. These people centred their lives, says Jeremiah, on a nothing, and they became nothing. They followed what was trivial, and became trivial. We become like what we worship.

2.6–7   spells out what God has done for Israel. The word 'land' is the theme word of these verses; a fact which REB obscures. God rescued Israel from the land of Egypt; brought her through the inhospitable land of the wilderness, and led her into the rich and *fertile land* of promise, which she promptly ruined. The thinking here is strongly reminiscent of Deuteronomy. See, e.g., Deut. 8.

2.8   puts the blame on the nation's leaders, three categories of them. First the *priests*, described here as *those who handled the law.* This was the priests' principal function in Israel, not offering sacrifice, but teaching the law, through which Israel was to know God. But these guardians of the law themselves did not know God.

Second, *the shepherds*, i.e. the rulers. Not only in Israel but throughout the ancient near east 'shepherd' is a common, not to say commonplace, metaphor for a king or ruler. Cf. Ezek. 34. Part of the royal insignia of the Pharaoh of Egypt was a crook. The Israelite shepherd carried a 'rod and staff' (Ps. 23.4). The 'rod' is the crook with which the shepherd guides, or when necessary rescues, the sheep. The 'staff' is simply a cudgel or club with which to defend them against any assault by predators or thieves. This club is later elaborated into the mace of authority and the sceptre of the king. The connection between shepherds and rulers has always been a close one.

The third category of leaders of society is that of *the prophets*. As the priests preserve true tradition in the law, the prophet applies that tradition by means of the word (cf. Jer. 18.18). The prophets were the enthusiasts for the Lord, whose job it was to defend the true faith in Israel's God against the alternative worship of Baal. This is what Elijah and Elisha, archetypal prophets, did so splendidly. The most dreadful thing a prophet could do was to be untrue to this task and to countenance the worship of Baal or other heathen gods. This is spelled out in Deut. 13.1–5, where it is declared a capital dereliction. But Jeremiah says: *The prophets prophesied in the name of Baal and followed gods who were powerless to help.*

30

2.9–13   Such behaviour is incredible. It does not, to Jeremiah, make any sense at all.

2.9   *Therefore I shall bring a charge against you.* The prophets quite frequently use the language of the law court, though this is not always readily recognizable in translation. They see themselves as God's advocates, bringing a case on his behalf against his people.

2.10   *Cross to the coasts and islands of Kittim.* Ancient Israelites' grasp of geography was in some ways restricted. They had a very sketchy knowledge of what lay to the west. *Kittim* is a rather imprecise term for the people of the Mediterranean islands. Here the word designates the distant West. *Kedar* similarly designates the people of the distant East. *Kedar* refers to the nomads of the eastern deserts and steppes. The prophet is saying: 'Look from one end of the world to the other and you will see nothing like this.'

2.11   *Has a nation ever exchanged its gods, and these no gods at all?* Even the idolators, thinks the prophet, are faithful to their second-rate deities. Israel cannot be faithful to her God, even though he is real. The prophet is in fact quite wrong about this. History offers numerous examples of nations and communities changing their religious allegiance.

My people have exchanged their glory for a god altogether powerless. An alternative rendering of the Hebrew would be: 'They have exchanged their wealth for what is worthless.'

2.13   offers another image expressing the prophet's incredulity at the perversity of his people's behaviour. Anyone who has ever tasted water from a water-butt will not need to be told how inferior stored, standing water is to the flowing water of a spring or stream, 'living water'. In ancient Israel many communities had to rely for a large part of the year on such stored water. But no one would actually choose water from a storage cistern if living water was available. The Israelites pile perversity on perversity: they not only reject the living water in favour of the poor alternative from the cistern, but they rely on storage cisterns that are cracked and will not hold water anyway.

There are some obscurities to us in the passage 2.14–19, but the theme of these verses seems to revolve around Egypt and slavery. Israel's history began with her deliverance from slavery in Egypt. 'To look at her now', the prophet is saying, 'you would think that that liberation had never happened.' She is still being browbeaten, and, of all things, willing to subject herself to Egyptian domination, to *make off to Egypt to drink the waters of the Nile* (2.18). There will be no joy in that, *the people of Noph and Tahpanhes will break your heads*. (For the Egyptian cities *Noph and Tahpanhes* see the note on 44.1.) For Israel to *make off to Egypt* is heavy with irony. Escaping from Egypt was the beginning of nationhood: for her to be ready to return there implies the abandonment of all she has become.

2.18 *Or why make off to Assyria?* After the battle of Carchemish in 605, at which Assyria and Egypt in alliance were very heavily defeated by the Babylonians, Assyria was no longer in contention as a world power. This oracle, therefore, seems to presuppose a date before 605. It can hardly be criticizing the policies of Josiah, since he was actually resisting an Egyptian army advancing to Assyria's aid when he was killed in 609. So perhaps it was uttered between these two events, i.e. early in the reign of Josiah's successor, Jehoiakim.

... to drink the waters of the Nile ... to drink the waters of the Euphrates. There is a link between the imagery here and that of v.13 in the preceding oracle; which is no doubt why the two oracles have been juxtaposed. Israel has rejected the living water offered by her God. She now looks to supply herself by resorting to other suppliers and other masters. We who are used to turning on taps need to remind ourselves how dependent human societies are on finding adequate and wholesome sources of water. The prophet is using an image here of something fundamental to existence. Isa. 8.6–8 plays with the same image, but in a rather different way, contrasting Jerusalem's God-given water supply in the pure and manageable spring of Gihon (which he calls 'the waters of Shiloah') with the torrent of Euphrates which can burst its banks and overwhelm all in its path.

The imagery of water and springs and cisterns is not as remote as may at first sight appear from the imagery of marriage and adultery that runs through the rest of this section of the book. Prov. 5.15–23 and 9.19 suggest that 'stolen water' may have been a conventional metaphor for infidelity, and 'drinking from one's own spring' a recognized metaphor for marital faithfulness.

2.20–28 presents us with a kaleidoscope of images. 2.20 *You shattered your yoke and snapped your traces*. The image here is of an ass or ox, seemingly domesticated, but eventually 'going wild'. Then abruptly, in the second half of the verse, we have Israel pictured *sprawled in promiscuous vice*. The two images are not unconnected. This is Israel's way of 'going wild', of rejecting her proper master. The sprawling in promiscuous vice is of course a reference to Baal worship. This worship happened at so-called 'high places', which were characteristically, though by no means invariably, on *hilltops*, and were normally surrounded by groves of sacred trees.

The temple in the ancient near east had many functions. It was a place of worship; but it was also a slaughter house, an eating place, a centre for the administration of law, a bank and a place of public assembly. And in most countries it was also a brothel. In Assyria and Babylonia the temples were major slave-owners. The male slaves worked the temple estates, the female slaves acted as prostitutes. The supply of slaves was kept up partly by donations of unwanted children. The Baal shrines of Palestine, about which we have less direct evidence, no doubt operated on a smaller scale, but the prophets' criticisms make it clear that they functioned in many of the same ways. Sexual rites were apparently regarded as part of the worship. The books of the Old Testament are full of sexual imagery employed as a metaphor for religious apostasy. The metaphor was a very obvious and appropriate one. Jeremiah makes more use than most of such imagery. It may not be altogether irrelevant to recall that Jeremiah was unmarried, not from choice, but because he believed God had imposed upon him this way of life. Is his fondness for sexual imagery prompted by his own frustrations?

There is another abrupt change of image in 2.21. Israel is a vine, apparently of good stock, but it has reverted to a wild form (again the 'going wild' theme). And once more the point is being made about Israel's perversity. She does not meet reasonable expectations. The image of Israel as the vine is a very well established one in scripture. See, e.g., Hos. 10.1, Ps. 80.8–6. Sometimes it is developed in extraordinary ways, as in Ezek. 17.1–10. The most striking development of all, in which Israel is not so much the vine as the vineyard, is in Isa. 5.1–7. The New Testament writers show equal originality in developing it; e.g. John 15, Matt. 21.33–43 and parallels, and Rom. 11.13ff (though in this last passage the vine has become an olive).

2.22   Yet another image, this time making a fresh point. Israel's guilt is ineradicable. The strongest cleansing agent cannot remove it.

The thought in 2.23 seems to follow from that of the previous verse, though the insertion of the formula *this is the word of the Lord God* suggests the beginning of a separate oracle.

How can you say, 'I am not defiled'? V.22 has just asserted that the stain is still manifest. It looks as if there was some difference of perspective between Jeremiah and his audience about what they were doing in their worship. There may have been practices which the prophet saw as baalistic but which they protested were legitimate features of Yahwism.

Look at your conduct in the valley. Another metaphor, this time of animal lust. Israel, says the prophet, is like a she-animal on heat. The point here is that Israel is out of control. Sin has taken her over and she is apparently powerless to resist it.

2.25   reverts to the figure of human lust. The passage so far, with its varied images, has told us three things about Israel's sin, as the prophet sees it: it is unreasonable and perverse; God had a right to expect better of her. It marks her with a guilt which is too deep simply to be shrugged off. And it has taken control of her. She is in its grip and cannot free herself of its power.

2.26   *So the people of Israel feel ashamed.* REB translates the tense of the verb as present. It might be better to take it as the so-called 'prophetic perfect', relating to the future. I.e., Israel will feel ashamed and embarassed when the gods she worships turn out to be no good to her in a crisis. She will appeal to her own God then, and it will serve her right if he is not interested.

2.27   ... *a block of wood* ... *a stone.* The words refer to the regular items of cultic furniture at the 'high places'. There would normally be several *mazzeboth*, or standing stones. These came in various sizes, from no more than a foot or so, up to the height of a man. There was probably only one *asherah* at each sanctuary. The *asherah* was a wooden pole, which may have originated as a stylized tree. An oddity of the text here is that elsewhere it is the stone *mazzebah* which is thought of as embodying the male principal of deity, the wooden *asherah* which represents the female. Here they are put the other way round.

The next unit runs from 2.29–2.37.

2.29   *Why argue your case with me?* Evidently they did argue. They cannot see it the prophet's way. 'What are we doing wrong?' they seem to be asking. The prophet is apparently challenging traditions and practices which they have long been accustomed to regard as acceptable. What seems to the prophet to be obviously wrong does not seem so to them.

2.30   *In vain I punished your people.* God has, says the prophet, already made attempts to bring the people to their senses by inflicting punishments on them. We are not told, however, what these punishments were (though cf. 3.3). Amos, who uses a similar argument in 4.6–11 goes into some detail about a series of disasters from which lessons have not been learnt. *Your sword devoured your prophets*. It is not easy to see how this relates to the first half of the verse. The destruction of the prophets is not one of the punishments God has inflicted on them. It is something they have done themselves. Is it implied that the prophets were killed because they were rightly interpreting the punishments? At all events, persecution of prophets in the seventh century was not unknown. There is a tradition that king Manasseh killed numbers of them, including Isaiah, though neither Kings nor Chronicles actually charges him with prophet killing (even though he did 'shed much innocent blood' – II Kings 21.16). Jer. 26.20–23 details one instance of a prophet put to death by Jehoiakim.

2.32 *Will a girl forget her finery or a bride her wedding ribbons?* Can one imagine a bride forgetting her wedding dress, or showing no interest in her ring? As incredibly as that, Israel neglects her God. Despite the fact that this chapter includes an astonishing variety of images, the figure of the marriage between God and Israel, whose hopeful beginning was recalled in 2.1–2, is the one that keeps recurring.

2.33 The prophet is saying to his people: 'Even the prostitutes could take lessons from you.' In 2.34 it is not only adultery they are accused of, but murder. Here we have the indelible stain again, but this time a blood-stain. They are guilty of the blood of the poor.

2.34 *You did not catch them housebreaking*. In ancient near eastern law a householder who killed in defence of his property could not be held guilty of murder. The people addressed here have not that excuse, or any excuse.

2.35 *You say, 'I am innocent'*. Another recurring theme: they still cannot see what they are doing wrong.

2.36 *Why do you so lightly change your course? You will be let down by Egypt as you were by Assyria*. As the Assyrian empire broke up in the second half of the seventh century and the Babylonians eventually began to take over as the leading power of the near east, the government in Judah had no firm foreign policy. They were constantly tempted to appeal to the Egyptians for support, though history offered them no encouragement. Egypt traditionally had been interested in de-stabilizing the small western Asiatic states, but had rarely been of any real help when the Mesopotamian power got tough with them. Jeremiah consistently advocated compliance with Babylonian rule.

3.1 How can Israel expect forgiveness? She has passed the point of no return. The prophet cites the curious case of a woman who is divorced, marries again, but later wishes to return to her former husband. Would such a thing be allowed? In our own society such a re-marriage does occasionally happen. We regard it as odd, and it is usually deemed worthy of mention in the newspapers, but we are not scandalized by it. Ancient Israelites apparently were scandalized.

Rather curiously, in the only place in the Pentateuch where the law of divorce is cited (Deut.24.1–4) it is cited in connection with the same, surely rather unusual, circumstance, of a previously divorced couple wishing to remarry, after an intervening second marriage by the wife. Both Deut. 24.1–4 and Jer. 3.1 use similar strong language, speaking of 'abomination' and 'uncleanness' or 'defilement'. And in both cases it is not simply the couple concerned, but the land which would be defiled if such conduct were allowed. REB translates: *Is not that woman defiled?* The Hebrew text does not say this, though the Greek Jeremiah does. The Hebrew reads: 'Would not that land be defiled?' This may seem unexpected but is almost certainly correct. Deut. 24.1–4 says that the result of such a re-marriage would be a defilement of the land, and in our present passage the very next verse (3.2) speaks of Israel defiling the land by her promiscuous behaviour. Given that Deuteronomy is generally thought of as a late seventh-century publication, one wonders whether there was perhaps some seventh-century *cause célèbre*, which prompted both Deuteronomy's law and Jeremiah's oracle. The point of all this is that according to this analogy, for God to restore his relationship with the apostate Israel is impossible. Even if she wished it, there would be a terrible impropriety about such a restoration.

3.2–5   is probably placed here precisely because v.2 picks up the theme of behaviour that defiles the land. 3.3 reverts to the argument of 2.30. The country has suffered drought (they defiled the land, so the land was afflicted) but the people have not interpreted this as discipline. They have brazenly persisted in their behaviour. Eventually, of course, though at this point the prophet does not spell it out, those who persist in defiling the land will lose the land.

You were resolved to show no shame. This confirms the picture we are building up, of a total difference in perspective between prophet and people. They behave in ways that he finds disgusting and embarassing, but which they regard as normal and acceptable.

3.4   *Not so long since you called me 'Father'.* One occasionally hears it said that the idea that God is our Father is peculiarly Christian. This is, of course, nonsense. The concept of God as 'father' is a commonplace in a wide variety of religions. The Canaanites, about whose religion Jeremiah and the other prophets are so scathing, not only worshipped Baal, but also a high god called El, one of whose regular titles is 'Father of gods and men'. He is also, incidentally, regularly described as 'El the kindly and the merciful', and is said to have created the world. 'Baal', which is not a name but a title, 'The Lord' (his actual name was Hadad) is the divine son of this divine father. 'The Lord' fought a battle with Death, and seemed to have been defeated. He descended into Hades. But eventually he rose again from the dead, was restored to his place in heaven, and lives to give life to his people and to his land. The Canaanites' faith bears witness to the conviction that the world cannot be saved, except a god should die. When the prophets spoke of Baal-worship they seized on its uncongenial aspects and condemned it. But not everything in Baal-worship is to be despised.

'Father' in Old Testament usage is a title of respect. In II Kings 6.21 the king addresses Elisha the prophet as 'My father', and in II Kings 2.12 Elisha himself applies the same title to his master Elijah.

3.6–11 Though it is written in the first person and is thus presented as the words of Jeremiah himself, this little prose section is regarded by many commentators as not being by Jeremiah at all. The doubts are based mainly on the language, which is said to reflect later Hebrew usage. It pursues the imagery of apostasy/adultery which preoccupies the preceding verses, so we can see why it is placed in this context. It can also be readily seen as a prose introduction to the poetic oracle in 3.12–13. One of its oddities is that it uses the name 'Israel' in the restrictive sense, to designate the Northern Kingdom, not the whole nation, which is not the sense it normally bears in the book of Jeremiah.

There are strong similarities between Jer. 3.6–11 and ch.23 of the book of Ezekiel. These are so close that the two cannot possibly be independent of each other. If 3.6–11 is really by Jeremiah then Ezekiel presumably used Jeremiah's words as the jumping off point for his own work. This would not be surprising, as Ezekiel quite often seems to do exactly this, taking up an idea or image briefly alluded to in Jeremiah and developing it at greater length. If, on the other hand, 3.6–11 is not by Jeremiah, then the borrowing must be in the other direction, and the passage must be based on Ezek. 23 and have been added to the book of Jeremiah at a later stage.

Israel and Judah are spoken of separately, as two sisters, in the same manner as Ezek. 23. Both sisters are clearly being thought of as wives of the Lord. Both are described as committing adultery and 'not coming back to' their divine partner. The implication is that what is being envisaged is a polygamous marriage.

3.8   *I have put apostate Israel away and given her a certificate of divorce.* This is a reference back to the events of 722/1 when Northern Israel was destroyed by the Assyrians. It is a common theme among the prophets that Judah should have learned from this warning example, but did not.

3.10   *In spite of all this, Judah, that faithless woman, has not come back to me in sincerity, out only in pretence.* Is this a reference to Josiah's reforms? Is it an indication that the prophet, or whoever composed the passage, was not impressed by what Josiah seemed to have achieved?

3.11   *Apostate Israel is less to blame than that faithless woman Judah.* What the Hebrew literally says is that 'Apostate Israel is more righteous than faithless Israel.' But in biblical Hebrew 'righteous' is a comparative and formal status. The word is basically a legal word, and in a court of law the litigant in whose favour judgment is given may be only marginally less blame-worthy than his opponent: nevertheless he is declared *tsaddiq*, 'righteous'. This does not necessarily mean that he is free from blame, only that he is less guilty than his antagonist. Something similar is true in most legal systems. In English usage for someone to be declared 'not guilty' does not mean that he is not at fault, only that nothing has been proved against him. 'Not guilty' does not mean free of blame, but free of any legal penalty. REB's translation, though not a literal one, exactly represents the meaning.

3.12–18   *Proclaim this message towards the north.* There had been no independent state of Northern Israel for over a hundred years. It had simply been a province of the Assyrian empire, and those whom the Assyrians had deported from it never returned. But of course it was still an identifiable area of the country and there is little doubt that one of the aims of Josiah's policies was to extend his control over the North and to re-unify the country as in the days of David and Solomon. For the prophet to offer a way back to a repentant Northern Israel was therefore, perhaps, a timely thing to do.

The phrase *apostate Israel* is a linking phrase which holds these short passages together. It appears in vv.12–13, on the one hand, and in the preceding prose passage of vv.6–11. The same phrase introduces the next section, vv.14–18, which is also in prose.

3.14–18   These verses seem to be speaking of a return from exile.

It is not clear to whom they are addressed. The words about the ark of the covenant in v.16 make it unlikely that they are meant for Northerners, since the ark was a Jerusalemite object of reverence. It is widely agreed that the prophet Jeremiah is unlikely to be responsible for this passage in its present form.

3.15 *There I shall give them shepherds after my own heart.* Ezekiel elaborates this theme in Ezek. 34. See especially 34.11–31.

3.16 *No one will speak any more of the Ark of the Covenant of the Lord; no one will think of it or remember it or resort to it.* The ark was a very ancient holy object, whose construction was said to go back to the wilderness period. It was basically a wooden box. It is said to have contained the tablets of stone with the ten commandments engraved on them. In the settlement period it seems to have been seen as the symbol of unity of the tribes, and was housed in the tabernacle, the national tent sanctuary (which did not always remain in the same place). Around the time of the beginning of the kingdom it was carried into battle when there was a war. I Sam 4.1–11 makes it sound as if this was exceptional, but II Sam 11.11 suggests that the use of the ark in warfare was routine.

After the building of the temple the ark was kept in the Holy of Holies, the innermost room of the sanctuary, flanked by two cherubim (probably winged bulls) carved out of olive wood. God is sometimes spoken of as 'enthroned between the cherubim', i.e. on or above the ark. This throne language, however, must be a later interpretation of the ark's significance, for there is nothing throne-shaped about its construction. In Jer. 3.17 this idea seems to be alluded to. The ark will no longer be needed as the Lord's throne, for the whole city will be the Lord's throne.

We are never explicitly told that the ark disappeared at the time of the Babylonian conquest in 586, but we have to assume so, since in the second temple the Holy of Holies was empty.

The precise significance of the ark is difficult to be sure about. Its significance may indeed have been seen differently at different periods, or by different people. But it is probably safe to say that it stood for the Lord's presence. When in I Sam. 4.21f. the ark is captured by the Philistines it is said that 'The glory has departed'. Now this glory (*kabod* in Hebrew) is identified with the real presence of the deity.

According to Jer. 3.16, however historic the ark may be, God's people will learn to do without it. No material symbol of the divine presence is indispensable. One of the biggest questions which Israel and her prophets had to face at the time of the exile was: What are the indispensables? What are the indispensables of faith, without which we could not go on believing in God any more; without which we would not be the people of God any more? What are the things without which we could not go on being ourselves any more; without which we would no longer be 'Israel'? Can we do without an ark? Can we get by without cherubim? Do we need a temple, or sacrifices, or a priesthood? Do we have to have a holy city? Can we cope without a king, and without our independence? Do we need a land to call our own?

At the exile Israel, faced with the loss of almost everything, found that the indispensables were fewer than she had thought. She needed her history, the story of what God had done for her. If we are to have a future, we need to know our past. If we are not sure where we are going, it becomes terribly important to know where we have come from. She needed the law, to remind her of what God required of her. And she needed her prophets, to interpret all these things to her, and to help her work out her priorities; to help her to see what mattered, and what did not.

We need to be aware that before the prophets' words ever came to be written down they had to be remembered. There was, for all the prophets at least before Ezekiel and Deutero-Isaiah, an oral phase in the transmission of the material. When people are recalling oral material their memories are triggered by catchwords. The key word in one oracle will recall another oracle in which the same word figures. An image may act in the same way. We have already seen several examples of this in the material we have considered so far. The links on to which the memory fastens are not always similarities of content, subject matter or meaning. They may be accidental or superficial features of the material concerned.

3.19–20   looks like a distinct short oracle. It is linked with its context by the way its wistful phrase *You would call me 'Father', I thought*, recalls the similar one in 3.4. Likewise 3.20 again uses the metaphor of the adulterous wife which runs repeatedly through these chapters.

All the prophets learned from each other. Either they pick up ideas and images from each other and develop them in different ways, or the people who edited the prophetic books deliberately highlighted similarities of theme and echoes of language. Jeremiah's language about God as Israel's father strongly recalls the image which is so prominent in Hosea. Cf., e.g., Hos. 11.1–4.

3.21–25   What is probably happening here is that the prophet listens to the noises of worship coming from the 'high place' and in his own mind reinterprets them. *Weeping is heard on the bare places*, i.e. 'the bare heights' where the *bamah* would be. The weeping (which was probably loud and vociferous) would actually be the ritual weeping for the dead Baal as he lost his yearly battle with the god of the underworld and the vegetation died in consequence. The prophet hears it as a weeping of contrition, wishing upon his people a repentance they did not in fact own.

The word *apostate people* in v.22 is probably the catch-word that accounts for the oracle's position here. Cf. vv.8, 11, 12, 14.

The repentance which the prophet wishes upon his people is spelled out in vv.22b–25. In his imagination they recognize the futility of *clamour on the heights*. In 3.24 REB reads *Baal* where the Hebrew text has *bosheth*, 'shame'. The two words are associated closely in the Old Testament and are often treated as if they were interchangeable.

Baal was supposed to be the giver of fertility, the donor of the rain, the lord of the harvest. 'Quite the reverse!' Jeremiah is saying: 'We have wasted the best of our harvests and of our livestock in offering sacrifices to him.'

The reference to *sons and daughters* may be a reference to human sacrifice, though the offering of human sacrifices to Baal was not, as far as we know, normal. It could be a reference to the dedication of children as slaves to the sanctuary. 3.25 *Let us lie down in our shame*. Again, shame is projected on to the people by the prophet himself. In reality they feel no shame at the sexual rites in which they engage.

4.1–2 may be a continuation of the same oracle. If in reality Israel were to turn and repent this is what it would mean: first a religious conversion, turning away from *your loathsome idols*; second, a moral conversion to value *truth, justice, and uprightness*.

Then the nations will pray to be blessed like you. This looks like a reference to the covenant with the patriarchs (cf. Gen. 18.18, 22.18, 26.4, 28.14). Such references are actually rather rare in the prophets.

4.3a *These are the words of the Lord to the people of Judah and Jerusalem.* This may be intended as a heading not for the oracle which immediately follows, but for the whole collection which begins with v.5. If so, the heading has been slightly displaced, since most commentators take 4.3b–4 as ending the previous collection.

4.3b–4 *Your ground that lies unploughed.* The Hebrew word used here (*nir*) is a rare one and we are unsure as to whether it refers to fallow ground or to virgin soil. REB carefully chooses a translation that leaves the question open. Ploughing was done in the autumn, after the autumn rains softened the ground. Ancient ploughs did not efficiently turn over the soil, like modern ones. They merely broke it up in preparation for sowing. The ploughing was expected, however, to deter weeds.

Up to now the prophet has spoken of the people's conversion as a return, a turning back to their former loyalty. Here he presents it differently, as 'breaking new ground' and giving an allegiance to God never previously truly given. The interpretation of *nir* as 'virgin soil' fits this sense better, and fits better the parallel image of circumcision in v.4. To be circumcised is what one does (as a Jew) when one first expresses one's belonging to the God of Israel. The required 'circumcision of the heart', i.e. of mind and will, of which the prophet speaks, implies that any earlier circumcision had not been genuine. Carroll, in his commentary, notes that the image of the people as unacceptable to God because not properly circumcised is picturing them, collectively, as a male. The image of the people as abhorrent to God because of sexual promiscuity pictures them, collectively, as female. He rightly observes that scripture is fairly even-handed in its use of male and female images, whether these are used positively or negatively.

4.4   *Or the fire of my fury may blaze up and burn unquenched.* The *thorns* which are causing the problem at the end of v.3 may not be the new green ones which will compete with the crop, but the dried remains of the old ones from the previous year, which can cover the field in autumn, and which may threaten the new crop by catching fire. That fire starting in thorns was a recognized risk is illustrated by Ex. 22.6, Judg. 9.15, Ps. 118.12; cf. Isa.9.18ff and 10.17–19. Thorns are very combustible and are several times referred to as being used for kindling (Ps. 58.9, Eccles. 7.6, Isa. 32.12). The writer has himself seen whole hillsides in Galilee burning out of control in the dry summer, having been accidentally set ablaze.

4.4   concludes the initial major unit, which has described the call of Jeremiah and then set out a series of accusations, largely couched in terms of the imagery of sexual infidelity, but betraying little sign that the prophet expected any imminent consequences of the people's behaviour. For this reason it has been common to see this collection as reflecting Jeremiah's message during the early part of his ministry, i.e. in the reign of Josiah.

Threats of imminent destruction
4.5–6.50

4.5–6.30 From 4.5 a second major group of oracles begins. Where, precisely, it should be regarded as ending is more debatable, but the likeliest finishing point is the end of chapter 6. Most of the oracles in these three next chapters have in common the fact that they are addressed to Judah and Jerusalem and have as their theme the imminent doom of the city. Though no specific date is indicated we may reasonably guess that most of them come from a period late in the reign of Jehoiakim when the Babylonian attack was expected fairly shortly. Throughout most of this section the note of urgency is unmistakable. Most of the oracles focus on the threat of an 'enemy from the north'. Within the section it is not always clear where individual oracles begin and end, and commentators and editors differ.

4.5–9 offers an alarming picture of imminent attack by the invader. When such an attack was anticipated the people living in the villages and the countryside would crowd into the cities, taking with them whatever they could save. Within the city they would hope to withstand any siege. What was outside was simply abandoned to the enemy.

4.7 recalls the experience of the nation a century earlier, in the time of Isaiah, when the Assyrians ravaged not only the country areas, but one by one the lesser cities of Judah, leaving only Zion 'like a shed in an allotment' (Isa. 1.8).

Compare Jer. 8.14 where the move to the city is not undertaken with much conviction. If even the fortified cities were not felt to be secure, and people had no confidence that they could withstand a siege, then instead of streaming into the cities they would flee in the opposite direction, to the mountains and to the wilderness, hoping to hide in caves and holes in the rocks. This is the picture in Jer 4.29 and in Mark 13.14ff.

4.8 Impending disaster would be met by demonstrations of grief and appeals to God. Much of this would of course be spontaneous, but there may also have been formalized rites for such occasions. One way of understanding the book of Joel, for instance, is to see it as a liturgy designed for just such times of disaster.

4.9 The failure of the leadership. The three principal institutions which hold society together will lose their nerve in the coming crisis; the king and governing authorities; the priesthood, and the prophets.

None of them will have any answers, or be able to cope with the catastrophe.

4.10 This single verse looks like an isolated brief oracle. *You surely deceived this people … in promising peace.* When did the Lord promise peace? This is very likely a reference to the words of the false prophets, who say 'Peace, peace', when there is no peace (6.14, 8.11), and whose word has been accepted as the Lord's word.

I said: Ah, Lord God … Some manuscripts of the Greek Jeremiah read 'They said …', thus putting the words not into the mouth of Jeremiah but of the deceived leaders. This makes easier sense but is not necessarily therefore correct. The problem of interpreting 4.10 is bound up with the larger problem of false prophecy, which is a very important one in the book of Jeremiah.

Why is God being credited here with the words of the false prophets? If they were false, surely it was not his message but theirs? But, difficult as it may be for us to accept, some Old Testament writers explain false prophecy not as prophecy which was uninspired by God or dreamt up by the prophets themselves, but as false messages which God deliberately put into their mouths. This is spelled out explicitly in I Kings 22 where the Lord allows a 'lying spirit' to mislead his prophets. And Jeremiah himself contemplates the possibility that God has given him a false message to proclaim (e.g. 20.7ff). The question of false prophecy is pursued elsewhere in this volume.

4.11–12 *A scorching wind from the desert heights …* The prevailing winds in Israel are from the west and come across the Mediterranean. Just occasionally an easterly wind blows, which comes across hundreds of miles of desert and is hot, dry and extremely unpleasant. A good wind was useful, indeed necessary, in order to winnow the cereal crops. The barley or wheat was taken to the threshing floor, an open space, often on a hilltop, and thrown into the air with shovels. The chaff was swept away by the wind while the denser grain fell back to earth (cf. Ps. 1.4). But the oracle here threatens *a wind too strong* for this; a wind which will sweep away chaff and grain alike.

In scripture there are two different pictures used of divine judgment. There is the judgment which is discriminatory, which punishes the wicked but saves the innocent. And there is the terrible judgment which sweeps away everything that is before it.

4.13–14 Another fragment describing an advancing army, and ending in an appeal for repentance and reform; … *and you may yet be saved.* The rest of the context suggests that it is rather too late for that. Might this be a fragment of just such a 'liturgy for times of terror' as was referred to above?

4.15–18 The passage pictures the news of the invader's progress filtering through from the localities to the north. Compare the more detailed picture of such a progress given in Isa. 10.27–32. *Dan* was the most northerly city of Israel and would encounter the trouble first. *Mount Ephraim* was the highland area south of the plain of Esdraelon. An army which had reached this region was ominously close to Jerusalem itself.

4.19–22 *Oh, how I writhe in anguish* ... Who is the speaker here? We might most naturally assume that the prophet is speaking, but some interpreters understand the speaker to be the nation, or the city of Jerusalem. Perhaps we could have it both ways and suggest that the prophet is speaking, but on the people's behalf, expressing an anguish which is both his and theirs. 4.22 seems to be an appended comment. If the prophet is still the speaker then he detaches himself from the people and blames the disaster on their own folly.

4.23–28 is a passage of almost apocalyptic flavour, representing the coming catastrophe not so much as a national one as a cosmic one.

4.23 *I looked at the earth, and it was chaos.* The Hebrew expression used here is the same as is applied in Gen. 1.2 to the pre-existent chaos before God began his creative work. The author of 4.23–28 sees the threatened disaster as a reversal of the creative process, an undoing of the work of God. This theme is pursued throughout the passage.

... *at the heavens, and their light was gone.* God's first creative act according to Gen 1 was the making of the light. Now he is unmaking it.

4.24 ... *at the mountains, and they were reeling.* Other Old Testament passages about creation (other than Gen. 1, that is) speak of God 'establishing' or 'making firm' the mountains, whose foundations go down into the primæval waters (e.g. Ps. 65.6, cf. Prov. 8.25). The prophet sees these firmest elements of God's creation becoming unstable.

4.25 *I looked: no one was there.* REB is a little weak here. The Hebrew suggests something altogether more portentous. 'I looked – No human race!'

All the birds of heaven had taken wing. The birds which, since the first Thursday of creation God had ordained to 'fly above the earth across the vault of the heavens' (Gen. 1.20) have disappeared.

4.26   *I looked: the fertile land was wilderness.* The earth, which since the first Tuesday had 'produced growing things; plants bearing their own kind of seed and trees bearing fruit' (Gen. 1.12) had reverted to barrenness.

4.27   *And I shall make an end of it.* The sentence is extremely ambiguous. Some translate 'And I shall not make a full end.' But this, in the context, simply contradicts everything the passage is saying. Holladay suggests in his commentary a different vocalization of the Hebrew and translates: 'And none of it I shall remake.' This is an attractive suggestion.

'In the beginning God created the heavens and the earth' (Gen. 1.1). That is all there was. Now it is all there is. The rest of creation stage by stage has been dismantled. All that is left is the heaven and the earth themselves, left to mourn the undoing of the work of God.

Perhaps the fundamental ambiguity of v.27 is a deliberate one. It uses the same verb as in Gen. 2.2. There it says that God 'finished all his work'. Now once more he says of his creation: 'It is finished'.

4.29   looks like a new departure, and some commentators take the verse as beginning the next section, not as following on from the previous poem about the reversal of creation. Its subject, however, is still the terror of the coming invasion. An earlier oracle in 4.5 spoke of the people fleeing to the fortified cities. 4.29, more terrifyingly, is speaking of them fleeing from the cities. The fortifications are not expected to hold back the enemy, so the cities are left empty and their populations prefer to take their chance in *the thickets* or *up among the crags.*

4.30–31   A rather abrupt change of focus. We now revert to an image common in the prophets, especially Jeremiah himself, Ezekiel and Hosea, picturing the nation as a woman who has flirted with the heathen empires, her lovers, but who finds that when she needs their support they not only fail to look after her (Hos. 1.5–7) but turn on her and destroy her (Ezek. 16.35ff., 23.22ff.).

4.30   *And you, what are you doing? When you dress yourself in scarlet, deck yourself out with gold ornaments, and enlarge your eyes with antimony, you are beautifying yourself to no purpose. Your lovers spurn you and seek your life.* McKane thinks that what is at issue is the nation's lack of realism, like a woman dressing up as for a party, when what she is really facing is her death. This is a comment that curiously recalls the story in II Kings 9.30 of the death of Jezebel, who, at the approach of the avenging Jehu 'made up her eyes and did her hair'.

The difference, of course, is that Jezebel knew what was coming to her. Judah, seated at her dressing table, does not know, or will not hear, that the Babylonians are advancing, driving furiously.

4.32 A sharp and deliberate contrast of images. The woman glamorizing herself to meet her lovers gives way to the picture of a woman in severe distress in childbirth. It is not clearly stated, but we may be meant to understand that it is also her death-bed.

5.1 *Search through her wide squares.* In the story of the atrocity at Gibeah (Judg. 19) the travelling levite finds no hospitality in Gibeah, and prepares to spend the night in the town square. But there, in the square, an old man coming home from work sees him and invites him in. In Gen. 18 there is a famous argument between Abraham and the Lord. How many righteous people would it take for the Lord to spare a wicked and condemned city? Fifty? Forty-five? Thirty? Twenty? Ten? 'Even for the sake of ten', says the Lord, 'I will not destroy it.' Abraham dares beat the Lord down no further. But in the event, when the destroying angels get to Sodom, there is no question of finding even ten. They too, like the levite at Gibeah, camp out in the town square. There, in the square, they find the one righteous man, Lot. Even in atrocious Gibeah and lawless Sodom, Jeremiah is saying, one righteous person could be found, in the square. But in the squares of Jerusalem? Not even one.

5.1–6 This little passage illustrates how hard it is sometimes to arrive at a precise understanding of the text. If we keep asking the questions, who is speaking and who is being addressed, there are a number of points in these few verses in which the answers are far from certain. In v.1 the speaker is evidently the Lord, but to whom is he speaking? Not to Jeremiah, certainly, for in the Hebrew the verbs are all plural. Perhaps we do not need to ask. Nobody is actually being expected to undertake this piece of research. It is the prophet's way of asserting that if anyone were to make such a search the result would be entirely negative. In vv.3–5 it is definitely the prophet speaking, but is v.2 part of his speech, or the end of the Lord's? And who is the speaker in v.6? Most commentators assume that this is the Lord's reply, but this is far from certain. It is reassuring that these uncertainties do not prevent us from understanding the main thrust of what the prophet is saying.

5.4–5 *I said, 'After all, these are the poor, these are folk without under-standing,* the lower classes: one can't expect too much of them. *I shall go to the great ones and speak with them.'* The tone is of course ironic. The prophet represents himself as rather pathetically expecting a better reception from society's leaders. Elsewhere he focusses on the leaders as the very ones who encourage apostasy, e.g. 2.8.

5.5 *But they too have broken the yoke and snapped their traces.* Reverting to an image used in 2.20.

5.6 ... *a lion* ... *a wolf* ... *a leopard* ... In biblical times there were still plenty of wild animals, including predatory ones, in western Asia. These were not normally much of a threat in settled areas, at least to human beings, though they were an active threat to livestock. (See, e.g., I Sam. 17.34–37, II Kings 2.23f., Amos 3.12.) But any disaster which reduced the human population was likely to see wild animals not only increasing but moving into settled or even urban areas (II Kings 17.24f.). This is the situation at which v.6 is hinting. See also the note on Jer. 49.19–20. *A leopard will prowl.* The verb here translated *prowl* is more literally rendered 'to watch'. It is the same verb (*shoqed*) as appears in 1.12, where the Lord says he is 'on the watch to carry out my threat'. Anyone who has seen a cat stalking prey will recognize the fearsome intensity of that 'watching'.

5.7–11 The imagery here echoes the prevailing theme of the previous section (1.1–4.4), accusing the people of religious apostasy under the figure of adultery and (as in v.8) animal lust.

The formula in v.11, *this is the word of the Lord,* seems designed to indicate the end of the oracle. If this is so, then the next oracle runs from vv.12–14. The paragraphing in REB suggests that its editors analysed the passage differently. If vv.12–14 do belong together v.13 is crucial to their interpretation; *The prophets will prove mere wind; the word is not in them.* Is this part of the people's speech? If so, it refers to Jeremiah and other prophets like him, who prophesied doom. The people are saying, 'They are windbags. We needn't take their threats seriously.' Alternatively, v.13 may be read as part of Jeremiah's own speech, in which case it refers to the prophets who prophesy 'Peace, peace'. These prophets, Jeremiah would then be saying, have misled the people and encouraged their complacency.

5.15–17 is a threat of foreign conquest. The oracle is typical in its content of the material in this section. It is characteristic of oracular speech to express such threats in oblique terms, not explicitly identifying the anticipated aggressor. In its form this passage is a very strongly rhythmic little poem, structured around the word 'nation' four times repeated, and prominently stressed, in v.15. This balances the four times repeated and similarly stressed 'devour' in v.17. REB does not clearly bring out this structure, at least in v.15. The effect in Hebrew is like hammering.

Any reader who doubts the interdependence of the book of Jeremiah and that of Deuteronomy may read and compare with the present passage Deut. 28.49ff. The Deuteronomy passage is a prose equivalent, but as powerfully terrifying as the Jeremianic parallel.

5.18–19   This is a prose comment, from the exilic period, asserting (after the event) that the destruction was not, after all, total, and attempting to explain why the exile happened.

5.20–25   The Lord is evidently the speaker here, and he is addressing unspecified hearers, who in their turn are directed to pass on his message to the *people of Jacob*. A reader of the English translation might naturally assume that the Lord was speaking to the prophet, but this cannot be, because in the Hebrew the verbs are plural. In v.25 the Lord seems to forget his original audience of intermediaries and addresses the people directly. The thinking of this passage has much in common with that of the wisdom writers. It is addressed to *foolish and senseless people*, in the hope that they will learn. But there is a kind of foolishness that cannot learn or will not learn, the foolishness which is perversity. People of this kind *have eyes and see nothing, ears and hear nothing*.

'The wise' believed that nature taught its own lessons, and that they were obvious to anyone who had the sense to read them. To be wise and to be virtuous (they acknowledged little distinction between the two) was to live in accordance with the natural order. This natural order was a moral order and a divine order. It is the order of the creator, who made and who sustains the universe, and *who gives the rains of autumn and spring showers in their turn*. But Israel neither perceives this order nor lives by it.

5.22   cites one (classic) example of God's power. He confines the sea to its limits. The sea in ancient mythology is the archetype of chaos and disorder. That God can rule and restrain it is the greatest tribute to his power and order-making capacity. Only God can impose rules on the sea (Job 38.8–11). The question in Mark 4.41, 'Who then is this, that even the winds and the sea obey him?' can only have one possible answer.

Job 38.8–11 illustrates the thinking. The ancients had not articulated the principles of hydrodynamics. They observed the sea perpetually throwing its waves against the land, sometimes violently, as if determined to sweep all before them. Why didn't they? The line of sand that marked the sea's edge was obviously too insubstantial to be a barrier. It must simply be a marker, beyond which God had commanded the waves not to pass. In Gen. 1.9f. he had given it, the sea, its instructions. But Israel do not learn the obvious lessons of nature. The ocean is turbulent, but it knows where to stop. *Its waves may heave and toss, but they are powerless.* But Israel's turbulence knows no stopping place.

5.23–24   If God ever does appear to falter in maintaining the regularity of nature it is because human sin and wickedness have disrupted things. *Your wrongdoing has upset nature's order, and your sins have kept away her bounty.* The theme of this section, 4.5–6.30, viz., the threat of imminent military attack, is lost sight of in this oracle, which seems to hint at a famine due not to invasion but to natural causes.

5.26–29   *For among my people there are scoundrels.* The word *For* seems to link these verses with what precedes, though some commentators treat them as an independent oracle. In content the verses are an expansion of v.25.

5.26   *Like fowlers.* An image common in the wisdom writings. The unscrupulous ensnare their fellows with deep-laid plots.

5.27   *Their houses are full of fraud, as a cage is full of birds.* Some interpreters punctuate differently, and read 'Like a cage full of birds they grow great and rich.' This sees the cage of birds as a cage in which birds are fattened. The scoundrels become *sleek and bloated.* In biblical times to be fat was regarded as desirable and enviable. The fat person was advertising his prosperity, demonstrating that he could afford to eat and to over-eat; cf. Ps. 73.4. The poor advertised their poverty by being thin.

5.30–31   These two verses do not link naturally with what immediately precedes, but rather take up the theme of vv. 12–13, a common one in Jeremiah. The prophets, who are supposed to keep the nation on the true path, actively mislead them and prophesy *sheqer*, 'what is false'.

5.31   *The priests are in league with them.* The word translated by REB as *are in league with* is obscure, but the overall sense is clear enough. The prophets mislead, and the other class of religious leaders, the priests, do nothing to counteract their influence, but join them in their errors.

6.1–8   This unit is defined by the formula with which it begins, and by the fact that the formula in v.9 introduces a new oracle. Attack is imminent, *calamity looms from the north.*

6.6   *Cut down the trees of Jerusalem.* In Deut.20.19 Israel's own rules of warfare forbid the cutting down of an enemy's trees during a siege. Trees take a very long time to replace, and clearly it was felt that to cut down trees was going too far, even in war. But Jerusalem's trees are to be hewn down. This is total, unforgiving warfare. The trees would be used either as fuel, or, more likely, for the making of such things as siege towers and protective shielding for the attackers.

Cast up siege-ramps against her. There were various methods of forcing a way into a fortified city. Besiegers could tunnel under the walls; breach them with battering rams; bring up portable towers on wheels, which allowed the attackers to get on a level with the top of the walls; or, a very common method, they could laboriously pile up earth against the wall until there was a ramp up which the attackers could charge. A famous Roman siege ramp at Masada near the Dead Sea is still visible.

6.7 The well of fresh water is nearly always an image of virtue and healthfulness. See, e.g., Prov. 10.11, 16.22, 18.4. Here, unusually, it is used negatively. Contrast Jesus' words in John 4.14.

6.9–12 Another threat, emphasizing the thoroughness of the destruction to come. This answers the thoroughness of the people's disaffection.

6.9 *Glean like a vine the remnant of Israel.* The figure of gleaning conveys the totality of the calamity. Just as the gleaner in the vineyard makes it his or her business to remove every last grape, leaving nothing worth picking, so there will be little left of Israel.

6.10 *Who will hear me? Their ears are blocked.* The prophet here speaks in the first person, on a theme common in the prophetic writings; cf Isa. 6.9ff. and Ezekiel's Watchman parable in Ezek. 3 and 33.

Their ears are blocked. The Hebrew is literally 'their ears are uncircumcised', i.e. covered, not ready to be put to their proper use.

6.11 *But I am full of the anger of the Lord, I cannot hold it back.* The people's scorn for the word of the Lord in v.10 is matched in v.11 by his wrath against them, transmitted to his prophet. The image is a telling one, of the prophet bursting with the indignation within him. But it is not his indignation; the indignation of an insignificant man, whom everybody ignores. It is the potent indignation of the Lord of hosts. When that indignation bursts out, it will sweep away children, young people, mature people, old people, women and men. The list of classes is determinedly comprehensive.

6.12 All that is closest to people's hearts they will be deprived of; homes, land and marriage partners; the conquerors will appropriate all three.

I shall raise my hand. Literally, 'I shall stretch out my hand'. For the 'stretched out hand' as a signal of judgment see Isa 9.8–10.4, where it appears in a four times repeated refrain.

6.13–15   The judgment is to be comprehensive, as we have heard in the previous oracle, because the corruption is comprehensive. The whole of society, *high and low*, is 'on the make'. The religious leaders, prophets and priests, are singled out for criticism because they are the ones who should have given a lead in a better direction. This oracle appears in almost identical form in 8.10–12.

6.14   These religious leaders do not appreciate the gravity of the situation. Society's ills are serious. They offer sticking plasters. They are guilty above all of complacency and encouraging complacency. They say, *'All is well'. All well? Nothing is well!* The words are two-edged. They suggest that the leaders are uncritical of the situation in front of them. ('There is nothing wrong.') And naively unaware of the consequences that threaten to engulf them. ('There's nothing to worry about.')

6.16–21   is a prose oracle which begins with two images expressing the people's wrong-headedness. They ignore the good roads and decline to travel by the established routes: they also refuse to pay attention to the watchmen appointed to warn them of danger. This second image, so briefly mentioned here, is taken up and expanded in Ezek. 3 and 33.

6.19   *I am about to bring ruin on them, the fruit of all their scheming.* The coming disaster is at the same time something which God inflicts on his people and something which they have brought upon themselves. *For they have given no heed to my words and have spurned my instruction.* The word translated *instruction* is the one usually translated as 'law' (torah). Such appeal to law or torah is, in the pre-exilic prophets, surprisingly uncommon.

6.20   *Your whole-offerings are not acceptable to me, your sacrifices do not please me.* Most of the pre-exilic prophets make comparable statements about the uselessness of conventional worship. Neither incense nor sacrifice is of any value. Cf. Jer. 7.22, Amos 5.25, Hos. 6.6, Isa. 1.11–15.

6.22–26   Another oracle referring explicitly to an 'enemy from the north'. The prospect of attack by this dread enemy does not arouse people to resistance but only to panic and despair. Curiously, in 50.41–43 the same oracle is delivered against Babylon.

6.27–30   It is unusual, though not unique, for a prophet to use the imagery of metal refining. The mention of *copper and iron* in v.28 rather confuses the issue. The rest of the oracle offers us a consistent picture of the refining of silver. Silver normally occurs as a minor component of the ore of lead. There are two stages in the process of refining. First the ore had to be reduced to metal, which at this stage would be mostly lead, with a small admixture of silver. Second, the lead had to be laboriously burned away until something like pure silver was left. At various stages the metal had to be tested to assess how the refining was progressing and the end product was tested again to confirm that it was reasonably pure. The process was not always successful and sometimes the sample ended by being thrown away. The prophet is compared to the assayer or tester, who in this case decides that the operation has been a failure and the residue should be written off.

Jeremiah's temple speech and associated prophecies
7.1–8.3

Chapter 7 needs to be discussed in close conjunction with chapter 26. The two chapters look like separate accounts of the same happening, the delivery of a speech (or sermon) by Jeremiah in the temple precincts. Some commentators treat the two accounts quite separately, but to regard them as independent narratives strains credulity more than to see them as alternative reports of the same occasion. Though they differ in their perspective, there are no significant factual discrepancies between the two narratives, and the key words of the prophet's address are the same in both. It is very clear, however, that in the two cases the reasons for telling the story are quite different.

Whoever is telling the chapter 7 version of the story is interested primarily in what Jeremiah said, i.e. in the content of the speech. Apart from the first two verses, which tell us that the prophet was commanded by God to *stand at the gate of the Lord's house* and proclaim his message there, there is no real 'story' at all; no narrative; only a record of what Jeremiah is supposed to have said. We are not told how his message was received, or what people's reaction to it was, or even whether anybody actually stopped to listen. Nothing is said of how the prophet ended, or if any consequences followed. Indeed, the speech is left so far 'hanging in the air' that it is not immediately obvious where we are to regard it as ending. (It should probably be understood to end with v.15.)

In chapter 26, by contrast, the content of the speech is given in a very brief summary in a mere three verses (26.4–6). The memorable part of the speech seems to have been Jeremiah's threat, on the Lord's behalf, that 'I shall do to this house as I did to Shiloh' (26.6). He is reported as saying the same, a little more expansively, in 7.12–14. What interests the storyteller of ch.26 most is how people reacted to what they heard. Most of the chapter is spent on an account of how Jeremiah was put on trial for 'prophesying against this city' (26.11); and we have a fairly detailed summary of the arguments used by both the prosecution and the defence. In ch.26 the story is rounded off by an indication of the outcome of the trial.

It is evident that the delivery of the temple speech made a major impact. It may have been something of a landmark in Jeremiah's career, and for all we know, may have been the incident that first brought him to public attention. It aroused serious opposition, and put the prophet at risk of his life. It looks as if the part of the speech which stuck in people's minds, and which formed the substance of the charges against him at his trial, was the threat that 'this house will become like Shiloh'.

Chapters 7 and 26 together allow us a fascinating insight into the way the prophetic tradition could take the same basic material and handle it in quite different ways in order to highlight different issues and to proclaim different, though related, messages. Though there are no significant discrepancies between the two accounts, they complement each other extraordinarily well.

7.1 *This word came from the Lord to Jeremiah.* In ch.7 no date is indicated, but 26.1 says that these things happened 'at the beginning of the reign of Jehoiakim', i.e., probably 609 or 608. If Jeremiah's call really did take place in 626 (as 1.2 asserts) then at the time of the delivery of the temple address Jeremiah had been prophesying for nearly twenty years.

7.2 *Stand at the gate of the Lord's house.* In 26.2 Jeremiah is commanded to 'stand in the court of the Lord's house'. Ancient near eastern cities were cramped and crowded places with few or no public open spaces. The temple mount in Jerusalem was an exception. It was the obvious place for a public speech or any public gathering or demonstration. The visitor to old Jerusalem today finds the temple mount a large, almost rectangular area, the size of several football fields. This is the temple area as defined by Herod the Great in his reconstruction; the temple mount as it would be known to Jesus and the apostles. The temple of Jeremiah's day was Solomon's temple, and the area of the temple mount would have been somewhat smaller, though still impressively large, perhaps two-thirds or three-quarters of the area we see today.

... *at the gate.* There were in fact several gates giving entrance to the temple court.

7.3   Verse 3 puts the message in a nutshell, which the rest of the temple address expands: *Amend your ways and your deeds, that I may let you live in this place.* Israel's confidence was rooted in what God had done for her in the past. He had brought her out of Egypt and given her the land. She had eventually established Jerusalem as her capital, the place of her king and of the temple. As Jeremiah's contemporaries saw it, they had 'arrived'. Jeremiah's words, *that I may let you live*, make it clear that in his mind her continued possession of land, city and temple is conditional.

There is a certain amount of evidence that at this period around the end of the seventh century there was an idea widespread in Israel that the temple and the holy city were some sort of guarantee of divine protection for the nation. Because the temple was God's own dwelling he would not allow it, could not allow it, or the city that housed it, to come to serious harm. The story of Jerusalem's miraculous deliverance from attack by Sennacherib at the end of the previous century (II Kings 18.13–19.37, cf. Isa. 36–37) may have been used as evidence supporting the theory, and the prophet Isaiah of Jerusalem himself may even have been credited with giving it his approval. The cryptic slogan quoted in Jer. 7.4 may be an expression of such ideas.

7.4   *This slogan of yours is a lie; put no trust in it.* The word *lie* (*sheqer*) occurs frequently in Jeremiah. Jeremiah's war is against a people who are convinced that nothing is wrong. They do have faith, 'trust' in REB, but it is a complacent faith built on *sheqer*, illusion. The slogan itself, in Hebrew, is a rhythmic little jingle, like an advertising slogan or a quotation from a song. We do not know who used it or what it is quoted from.

7.5–6   summarizes what 'amending your ways and your deeds' actually amounts to. This may be the prophet's own summary or that of the book's deuteronomic editors. It means to 'deal fairly' (in Hebrew, 'to do *mishpat*'). The identical phrase is used by Micah in 6.8 (though at that point REB translates 'justly'), and this in turn is spelled out as ceasing to act oppressively towards the vulnerable members of society, *the alien, the fatherless, and the widow.*

Note how the Bible's immediacy constantly falls victim to our attempts to translate it. Even a very good modern translation like the

REB opts for words that distance the message from us: 'alien', 'fatherless' and 'widow'. A genuinely contemporary rendering would speak here of 'ethnic minorities and single-parent families'.

7.6   *Shed no innocent blood in this place.* Miscarriages of justice are all too common. The words *in this place* are ironic. The *place* in whose sacredness they put such confidence is the very place they defile with bloodshed and injustice. The remedying of social ills is put first; the purely religious derelictions are in second place. *Do not run after other gods to your own ruin.* This is very much what the deuteronomists understand by faithfulness: social justice plus the worship of the one God (though Deut. 6.4ff., a classic text, puts the religious and ethical in the opposite order).

7.7   *Long ago … for all time.* God's gift to Israel of land and nationhood is intended to be eternal, but it is still conditional.

7.8–11   expands the same theme of false confidence.

7.9   *You steal, you murder, you commit adultery and perjury.* This is one of the very few places where it looks as if a prophet may be echoing the ten commandments. But is he? The words are certainly not a direct quotation of the ten commandments in the form in which we find them in Ex. 20 and Deut. 5. The Jeremiah passage alludes to only four out of the ten commandments. The four do stand next to each other in Deut. 5.17–20 and Ex. 20.13–16, but not in this order. So he may simply be cataloguing a selection of serious offences without there being any question of quoting an existing list.

The argument is that the people do all these things, and worship Baal and other gods, and yet still believe that the Lord will guarantee their safety, though they are flouting every demand he makes on them.

7.10   *This house which bears my name.* A characteristically deuteronomic phrase.

7.11   *Do you regard this house which bears my name as a bandits' cave?* The allusion to these words in Matt. 21.13, Mark 11.17 and Luke 19.46 (John 2.16 is different) is deliberate. When we read the story of the cleansing of the temple we are meant to be reminded of Jeremiah. There are some curious parallels between the trial of Jeremiah and the trial of Jesus. According to Jer. 26 Jeremiah is put on trial for his life because he has uttered threats of destruction against the temple and the holy city. In the synoptic accounts of the passion Jesus' attitude to the temple and holy city has a similarly prominent part. His cleansing of the temple provokes the hostility of the religious leaders. He prophesies and laments the destruction of the city. He explicitly predicts the destruction of the temple. In Matthew's account of the trial before the Jews the only charge actually brought is that of threatening the temple's destruction.

The two trials differ, of course, in their outcome. The court in Jer. 26 draws back from the death sentence for fear that it will bring the guilt of innocent blood upon the people. In Matthew's account of the trial of Jesus (Matt. 27.25) the people consciously accept this risk. 'His blood be on us and on our children', and when Judas in remorse claims that an innocent man has been condemned, his argument is dismissed contemptuously (Matt. 27.4).

7.12 *Go to my shrine at Shiloh, which I once made a dwelling for my name.* Again the thought here is characteristic of Deuteronomy. According to deuteronomistic thinking there was only one legitimate place of sacrifice; but historically it had not always been the same place. After Joshua's conquest and throughout the period of the judges it had for a while been Gilgal, and at another time, Shechem. The place seems to have been wherever the ark was held at the time. By the end of the period of the judges the ark was at Shiloh, and it was there that Samuel had been apprenticed, (and there, incidentally, that Jeremiah's own ancestors had been priests in charge). After David came to the throne he brought the ark to Jerusalem, and from then on, in unbroken succession, Jerusalem, and the temple mount on which Jeremiah was delivering his address, had been the place chosen by God to put his name there.

We do not know for certain when Shiloh was destroyed. It is likely that it was demolished by the Philistines when they captured the ark in the events described in I Sam. 4, though this is never explicitly stated. The point being made is that Shiloh in its day had the same status as that which Jerusalem now held. It was the place of the ark, the one sanctuary above all other sanctuaries which the Lord had made a dwelling for his name. That high status had not saved it from destruction when its priesthood became negligent and corrupt.

Some commentators suggest that Shiloh had survived until Jeremiah's own time and that he is referring to a more recent destruction by the Babylonians. This is possible, but the argument loses some of its force unless Shiloh had been destroyed while still holding the status of principal sanctuary.

Jeremiah and Samuel are parallel figures; each called in youth and each called to deliver a message of doom. Samuel, in I Sam. 3.50, is reluctant to deliver it, as Jeremiah was reluctant. We are told little of the content of the word God spoke to Samuel at the time of his call.

57

What we are told focusses not on the sanctuary but on the priest-hood. But Jeremiah may have inherited a tradition which spoke not just of the judgment of the Shiloh priesthood but of the end of the Shiloh sanctuary too.

See what I did to it because of the wickedness of my people Israel. Again the perspective differs from that of the account in I Samuel, which has nothing to say of the wickedness of the people, only of that of the priesthood.

7.15   refers back to Assyria's conquest of Samaria and the deport-ation of the Northerners, *all Ephraim's offspring.*

Up to now it is the people who have been addressed. Abruptly in v.16 it is the prophet himself who is being spoken to. This would sug-gest that the prophet's temple speech is to be thought of as ending with v.15. The prophecy about making this house like Shiloh (v.14) would certainly make a fitting climax. The next unit therefore will be 7.16–20.

7.16   *Offer up no prayer for this people.* The instruction not to pray for the people is an extremely serious one. Intercession was a major part of a prophet's job. It is indeed half of his task. The one half is to speak to the people on behalf of God, the other is to speak to God on behalf of the people. This instruction appears also at 11.14, 14.11–12 and 15.1. (A comparable statement made by a prophet is in Isa. 1.15.) Prayer would be a waste of time. God is already set on judgment. The people are past praying for. This is another reason for not seeing these verses as part of the temple speech, for in the temple speech, according to 7.1–7, the prophet is still appealing for repentance, assuming that repentance is still possible and that it is not too late.

7.17–20   God will listen to no intercession because he is so incensed by what the people are doing. The oracle stresses the comprehensive involvement of the whole nation in idolatrous worship. It is going on *in the towns of Judah and in the streets of Jerusalem.* There are no localities free of it. It involves the entire pop-ulation, men, women and children (7.18).

7.18   *The queen of heaven.* It is not absolutely certain which goddess is meant here, but most likely it is the Canaanite Astarte, who was regarded as the consort of the high god El. See also 44.17.

Crescent-cakes. The translators are guessing here. We do not really know what these cakes were. Some suggest they were cakes in the shape of the goddess herself, like little gingerbread men, or women.

According to Deut. 13, if a prophet attempts to seduce people to idol worship, whatever other signs of true prophecy he might display, he is to be put to death (Deut. 13.1–5). If any other individual suggests taking part in such worship, even though he or she be one's nearest and dearest, they are to be denounced and stoned (Deut. 13.6–11). If a whole community is led astray into idolatry then the entire population and all its possessions are to be destroyed (Deut. 13.12–18). It is this last situation that Jeremiah conceives of here, except that Deut. 13 envisages the possibility that one odd town or city might so apostatize; Jeremiah is saying that every town and city is guilty in this way. Deut. 13 lays it down that the deviant community is to be punished by the rest; but if all have gone astray, what can they expect but a judgment by God himself?

7.20 *My anger and my fury will pour out on this place, on man and beast, on trees and crops, and it will burn unquenched.* As in Deut. 13, the consequence of judgment is not just the death of the people but the destruction of everything. This is the so-called 'ban'; the total destruction of a city and everyone and everything in it, sparing nothing. This is the fate to which Jericho was subjected at the time of the conquest (Josh 6.17–19).

On trees and crops ... When a land was attacked, quite apart from the threat to lives and homes the destruction of crops was one of the most serious consequences. A population might survive the attack itself but then be decimated by the famine which followed. The destruction of trees was in the long term even more serious because they could not quickly be replaced. Deut. 20.19–20 forbids the cutting down of trees in war. See the note on 6.6. That God pours out his fury on trees and crops thus illustrates the exceptional and ferocious nature of the judgment.

7.21–23 has some striking things to say about sacrifice. If these verses were not originally part of the temple address they have nevertheless been placed here most appropriately. Several of the prophets have very critical things to say about sacrifice and about temple worship in general, e.g., Isa. 1.10–16, Hos. 6.6, Micah 6.6–8, and cf. Ps. 50.9–15. So there evidently were those in Israel who did not give a high priority to sacrifice or see it as a vital feature of true religion. But Jeremiah is more critical than most.

It is also very striking that Solomon's prayer at the dedication of the temple in I Kings 8, which is usually regarded as a deuteronomic composition, though it is very expansive and has a great deal to say about how the temple will function in the life of the nation, does not have a single word to say about sacrifice, but speaks of the temple throughout as primarily a place of prayer. The deuteronomic reform certainly bestowed enormous importance and centrality on the Jerusalem temple, and the deuteronomic law legitimates the sacrificial system and affirms it as a proper constituent of the worship of Yahweh, as Jeremiah seems not to be prepared to do, but it does not give the sacrificial system anything like the prominence given to it by the priestly writings or Ezekiel. Though they do not go so far as Jeremiah in actually rejecting sacrifice, it is probably fair to say that the deuteronomic school are more concerned to control it than to extol it.

7.21   *Add your whole-offerings to your sacrifices and eat the flesh yourselves.* A shocking suggestion. The word 'sacrifices' here is being used in its restrictive sense, as a synonym for what are otherwise called 'peace-offerings'. The peace-offering was eaten mostly by the worshippers. The blood was poured out, the fattier parts burnt; the priest would take a cut, and the rest was for the worshippers to enjoy themselves. But the whole-offering was very different. Again the blood was poured out and the animal cut up, but every bit of the carcase was burnt. Even the priests got no share. It all belonged to God. For anyone to eat of the whole-offering would have been a scandal and a blasphemy. Jeremiah is saying: 'You might as well eat the lot. It's only meat.'

The prophet goes on in v.22 to make the unexpected assertion that sacrifice is no part of true Israelite religion. *When I brought your forefathers out of Egypt, I gave them no instructions or commands about whole-offerings or sacrifice.* Now according to the books of Exodus, Leviticus, Numbers and Deuteronomy God spent a great deal of time doing exactly that. Clearly Jeremiah has inherited a tradition very sharply at variance with those enshrined in our Pentateuch, which trace the sacrificial system back to God's commands to Moses in the wilderness. And this is not just a quirk of Jeremiah's. Amos had evidently inherited the same understanding, because in Amos 5.25 he asks: 'Did you, people of Israel, bring me sacrifices and offerings those forty years in the wilderness?' And it is a rhetorical question, i.e. the prophet assumes that the answer is 'No!', and assumes that his hearers know that the answer is 'No!' This suggests that Jeremiah is by no means exceptional in his devaluing of the sacrificial system and that the tracing of the institution of sacrifice back to the wilderness period may be quite a late development.

7.23   *What I did command them was this: Obey me, and I shall be your God and you will be my people.* The sentiments, though not the words, are closely parallel to those credited to Samuel in I Sam. 15.22. This is the same Samuel who was a prophet at Shiloh, and presumably himself a priest after the order of Abiathar, and who prophesied of Shiloh's priesthood that 'their abuse of sacrifices and offerings will never be expiated' (I Sam. 3.14 REB).

I shall be your God and you will be my people is a basic summary of the covenant.

7.24–28 *Again and again I sent to them all my servants the prophets.* The Deuteronomic History which we have in the books of Joshua, Judges, Samuel and Kings is structured round a series of prophets. They were sent to keep God's people true to him. All the people had to do was listen to them. Israel and her kings did not listen. This passage of Jeremiah is offering us the same view-point. The parable of the Wicked Husbandmen in the gospels is an elaboration of this same understanding of Israel's history. Indeed, the parable might have been conceived as an illustration for a sermon on Jer. 7.24–27.

7.29 *Jerusalem, cut off your hair and throw it away.* The word *Jerusalem* does not appear in the Hebrew text. It is inserted by the translators, presumably to make it clear that the verbs are in feminine singular form and therefore must be addressed to the personified city or nation. The significance of the command to *cut off your hair* is not immediately obvious to us. One ancient explanation connects it with the custom of making Nazirite vows. See Num. 6 where the law relating to Nazirites is set out in some detail, and cf. Ex. 21.23–26. The Nazirite had to allow the hair to grow unchecked during the period of the vow. At the end of the period, sacrifices were offered, the head was shaved and the hair burnt on the altar along with the sacrifices; the hair thus being treated as sacred. If, however, the Nazirite was for any reason defiled before the term of the vow was fulfilled, the hair had to be cut there and then. It was not consecrated, and the period of the vow had to begin again from the beginning. In these circumstances, to *cut off your hair and throw it away* would be a sign of defilement. It may be worth noting, too, that in Lev. 14.8–9 the shaving off of all body hair is part of a purificatory rite.

An alternative explanation of Jeremiah's words sees the cutting of the hair as a mourning rite. There is plenty of evidence that the Israelites (and people of neighbouring countries too) did do this as part of funerary ritual. See, e.g., Isa. 22.12, Jer. 16.6, 48.37, Ezek. 27.31, Micah 1.16. This explanation is supported by the words which follow immediately in 7.29, *cut off your hair … raise a lament on the bare heights.* The weakness of this suggestion, however, is that it does not, at least at first sight, explain why the hair is to be thrown away.

61

Ezek. 5.1–4 may offer us a clue. In this passage the cutting off of the hair, and its dispersal, signifies divine judgment. Why should this be so? The Old Testament several times speaks of the cutting off of hair as a mourning rite or sign of acute distress, but in the specific context of military defeat, the sacking of cities and the taking of prisoners. See, e.g., Isa. 3.24, 15.2, Jer. 47.5, Ezek. 7.18. Was this something that was routinely done to war captives? Deut. 21.10–14 seems to suggest so. Or was it something the defeated did to themselves in anticipation? Either way, it looks as if the shaving of heads could be used as a shorthand image for military defeat and for divine judgment expressed through such defeat. Isa. 7.20 speaks of a threatened attack by the Assyrians. The Lord, he says, 'will shave the head and body with a razor hired on the banks of the Euphrates', viz. the Assyrians. Jer. 7.29, though less explicitly, may be alluding to the same image.

7.30–34   With this passage compare 19.1–20.6.

7.30   *They set up their loathsome idols in the house which bears my name.* Note again the deuteronomic language. If this is an oracle of Jeremiah it either refers to past derelictions, which Josiah's reform dealt with, or it comes from the reign of Jehoiakim, who may have reversed some of his father's policies.

7.31   The *valley of Ben-hinnom* is the valley to the west of Jerusalem's western hill, which is today a pleasant place (apart from the traffic) with some fine gardens, but was in biblical times a place of ill repute. In the New Testament period it was a rubbish dump, and it was said that fires burned there more or less permanently. The Hebrew 'Ge-hinnom', 'valley of hinnom', becomes in Greek 'Gehenna'. Earlier, in Old Testament times, it was associated with human sacrifice. The victims were usually children. These rites apparently received at some periods official approval in that kings involved themselves in them. See, e.g., II Kings 16.3, 21.6. The human sacrifices seem to have been part of the worship of the god of the underworld, whose name is usually vocalized in the Old Testament as Moloch, but it is possible that some Israelites saw them as part of the worship of Yahweh himself. Jer. 7.31 (cf. 19.2) effectively implies this. The prophet would hardly need to assert, on the Lord's behalf, *That was no command of mine; indeed it never entered my mind,* unless some people were saying otherwise. Josiah is specifically said to have suppressed human sacrifice (II Kings 23.10), which he could not have done unless it was happening. Ezekiel, a contemporary of Jeremiah, condemns it in 16.21 and 23.37. The laws of Lev. 18.21 and 20.2–5 expressly forbid it. Law never forbids what nobody wishes to do.

7.32–34 Since the valley of Ben-hinnom has been the scene of such horrifying wickedness, it will be the scene of mass burials when judgment is inflicted on the nation; or rather, not even burial, for the corpses will lie unburied, and no one even there to chase off predators.

8.1–3 A prose oracle, probably placed here because its theme connects with that at the end of chapter 7. The proper treatment of the bodies of the dead is a sensitive matter in all societies, including those of the modern West, but to the people of Old Testament times, and to most people in the Middle East today, it is a matter of even more intense concern. To remain unburied was in biblical times considered a shocking fate (cf. II Sam. 21.1–14). To throw the bodies of one's enemies out of their tombs and not rebury them was to treat them with the maximum of contempt and vindictiveness. The prophet envisages the corpses of the nation's leaders being turned out of their tombs in this way, and he sees a dreadful appropriateness in their fate, exposed to the gaze of the sun, moon and stars which they had worshipped, and in whom there had been no salvation.

8.3 In spite of the dishonoured state of the dead, the state of the living will be so bad that they will wish themselves dead too. The threats made in these verses are fulfilled in 33.10–13, at which point the prophet moves from threat to promise.

Miscellaneous short oracles
8.4–10.25

The next major unit runs from 8.4 to 10.25. This is a very diverse and heterogeneous section, with no discernible overall theme. It consists mostly of short oracles; in some cases probably only fragments of oracles. In some instances it seems clear that the catchword principle is operating, which suggests that we have here a little collection of material which has been passed on by word of mouth.

8.4–7 returns to a favourite theme; the perversity and nonsensical nature of Israel's behaviour. The prophet is arguing very like a wisdom writer, from the natural order. If somebody falls over, we expect him to get up again; if he wanders off the path we expect him to find his way back on to it. But Israel are 'all over the place'; no consistency, no sense, in their behaviour. They are insensitive to their own errors.

8.6 The Lord has listened carefully to them, but not a single one betrays any awareness of the mess they are in. They just rush on, nobody stopping to ask: 'Where are we going? What are we doing?'

8.7 As he often does, the prophet compares his people unfavourably with creatures of the animal world. The migrating birds know infallibly how to keep the rules laid down for their behaviour. Why cannot his people, with all the benefits of reason and articulate speech, recognize the rules laid down for them? McKane translates the end of v.7 very astutely: '... but my people do not know what Yahweh's order is'. 'Order' is a word nicely chosen. They do not recognize his 'order', his command; what he has told them to do. Neither do they recognize his 'order', his plan, the way he has designed the world to work. Jeremiah would not have used a phrase like 'the laws of nature', but that is what, in our terms, he is talking about. These people are trying to defy the laws of nature, which God has programmed into the cosmos. Such behaviour is self-evidently foolhardy, and indeed self-destructive.

8.8–9 is an oracle against 'the wise'. This follows naturally on the wisdom-style argument of the preceding verses. The prophet has shown that he can do what the professional 'wise' are supposed to do, i.e. draw lessons from experience and from the natural order. The professionals themselves, however, get things all wrong. The 'wise' or 'scribes' were the educated, literate classes, from whose ranks were drawn the civil servants and the government advisers. Their successors in post-exilic times came to be regarded as exponents of, and interpreters of, the religious law. 8.8 seems to reflect a time when this was already beginning to happen.

It has been claimed that the words of 8.8, *scribes with their lying pens have falsified it,* is a reference to Josiah's law book, and to the fact that Jeremiah knew it did not emanate from Moses but was a recent composition. This is reading a lot into a rather cryptic text. If this interpretation of the verse were correct, it would imply that Jeremiah disapproved strongly of the law book and of the reform of Josiah. If he did so disapprove, it is remarkable that the book does not contain clearer indications of his disapproval; and if he did not like the reform, it is surprising if he paid such a tribute to Josiah as he is credited with in 22.15–16.

8.10–12 These verses, an oracle of doom on the nation and its leaders, are a virtual duplicate of 6.12–15. They do not follow closely from the preceding verses. Vv. 8–9 concern a particular group, 'the wise', but vv. 10–12 are very general in their condemnation, and in so far as they focus on the leaders, do not single out the wise but the prophets and priests. All in all, they would seem to fit their context in ch.6 better than the context in which they are placed here.

8.13 is probably to be regarded as an isolated verse. It uses the harvest as a figure of judgment. In the Gospels this is a commonplace. Here we are told that the harvest/judgment will be so thorough that it will not only strip every vestige of fruit, but even the leaves off the trees.

8.14–17 Once more the theme of imminent invasion. The oracle is probably placed here on the catchword principle. The word translated 'gather' in v.13 and the one translated 'assemble' in v.14 are different forms of the same Hebrew verb.

In 4.5 the people were summoned to the fortified cities in the hope of saving themselves. Here again they are summoned to the city, but not with any great hope. They expect to meet their doom in any case.

8.14 *Our God has doomed us, giving us a draught of bitter poison.* This may be a reference to the practice of trial by ordeal, in which the accused is given a drink which, if he is innocent, is supposed not to harm him, but if he is guilty will act as a poison. The only reference to the use of such an ordeal in the Old Testament is in Num. 5, where it relates to the very specific situation of a woman suspected by her husband of adultery. This is enough to show, however, that Israel's law makers did know about such ordeal rituals and were, at least in this one case, prepared to make use of them. Such ordeals are known elsewhere in the ancient near east. An ordeal of this sort is at the same time a test of guilt and an exaction of the penalty for guilt. Cf. Jer. 9.15, 23.15, 25.15–29, 48.26.

8.16 *The snorting of their horses is heard from Dan.* Dan was the most northerly city. This is the enemy from the north again. *They devour the land and all its store.* A large invading army, living off the land, commandeered whatever it could find to eat, and its presence of course prevented the inhabitants carrying out normal agricultural operations. The result, even if the army eventually departed, was famine.

8.17 *I am sending snakes against you.* An unusual threat. The 'snakes' are presumably a metaphor for the invading enemy. This threat may be intended to recall the story recorded in Num 21. On that occasion the threat was neutralized by the pseudo-magical means of setting up a brass snake on a pole. 8.17 may be hinting that there will be no such get-out this time.

8.18–9.1 The chapter division in English Bibles is not satisfactory here. In the Hebrew, more logically, the verse which the English has as the first verse of ch. 9 is the last verse of ch. 8. The prophet speaks, uttering a lament. Jeremiah gets no satisfaction from prophesying doom and disaster. He is not a spectator of his people's suffering; he is involved in it and shares it.

8.19   *Hear my people's cry of distress from a distant land.* Either the words are spoken after the first deportation in 597, or they are earlier than that and the prophet is imagining them already in exile.

Is the Lord not in Zion? Ezekiel in his prophecy thought of the divine presence as actually leaving the temple and the holy city at the time of the exile and looked forward to its return at the time of restoration. See Ezek. 10.18–19, 11.22–23, 43.1–9.

Is her king no longer there? There was still a human king of Israel on the throne after the first deportation in 597. Though he was a Babylonian nominee, he was genuinely a descendant of David. After the second deportation, that of 586, Israel did not even have that satisfaction. The country was ruled by a civil governor. But Israel's true king was the Lord. The prophet is asking, rhetorically, has he too been dethroned?

8.20   *Harvest is past, summer is over, and we are not saved.* The last of the three harvest festivals of the year was the autumn festival of Tabernacles, also known as Booths, Succoth, Ingathering, etc. It was the fruit harvest, when olives were picked and crushed to provide oil for the coming year, and when the grapes were gathered and the new wine celebrated. After the harvest was a slack time while the people waited for the light autumn rains, the 'former rains', that soften the ground and make ploughing and sowing for next year possible. This was the regular season for war, when the king would lead his people in wars of conquest, or raids to appropriate the harvests of their enemies; or repulse foreign invaders trying to do the same to them. This is why the Old Testament so often links the images of harvest (or vintage) and warfare together. They came together in the cycle of the year. The people would give thanks for the fruits of the earth and the spoils of war simultaneously. See, e.g., Isa. 9.3, and note the vintage/war imagery of Isa. 63.1–8. It is not surprising therefore that the autumn festival was also a kingship festival, when the king was in all likelihood crowned afresh to begin another regnal year, and when his victories could be celebrated. In later times it was the feast at which Jews looked forward to the coming of the king messiah. What all this adds up to is that the autumn, when harvest was past and summer over, was the time of salvation, of victory, if there was any salvation or victory to be had. On this occasion, says the prophet, there is none to be had. There is no king in Zion to lead his people to success and prosperity.

8.19 *Why do they provoke me with their images and with their futile foreign gods?* A question by the Lord, in the middle of a lament by the prophet. It is curiously intrusive and is probably a scribal misplacement of something which really belongs elsewhere in the book. It is hard to imagine that any editor deliberately placed it just here. It anticipates the theme of 10.1–16.

8.22 *Is there no balm in Gilead, no physician there?* Gilead, in the northern trans-Jordan, was evidently famous for its medicines and its healers. But even they can do nothing for Judah's condition.

9.2–6 These verses are probably best regarded as an oracle which falls into two parts, each concluded with the phrase *This is the word of the Lord*. The theme is the thoroughgoing corruption of society. The oracle is almost certainly placed here not because of any connection of its subject matter with what precedes, but on the catchword principle. It opens with an almost identical phrase to the one that opens the final verse of the preceding oracle, *Would that ...*

9.2 The prophet (if indeed the prophet is the speaker) wishes he could 'drop out' of society altogether; he is so sickened by the state of things. He cannot find one good thing to say for his people. The second half of the oracle, vv.4–6, focusses on the widespread lack of trust and general faithlessness. These corrupt people do not even have any loyalty to each other.

We do not know enough about seventh/sixth-century Judah to say whether, by any objective standards, the prophet's complaints are justified. But many Christians (and not only Christians) will recognize the prophet's mood. There are times when we read our newspapers or watch the television news and are faced with what seems like a catalogue of declining standards of public morality, and every initiative the politicians suggest seems to take us another step backwards towards the dark ages. What would have been the unthinkable a decade ago becomes the taken-for-granted of today.

When Elijah gets into a similar depressed state (II Kings 19) he is told that from God's point of view things are far from being as bad as they look, and that if the prophet would just get on with his job God would take care of the outcome. When Jeremiah makes similar, though more detailed, complaints, the implication seems to be that from God's point of view things are as bad as they look, and that all God can do; or all that he will do; is to pronounce judgment on a degenerate society.

When we ourselves are despondent it is not always easy to know whether we are in an Elijah situation or a Jeremiah situation. It is so easy, even for the saints, to mistake their own low spirits for true hopelessness. It is also easy, even for the saints, to hope against hope, and not to recognize and not to say when the point of inevitable judgment has been reached.

Perceiving this distinction was no easier for the prophets than for ourselves. In assessing the state of affairs in their world, and discerning God's message to that world, they had exactly the same means at their disposal as we have in assessing the state of affairs in our world and discerning God's message to us and to our contemporaries. Jeremiah has no methods open to him of knowing the will of God that are not equally open to ourselves, and no 'hot line' to heaven to which we have not equal access. Jeremiah therefore stands exactly where we stand, and shares our dilemmas to the full. To appreciate that, is the better to understand his agony. It is also to strengthen ourselves, by observing what courage and com mitment can do. He wielded no tools that do not lie already under our hands.

9.7–9   This oracle follows closely on what precedes. It points to the consequences of the dreadful state of affairs just described. *I shall refine them and assay them.* We have already been introduced to this image in 6.27–30, but here it is not developed, merely referred to.

9.10–11   In v. 10 the prophet summons his people to lamentation. In v. ll, without any introductory formula, it is evidently the Lord speaking. The prophet's lamentation focusses on the desolation of the countryside. The Lord's threat addresses itself to the cities.

I shall raise weeping and wailing. Public displays of grief and the making of formal lamentations are not part of the cultural tradition of northern Europe, but there are many societies where they are. There are numerous examples in the Old Testament of such public displays. The 'lament' was a well-established form of communication, with its own rules of composition and a special poetic metre of its own. The book of Lamentations consists of five such formal laments on the destruction of Jerusalem. The book of Psalms contains numerous laments, some of them for highly specific occasions, some of more general application, some for the use of individuals, some communal. Much of the book of Job consists of lamentations by Job himself on his various misfortunes.

The nearest thing in modern western societies to the lament is the funeral oration, and even this is very different in its content, as well as being less rigidly defined. The funeral oration is normally expected to focus on the virtues of the deceased and to express thankgiving for his or her life. Regret at the death is rarely a principle feature of such addresses. They are normally eulogies rather than expressions of grief. We do not allow ourselves publicly and unrestrainedly to articulate feelings of loss and devastation. Ancient Israelites knew no such inhibitions.

9.10   The rather eerie description of silent countryside is of a land either awaiting the invaders' arrival, after the people of the villages have fled to the cities, or after the attack, when war has depopulated the region.

9.11   *I shall make Jerusalem a heap of ruins.* This, of course, is exactly what happened.

9.12–16   is a prose comment, expanding the picture of vv.10–11 in deuteronomic-sounding terms, and explaining the exile as due to neglect of the law. But if this is due to a deuteronomic commentator he has not only used deuteronomic language, but he has assimilated Jeremianic phrases too, such as the *wormwood and bitter poison* (v.15) picked up from 23.15 (cf. 8.14) and the description of the *scorched, untrodden land* (v.12) echoed from the oracle which now immediately precedes it (9.10).

9.17–22   This oracle takes up the theme of lamentation. The collector has doubtless placed it here because 9.10 recalled it.

9.17   *These are the words of the Lord of Hosts.* REB makes clear by the way it prints the text that its translators read these words as rounding off the foregoing oracle, not as introducing the next one. They are almost certainly right, as vv.17–22 read most naturally as a speech by Jeremiah, in his own person, not by the Lord.

Summon the wailing women. In v.10 the prophet himself raised the lamentation. Here he calls on the professionals, *the women skilled in keening.* The making of lamentation was characteristically, though by no means exclusively, a job for women rather than men. It is worth recording that women normally took the lead in public celebrations too. See, e.g., Ex. 15.19–21, I Sam. 18.6f. It is they who articulate the emotions of the community.

9.19   The people are called to lament, first of all, the loss of property, of lands and houses. Land is livelihood. Without land no one can be guaranteed a living. Land is self-respect. A landless person is dependent on others in a way that a landed person is not. Land is identity, because the person I am (at least if I am an ancient Israelite) is defined partly by where I belong.

9.21   Not until v.21 does the lament encompass loss of persons, the death of *children* and *young men*.

9.22   People will literally be 'mown down', falling in the fields as the grain falls to the sickle. The normal method of harvesting was for the reaper to cut the corn, then pass it back to a second person who bound it into sheaves. In Jeremiah's picture, when death reaps there will be none to gather.

The abrupt shift between vv.21 and 22 from one disturbing image to another is very powerful. The unrelatedness of the images makes them even more disconcerting. Those indoors are not safe, for *death has climbed in through our windows*. For those in the open, the reaper is waiting.

Though this large unit 8.4–10.25 is composed of very disparate materials, nevertheless references to 'wisdom' and 'the wise' run like a linking thread through the whole of it. In 8.8, in the middle of a typical 'wisdom-style' argument, we have *How can you say, 'We are wise'?* In 9.12, *Who is wise enough to understand this?* The present oracle, 9.23–24, is introduced by the words: *Let not the wise boast of their wisdom*. All three sayings are calling Israel's wisdom into question. Is there any wisdom in the land? Can anyone read the signs of the times? Does anybody know what is going on? Later, in ch. 10, (10.7b) there is a reflection that *the wisest of the nations* has not discovered God by its wisdom. Their wisdom has been perverted into the making of idols. Jeremiah seems constantly to project the feeling that he is the one sensible person in a kingdom of fools; the sane one in a mad house; in a nation trapped in error and delusion, the one person in touch with reality.

9.23   Wisdom is not the only human virtue called in question. 9.23–24   constitutes a very dense and tightly structured little poem; much more compact and tersely expressed in Hebrew than in English. There are thirty-three words in the Hebrew, sixty-eight in REB; more than twice as many. It tells us that neither intelligence, military prowess or economic resources will avail, but only faithfulness to Israel's proper God. Prophecy, like preaching, is about priorities. It is a call to make important the things that are important. The message of the prophets and the message of Jesus in the Gospels are alike in this, they face people with stark questions about what matters most to them, and thrust at them fierce demands about what ought to matter most to them. 'Seek first the kingdom of God and his righteousness' is a summary that encompasses most of prophecy and half the gospel.

9.25–26 There is no apparent connection between this prose oracle and its context. The way it is expressed is somewhat obscure, but the main thrust of its message is reasonably clear.

I shall punish all the uncircumcised. Circumcision is not a peculiarly Israelite or Jewish custom. Up to the rise of the Persian empire towards the end of the sixth century (nearly a hundred years after the birth of Jeremiah) almost all Israel's neighbours practised it, including all those mentioned in v.26, *Egypt ... and Edom, Ammon and Moab.* The Canaanites, the Syrians, the Assyrians and the Babylonians might all have been added, together with most of the peoples of Africa. The only exceptions were the Philistines, who were a non-Semitic people. In Jeremiah's time, therefore, circumcision was no distinction. Rather than marking Israel out, it was a custom she shared with the heathen. Circumcision was meant to be a sign of purification and fitness, but neither in the case of Israel herself, the prophet is saying, or of her heathen neighbours, does it mean anything at all. None of them are pure; none fit for the purposes of God. They are *uncircumcised in heart,* and their physical circumcision is no more than an outward and visible sign matched by no inward grace.

9.26 *All who live on the fringes of the desert.* There is a dispute as to the correct way to understand this phrase. Some scholars translate: 'the desert dwellers who crop the hair on their temples'. I.e., the phrase either refers to whereabouts in the desert these people live, or to some peculiarity of their hairstyle. The same phrase occurs in Jer. 25.23 and 49.32. Hairstyles were important in the biblical period. The book of Leviticus (19.27) goes to the trouble of laying down careful rules (which we do not accurately understand) about what kinds of haircut are permissible for those who worship Israel's God. There is some evidence that prophets advertised their profession by the way they cut their hair, possibly with a tonsure (cf. II Kings 2.23). In I Kings 20.41 a prophet is only recognized for what he is when he takes a bandage off his head. Nazirites advertised their commitment by not cutting their hair at all.

10.1–16 is a piece of polemic against the idols. It has many points of contact with the work of Deutero-Isaiah (Isa. 40–55), especially with Isa. 44. For this reason it is widely believed not to have originated with Jeremiah but to stem from the Jewish community in exile, somewhat after Jeremiah's time. There are three classic passages in scripture of anti-idol polemic: our present passage, Jer. 10.1–16, Isa. 44.9–20 and Wisd. 13–15 (cf. also Isa. 40.18–20, 41.6–7, 46.1–6). The three afford some interesting comparisons. They use several of the same arguments. Wisd. 13–15 is by far the best-considered and most far-ranging. The author of Wisdom is living in a Greek environment and is himself Greek by education and culture. He is throughout appreciative of the artistic skill of the makers of the idols. He also understands how readily people sensitive to the beauty of the forces of nature and of created things could be seduced into worshipping them. Neither Deutero-Isaiah nor the author of Jer. 10 makes any such sympathetic attempt to understand the idol-worshipper. All three passages mock the idolator for praying to a piece of wood, or pottery or metal, and none, not even the author of Wisdom, meets the obvious objection that the idol-worshipper is not really praying to the piece of wood etc., but to a postulated something, or someone, which the image represents. The Bible's anti-idol polemic is good knockabout stuff, but most of it is not serious argument. Read these passages, imagine you are an idolator and think up what arguments you would use in reply. It is not difficult to think of some. It is not likely that such passages ever convinced and converted any real idolators, and not likely that they were really designed to do so. The authors are actually addressing their fellow Jews, and trying to strengthen their conviction of the superiority of their own religious culture.

During the exile, and for most of the centuries after that, the people of God lived in a pluralistic society. There is little evidence in the Old Testament of any attempt to understand the other religions and alternative stances that they encountered. Israel was certainly influenced during her history by foreign cultures and foreign religions, sometimes profoundly, but rarely or never in ways that she acknowledged. In our own encounter with other faiths and ideologies, and our attempts to come to terms with them, the Bible gives us regrettably little lead.

10.2   *Do not be terrified by signs in the heavens.* Most ancient peoples were profoundly interested in astrology, and Israel's Babylonian neighbours more so than most. Particular conjunctions of stars, and the appearance of such unexpected phenomena as comets or super-novae were taken very seriously as predicting future events. One of the great practical advantages of biblical monotheism is that it frees its devotees from the terrors and worries of superstition of all sorts.

10.3–4   There were many different types of idols, of different sorts of materials. The kind being described here were made of wood, but had an overlay and trappings of precious metals, and were fixed to a wall. This is exactly the kind visualized in Isa. 40.18–20 and 41.6–7.

10.5 *They have always to be carried, for they cannot walk*. Deutero-Isaiah makes the point more elaborately in 46.1–7. It is rather ridiculous to rely for support on something which needs so badly to be supported. Israel's God carries his people; the heathen gods need to be carried.

10.6 *Where can one be found like you, Lord?* This sentiment is uncannily reminiscent of Deutero-Isaiah.

The 'wisdom' theme, which we have observed as a linking theme holding 8.4–10.25 together, reappears at this point. 10.7; *Where among the wisest of the nations* ...? The wisdom of the nations is not sufficient to enable them to know the true God. Cf. Paul's comment in I Cor. 1.21, 'As God in his wisdom ordained, the world failed to find him by its wisdom.' Instead the nations' 'wisdom' has been corrupted and perverted. They use their skill to make idols. The word translated *skilled workers* in v.9 is the same word in Hebrew as the one translated 'the wise'. The idols and their elaborate trappings are 'all of them works of "the wise"'. The irony is heavy here.

10.9 *Beaten silver is brought from Tarshish*. Tarshish was apparently somewhere at the western end of the Mediterranean, possibly in Spain. We are rather vague about its location, and the Israelites may have been so too. *And gold from Ophir*. The Hebrew text actually says 'gold from Uphaz'. The fact that we have heard of Ophir but not of Uphaz is not really a good enough reason for substituting one for the other. We do not know where either of these places was, and it would make no difference to our understanding of the passage if we did.

10.11 is a prose interjection in Aramaic. After the exile Hebrew ceased to be a spoken language in Palestine and was replaced as the vernacular by Aramaic. Some parts of the book of Ezra are written in Aramaic, and a substantial part of the book of Daniel. The language of this verse therefore betrays it as having been inserted into the book of Jeremiah in the post-exilic period. It proves that the book was still being modified well after Jeremiah's own time. This conclusion is supported by the fact that the Greek form of 10.1–16 differs considerably from the Hebrew. The Greek Jeremiah omits vv.6–8 and 10, and places v.9 in the middle of v.5. We have no way of being certain which of these text forms is the older.

10.12–13 These verses are duplicated in 51.15–16. We have been hearing about the idols, made by the second-rate wisdom of the heathen, and needing to be fixed to the wall. Israel's God, by contrast, is powerfully described here. By his wisdom he *fixed the world in place*. The fact that these verses appear twice in the book may suggest that they are a liturgical formula which is being quoted, rather like the 'doxologies' in the book of Amos.

10.14–15   is also duplicated, in 51.17–19. It reverts to the subject of the idols and their makers. By contrast with the wise God the idolators are *brutish and ignorant.*

The figures he casts are sham, there is no breath in them. The word *sham* represents the Hebrew *sheqer*, a word with which, we have already noted, Jeremiah is much preoccupied. *Sheqer* is 'illusion', 'falsity'. The idols are *sheqer* and a source of *sheqer*. There are ironies here which the English translation cannot easily bring out. The word *wind* in the last line of v.13 and the word *breath* in the last line of v.14 both represent the same Hebrew word, *ruach*. The true God *brings the* ruach *out of his storehouses.* But the *idols are a sham*: no *ruach* there! The true God can unleash the storm wind. But the idols? Not a puff!

10.17–25   These verses leave the subject of the idols and pick up the theme of 9.17–22 after the intrusion of 9.23–10.16. The passage appears to belong chronologically to the closing stages of the Babylonian siege in 597. The prophet speaks of the people's imminent deportation. He is telling them: 'Pack your bags' (10.17a). God is going to squeeze the population out of the land like someone squeezing juice out of a lemon (10.18). There are some obscurities in vv.17 and 18. What the REB translators offer is a probable sense.

10.17   *Gather up* ... The verb is feminine singular. The person addressed is the city or nation personified. ... *and flee the country.* REB's rendering is curious. The people are in no position to *flee the country.* They are under siege and hemmed in by the enemy. The prophet is calling on them to pack their bags and await deportation.

10.19   *Oh, the pain of my wounds* The speaker is feminine; presumably the one addressed in vv.17–18. She speaks in v.20 of *my children.*

10.20   Judah/Jerusalem is pictured here as a tent-dweller. Her tent is wrecked; her family have all been driven away and there is nobody to help her re-erect it. *My tent* is in Hebrew *oholi.* It may be this language which Ezekiel is picking up in Ezek. 23 when he represents Judah as a woman called 'Oholi-bah', 'my tent is in her'. If the *tent* referred to is meant to indicate the temple (which is only a possibility) then the oracle would reflect a time when the temple had been destroyed, and therefore would relate rather to the events of 586 than those of 597.

10.21   *The shepherds.* As often in Jeremiah, it is the people's leaders who are held chiefly responsible.

10.22   *From the land of the north.* The customary language of this
section of the book. It is from the north that the enemy comes.

10.23–25   It is not totally certain that these verses should be
regarded as part of the unit which begins at 10.16. Possibly they
ought to be seen as independent, though the first person form, which
seems to assume that the personified nation is speaking, links the
passage naturally with v.20. The passage seems to express the
people's response to the catastrophe of exile, or rather, a little
collection of responses. It echoes several other passages of scripture,
and it may be that it represents the people's pious attempts, using
scriptural or traditional language, to cope with the crisis.

10.23   expresses the view that 'there's nothing we can do about it';
cf. Prov. 16.9, 20.24. It seems to be piously asserting that everything
is in the hands of God, but the important thing is not what is being
asserted, but what, by silence, is being denied. What is being implicitly denied is any responsibility on Judah's part for her own fate.

10.24   quotes and expands Ps, 6.1 (and cf. Ps. 38.1). The perspective is different from that of 10.23. Here it is acknowledged that what
is being experienced is punishment, and it is implied that some discipline and/or correction was in order; but it also suggests that God
is over-reacting. Whoever said this was not, in the eyes of the
prophet, taking the matter seriously enough or recognizing the
enormity of what had gone wrong.

10.25   cites Ps. 79.6–7. It acknowledges no guilt, and neither does
it recognize God as responsible for the catastrophe. It lays the blame
on the foreign nations who have perpetrated the disaster. They are
*nations that have not acknowledged you ... tribes that have not invoked you
by name,* and who cannot, therefore, (so the intended inference seems
to be) be the agents of God's judgment. God is called on to make
them the objects of his judgment; to reassert his authority and defend
his own. The implied criticism here of God's handling of the situation is very severe.

Judgment, rejection and persecution; the prophet's complaints
11.1–20.18

Chapters 11–20, though again quite diverse in content, are held
together by a number of features. A quick glance at the printed text
shows these chapters to consist of prose sections interlaced with
pieces of poetry. Closer inspection reveals that much, though by no

means all, of the material fits into a pattern. In the prose sections deuteronomic language predominates. A situation is set out in which the prophet's message of judgment is presented. This is followed by opposition to and persecution of the prophet, to which he responds with lamentation and complaint to God.

Judah's covenant-breaking

11.1–17

11.1–14   raises in an acute form the question of Jeremiah's relation to Deuteronomy and his attitude to the Josianic reform. The deuteronomic language and sentiments in this passage are unmistakable. Any reader unconvinced of this should refer, for example, to Deut. 4.20, 7.8, 8.18, 26.8–9 and 31.20; though many other passages could be cited in addition. How may we explain these deuteronomic features in the book of Jeremiah? Some suggest that Jeremiah, who apparently lived through the reform and witnessed the publication of Josiah's law book, espoused its cause, took over much of its language and accepted the main lines of its theology and its interpretation of events. This would explain the deuteronomic-sounding language, and some of the theology, but it fails to explain why the book lacks any clear or wholehearted endorsement of the reform itself. Others assert that the book of Jeremiah, or rather the collection of material which it contains, was taken over at an early stage by people who belonged to the deuteronomic school or party. They edited the material, imposing on it their own point of view and some of their own linguistic peculiarities. Again, this would explain the language and some of the theology, but it is open to the objection that if the deuteronomic school were determined to impose their own outlook on the material they have not done a very thorough job. They have certainly stopped well short of representing Jeremiah as a strong advocate of Josiah's policies. We are left with the conclusion that the deuteronomic influence on the book of Jeremiah is real but limited. Allowance must be made for the fact that we now read his work through deuteronomic eyes, but we have some reassurance that the deuteronomic school have not completely hijacked the prophet and his message. We are still in touch, however uncertainly, with the man from Anathoth.

11.2   *Listen to the terms of this covenant.* When we read the Old Testament we feel as if we encounter the word 'covenant' everywhere. The relationship between Israel and her God is a covenant, or based on a covenant. The idea is not only apparently ubiquitous, it seems central to the Old Testament writers' thinking. It is easy to feel that if that pillar were taken away the Old Testament's theology would collapse like the Philistine temple about the ears of Samson.

But if we look only a little more closely we find our impressions to be misleading. Prophets before Jeremiah virtually never use the word 'covenant'. If they did see it as an important way of understanding the nation's relationship with God they are very reticent about spelling it out. The covenant idea is central only in deuteronomic literature, in Jeremiah, and in subsequent writings. It is hard to find examples of the word's theological use in any writing known to be earlier than the seventh century. We have to conclude that the Old Testament only bears witness to the centrality of the covenant idea because so much of the literature has been so thoroughly 'deuteronomized'.

This covenant. Which covenant? The text refers to *this covenant* as if to some covenant previously introduced or already known to the reader. But the idea has not in fact been previously introduced. If Jeremiah was already prophesying as early as the time of Josiah's reform and if this passage were accepted as authentically by him, then it might naturally be taken as referring to the covenant spoken of in II Kings 23.2–3 and as expressing the prophet's full support for the reform programme. Some will see this as the simplest interpretation and see no reason for not adopting it. The reason why others of us hesitate is that it is so difficult to find support for this elsewhere in the book. If Jeremiah did prophesy at the time of the reform and if he was an enthusiastic supporter of it, would we not expect to find far more material in the book making this clear? Why is the deuteronomic colouring and language apparent almost exclusively in prose passages? If Jeremiah's thinking was so steeped in, and so accepting of, the deuteronomic viewpoint and vocabulary, why does it have so little effect on the poetic oracles?

The lack of answers to these awkward questions suggests that the Jeremianic traditions have had a deuteronomic viewpoint imposed on them largely by the simple device of inserting into them prose sections with a strong deuteronomic flavour, rather than by reworking, in any extensive way, the poetic oracular material. This does not mean that the composers of the prose sections were simply making them up from scratch. There is evidence that they may have been working over and expanding genuine Jeremianic teaching. Jeremianic turns of phrase and imagery do appear in the prose constructions, though in the passage we are at the moment considering, 11.1–14, no one has yet successfully identified a Jeremianic kernel.

11.3   *A curse on everyone who does not observe the terms of this covenant.* Covenants in the ancient near east (not theological or religious covenants, but the secular sort) were regularly cemented by the addition of blessings and curses; blessings which would follow the keeping of the covenant and curses which would come home to roost if it were broken. Deut.27.15ff. envisages such curses as being attached to Israel's covenant with the Lord. See also Deut. 28, where we have both curses and blessings.

11.8   *So I brought on them all the penalties laid down in this covenant.* Cf. Josh. 24.20. Josh. 24 is another account of a covenant making or covenant renewal. Its language is echoed again in 11.10.

11.9 ... *have entered into a conspiracy.* The word *conspiracy* (*qesher* in Hebrew) is not especially common in the Old Testament, but when it does occur it tends to refer to rebellion against, or rejection of, the authority of one's overlord or king. I.e., it is not merely conspiracy; it is conspiracy with the flavour of treachery and rebellion. In II Kings 11.14 it was *qesher* which caused the overthrow of Athaliah (REB at that point translates as 'treason').

There is a particular type of covenant in the ancient near east, usually called a 'suzerainty treaty', which was made between an overlord and his vassal. The fact that such a treaty/covenant was imposed by the overlord, as the stronger party, made it no less binding. Moreover, such covenants/treaties were by no means entirely one-sided. The overlord did undertake obligations with regard to his vassal, e.g., to defend him against attack. Once the covenant/treaty was entered into, for the vassal to repudiate it was regarded as an act of treachery or *lèse-majesté*. A number of the Old Testament's formulations of the covenant between Israel and her Lord show strong points of similarity in their structure and content to the suzerainty treaty form. This is what makes the language of *qesher* appropriate to Israel's behaviour.

One of the conditions routinely written into suzerainty treaties is that the vassal undertakes to acknowledge no other overlord than the one with whom he is covenanting. Israel has repeatedly infringed this basic requirement; not confining her allegiance to her one divine master, but flirting with others. This is the stuff of *qesher*.

The Old Testament affords plentiful examples, actual or alleged, successful or unsuccessful, of *qesher*. *Qesher* is the challenge to what sees itself as legitimate authority. In Amos 7.10 the prophet is accused of 'conspiring' against the king. What his 'conspiracy' amounts to is that he has prophesied that the king 'will die by the sword'. This is not, in our normal sense of the word, 'conspiracy' at all, but it is, in the eyes of Amos's contemporaries, *lèse-majesté*, i.e., a challenge to the king's position and authority. A more regular example is found in II Kings 17.4, where it says that the king of Assyria (in whose empire at the time Israel was included) 'found *qesher* in Hoshea' king of Israel. REB translates (accurately) he 'discovered that Hoshea was being disloyal to him.' Other historical examples of *qesher* can be found also in I Sam. 15.12, Kings 16.20, II Kings 11.14, 12.21, 14.19 and 15.30.

11.11   *I am about to bring on them a disaster from which they cannot escape.* The talk about covenant-breaking and about *qesher* is building up to the conclusion not merely that exemplary disaster is about to overtake Israel, but that God is justified in inflicting it.

11.14   Cf. 14.11 and 15.1. *I shall not listen* ... This is what Israel repeatedly got wrong. They did not listen. This is what their covenant-breaking amounts to. In Hebrew to 'listen/ hear' and 'to obey' are the same verb. Not listening is therefore not obeying. This is now God's judgment on their behaviour. He will not listen.

11.15–16   These verses are very difficult to translate. The text seems to have been damaged at an early stage. The translators of the ancient versions clearly had the same problems as ourselves. These two verses are poetry, while 11.1–14 which precedes them is in prose. It has been suggested that the poetry is an authentic oracle of Jeremiah's, which has then been elaborated by deuteronomic editors into the speech of vv.1–14. But there are no real points of contact between the content of the poetry and that of the preceding prose, and it is hard to see how the one could have generated the other.

11.15   seems to be picking up Hosea's image of the faithless 'beloved', who by her behaviour has forfeited her place in her husband's home and heart and deserves only to be expelled. As the text stands, however, the word 'beloved' is masculine, not feminine. The thought moves on swiftly to the uselessness of sacrifice to avert the offender's just deserts. Scepticism about the efficacy of sacrifice is a common Jeremianic theme.

11.16   An abrupt and dramatic change of metaphor. Israel was once a flourishing olive tree, but now dried, withered and set on fire.

11.17   is a comment tying in vv.15–16 and their imagery to the train of thought of vv.1–14.

The first two 'confessions'

11.18–12.6

11.18–23 is the first of what are usually called Jeremiah's 'confessions'. (The others are 12.1–6, 15.10–21, 17.14–18, 18.18–23, 20.7–18.) The word 'confession' is by no means the most appropriate label that could be given them. In structure and phrasing they have much in common with the individual psalms of lament. They appear to be highly personal prayers in which the prophet reveals his inner struggles with his vocation.

It is useful to deal with these verses (11.18–23) and the immediately following ones (12.1–6) together. Though they are distinct units, and appear to presuppose rather different situations, or perhaps different phases in the one situation, they are alike in that both reflect circumstances in which the prophet is facing severe opposition from his own community at Anathoth. It is worth recalling here one of our comments on 1.1, that Benjaminites had a reputation for, and a tradition of, violence.

The precise reasons for the conflict between Jeremiah and the people of Anathoth are never explained, but we may guess at some of them. In 1.1 Jeremiah's family are described as 'priests, of Anathoth'. It seems that they did not belong to that circle of priestly families from which the staff of the Jerusalem sanctuary was drawn, but represented one of the provincial priesthoods attached to a local shrine. Josiah's reform closed all such local shrines. It closed down all sanctuaries other than the one at Jerusalem; not merely those which were centres of Baal worship, but the sanctuaries of Yahweh. Deuteronomy, which most scholars believe reflects the content of Josiah's law book, lays it down that the priests of the provincial sanctuaries should be invited, or permitted, to move to Jerusalem and find employment there, or be supported there. This, at any rate, seems to be the implication of Deut. 18.6–8. II Kings 23.9 suggests, however, that when Josiah carried out his reform this did not happen. The provincial priests were not treated as equals in Jerusalem. Perhaps their numbers were too great to be absorbed. Perhaps the Jerusalem priesthood, jealous of its privileges, successfully resisted the implementation of Deut. 18.6–8. The compilers of the law book may indeed have known that their suggestion was unrealistic, for Deuteronomy repeatedly commends levites (who included the provincial priesthoods) to the charity of its readers, classing them with the poor, the orphan and the refugee. Everything suggests, therefore, that the carrying through of the reform caused great hardship among the priests of the old provincial sanctuaries. We have no idea how many of them there were, but the frequency with which they figure in Deuteronomy's commendations to public charity suggests that they amounted to a major problem.

If Jeremiah's family and associates were caught up in this they would undoubtedly feel bitter. Such bitterness might vent itself on Jeremiah if they thought he had supported the reform movement, for they would readily have seen this as a betrayal of his family and community. Now, as we have seen, there is a distinct shortage of evidence that Jeremiah was an enthusiastic supporter of the reform movement; nevertheless, it might have been enough to give rise to accusations of betrayal if the people at Anathoth felt that he had not strenuously opposed it, and there is certainly no indication that he did this.

Whether this guess about the reasons (for it is no more than a guess) is correct or not, the text makes it clear that Jeremiah's own folk did oppose him very bitterly, to the extent that they threatened his life. Jeremiah had a job to do, which he felt God had given him, which was, humanly speaking, an immense one, and was bound to be a hugely unpopular one. He was set on a course which was bound, under every king subsequent to Josiah, to bring him into opposition to government policies. He asserted that the rising power of Babylon would inevitably overrun his country, and when it came to war, he prophesied defeat and advocated submission. He set his face against the nationalism and patriotism of the period and regarded most of the worship at the national shrine as a waste of time. Such stances won him few friends. He never married, and presumably lacked the support of any close partner. If in addition to all this his wider family and the people with whom he had been brought up also disowned and detested him his isolation must indeed have been great. Perhaps his 'confessions' fall into place here as attempts to work out on God the frustrations and anxieties that many of us unload on to our marriage partners, our friends or our psychiatrists.

In trying to imagine the situation in which the prophet finds himself it is worth reflecting on the intense pressure experienced by community leaders in acute conflict situations; people such as the early civil rights leaders in the USA, or those caught up in the conflicts of the apartheid era in South Africa. Anyone who in such circumstances publicly takes up a political position or makes public pronouncements inevitably not only attracts criticism but enters a situation of great personal danger. Such people are apt to become the focus of the anger of entire communities. Those of us who spend our lives in calmer waters can only guess at the stresses involved.

These first two 'confessions', though we have compared them with the psalms of lament, differ from them in one important respect. The psalms of lament were doubtless in many cases directed towards highly specific situations in which the author or user of the psalm was facing a very particular problem or threat. But in the psalms we usually do not know what the situations are except in somewhat general terms. In these first two 'confessions' of Jeremiah we do know something about the particular difficulty which was the occasion for them: they are much more specific than the psalms.

In both 11.18–23 and 12.1–6 we learn not merely that Jeremiah's family and close associates were plotting against his life but that they were not being open about their opposition to him. They were plotting behind his back but still speaking fair words to his face. This is clear from 11.19 and 12.6.

11.19   *I had been like a pet lamb.* That ancient Israelites did occasionally treat animals as pets is demonstrated by II Sam. 12.1–3, which describes in some detail the treatment of a pet lamb. However, whether REB is correct in interpreting the Hebrew phrase in 11.19 as meaning 'pet' is open to question. As is widely known, sheep in the middle east normally follow their shepherd; they are not driven but led. This being so, even when it comes to the time for slaughter they do not need to be dragged to the spot, but still follow where the shepherd leads. This is so whether they are pets or not.

11.21   *Prophesy no more in the name of the Lord or we shall kill you.* This quotation from the *men of Anathoth* makes it clear that their opposition was to Jeremiah's prophesying. It was what he said that upset them. Unfortunately the text does not go on to tell us exactly what he had said that they found so objectionable. Contrast ch. 26, where a public and judicial attempt is made to call Jeremiah to account, but where we are left in no doubt as to the nature of the words complained of. In any case, his opponents are not said here to be focussing on particular aspects of the message or trying to prevent him saying particular things; they are attempting to silence him altogether: *prophesy no more.* It seems to be the whole message which they are resisting.

If the guess outlined above is correct, and what they are chiefly enraged about is Jeremiah's failure to oppose the destruction of the local shrines in favour of the Jerusalem temple, it is ironic that later in the book (ch. 26) Jeremiah faces a threat to his life from people who are enraged because he is showing insufficient respect for the Jerusalem temple. The total picture presented by the book is that Jeremiah's message did not suit anybody. Though his opponents opposed him for many different reasons, even people who opposed each other nevertheless all opposed Jeremiah. As he complains later, in 15.10, he is 'a man doomed to strife, with the whole world against' him.

11.20 *Let me see your vengeance on them.* The attitude to enemies and opponents which is advocated in the New Testament is rarely evident in the Old. The psalms of lament frequently appeal to God for vengeance, and even quite virtuous characters in the Old Testament show no shame in displaying similar attitudes. Amos in 7.17 utters a damning prophecy against his opponent Amaziah as Jeremiah does against his antagonists here in 11.22–23.

This verse (11.20) appears also at 20.12. Here in ch. 11 it is a verse of poetry in an immediate context of prose. In ch. 20, where it appears in a context of poetry, it looks more at home.

12.1 Jeremiah at this point sounds very like Job. He is saying to God: 'I know it's no good arguing with you; all the same, I'm going to take you to task.' *You are always in the right* is not so much an acknowledgment as a complaint; 'You always win.' 'You're bigger than I am, but I'm going to take you on.'

This theme, of the saint who contends with God, is a prominent one in the Old Testament, and one too much neglected by preachers. It is not only anonymous psalmists who take God to task, but heroes of the faith like Abraham, who in Gen. 18 is very critical of divine plans to carry out judgment against the cities of the plain. Moses, not quite so outspokenly, pleads with God for Israel after the sin with the golden calf (Ex. 32.30–35). Jacob in a rather different way fights God (literally) in Gen. 32. And Job puts up the most heroic, and longest, struggle of all, questioning God's justice and his governance of the universe, and demanding to be answered. And perhaps the most awful struggle, though it becomes articulate only in a single cry, is that of Christ on the cross: 'My God, my God, why have you forsaken me?'

This struggle with God is of immense theological and religious importance. The stories referred to above are important first because they will have no truck with superficial piety. In the book of Job the answers of superficial piety are propounded at length, given every opportunity to be heard, and then exposed. Job, for his part, makes the most dreadful accusations against God; and yet God justifies him, condemning his friends' pieties. 'Unlike my servant Job, you have not spoken as you ought about me' (Job 42.7–8).

In every case God treats those who fight with him with great respect. They do not always get the answers they are looking for, maybe because they do not necessarily begin with the right questions, but in every instance God treats his critics with total seriousness.

These accounts make a vital theological assumption, that God not only judges, but that there is a sense in which he can be judged. If he demands certain standards of justice and righteousness then these can, in principle, be turned back on him and he can be asked whether his own behaviour matches up with them. God's actions are not, by definition, right, simply because it is God who has done them. There is an interesting reflection of this idea in the rabbinic statement that God created the law first, and then created the world according to the law. The perception here is that God does not make up the rules as he goes along. He laid down the rules, and after that, all that he himself does is governed by them.

But perhaps the most important observation of all is that the sharpest, and maybe the most awkward and damaging criticisms of the religious view of life are not the ones that proceed from unbelief, but those which spring from faith. It is the faithful who contend with him. We can only fight God if God is real to us.

12.1   *Why do the wicked prosper and the treacherous all live at ease?* This is posed as a general question and is echoed in a number of the psalms, but what prompts it is Jeremiah's own very specific situation.

12.2   *You are ever on their lips, yet far from their hearts.* Jeremiah's enemies, who he is so sure are also the wicked, are not irreligious people; quite the reverse.

12.3   *You know me, Lord …* As frequently in the psalms of lament the speaker protests that he is innocent, and appeals to the omniscient God who must know this, really. He asks that he and his enemies reap the reward of their true character. They are the ones who ought to be going like sheep to slaughter, and not led gently, but dragged bleating to the butcher's knife.

12.4   An abrupt change: the prophet's discomfort is not merely that he as an individual is under threat; the whole country is in trouble through drought (see also 14.1ff.). This can only be explained, the writer assumes, by the people's wickedness. Some commentators suggest that this verse is out of place here, which may be the case, though we should not too hastily assume so. The Old Testament does sometimes make these disconcerting jumps from the individual to the communal perspective, or vice versa. The Old Testament writers are not alone in this. The liturgical *non sequitur* is something that most worshipping communities take in their stride.

12.5–6 is God's answer to the prophet's complaints. It is an oblique one, not responding to the prophet's question in the terms in which it is put. 'You think you've got problems? You've seen nothing yet.'

12.5 *If you have raced with men running on foot* ... The metaphor is probably a military one, though the translators of REB evidently did not think so. 'If you can't keep up with the infantry, how will you cope with the cavalry?' This does address Jeremiah's immediate problem, which is that his own family and friends have turned against him. These are the infantry. If the prophet cannot stand a bit of opposition from his friends, how will he manage in the face of out and out enemies who owe him nothing?

At this point Jeremiah's 'confession' and the traditional lament part company. The traditional lament often includes, or ends with, a reassurance of God's deliverance. See, e.g., Ps. 12.5–7, 60.11–12 (parallel 108.12f.). Even where it does not, some scholars believe that in practice such a psalm, when uttered in the temple, was answered by a priestly or prophetic oracle of salvation. But God is not always into the reassurance business. The only reassurance he offers Jeremiah at this point is, 'Stop whingeing'.

12.5 *If in easy country* (literally, 'in a land of peace') *you fall headlong* ... The Hebrew actually reads, 'though in easy country you are secure ...' but most interpeters regard the text as mistaken and emend to the verb 'flee' or 'fall down'. *Jordan's dense thickets.* The lower course of the Jordan is a long way below sea level: the region is therefore very hot and the vegetation virtually tropical. On each side of the river is a strip of what is effectively jungle.

God's method of comforting people is sometimes not at all what they were hoping for.

Prophecies of doom

12.7–13.27

12.7–17 is a mainly poetic lament by the Lord himself, bewailing the devastation of his land, Israel, and followed by a prose section (vv.14–17) threatening the destruction of those neighbours of Israel who have taken advantage of her distressed condition. It is not certain which particular invasion is being described or predicted here. Whether it was the intention of the book's compiler or not, the juxtaposition of this passage with 12.1–6 is thought-provoking. When Jeremiah presents his lament for all that is going wrong God does not respond with an explanation, or a justification. He offers a lament of his own. God, too, has his problems. If 11.18–23 and 12.1–6 are to be called 'Confessions of Jeremiah' perhaps we should entitle 12.7–13 a 'Confession of Yahweh'. Jeremiah has complained of his treatment by the men of Anathoth. In reply the Lord points out (12.8) '*My* own people have turned on me ...'

12.9   There are acute translation problems here. What REB offers is only one of several possibilities.

12.14–17   When a country was attacked and overrun by a powerful empire it was always tempting for her smaller neighbours to take advantage of her disarray and infiltrate her territory. This certainly happened to Judah after 586 when the Edomites, in particular, took advantage in ways that led to long-lasting hatred. It looks as if that is what is being referred to here. 12.14 threatens to uproot the usurpers, though it also threatens the uprooting of Judah herself.

12.15   promises restoration, after exile, of the people of Judah to their ancestral land holdings. However, 12.16, curiously, offers the usurpers a permanent place in the land provided that they accept Judah's religion. See II Kings 17.24–28, which describes a rather similar state of affairs in Northern Israel following that country's takeover by the Assyrians. Whether any of these words are by Jeremiah is very doubtful. Vv.14–17 were probably added, piecemeal, after 586.

13.1–11   A prose account of an enacted prophecy. Such enactments are attested among the early (pre-literary) prophets, e.g. I Kings 11.29–39. They are rare in the records of the classical prophets of the eighth century, though they are not totally lacking. See, e.g., Isa. 20.2–6, Hos. 1.2ff, 3.1ff. But prophetic enactments are made much use of by Jeremiah and Ezekiel. Enactments are not different in substance from the prophetic 'word'. They put the word into dramatic form. This particular enactment, concerning the loin cloth, is one of the odder examples of the genre.

The prophet is instructed to buy a new loin cloth (or girdle), to wear it for a while, and then to take it to 'Perath' and hide it in a crevice in the rocks. *A long time afterwards* he is ordered to go and retrieve it, but he finds it spoilt, and good for nothing.

Where is 'Perath'? The word 'Perath' is the name normally used in Old Testament Hebrew for the river Euphrates. If the prophet was really expected to take his loin cloth all the way to the Euphrates it would have involved two double trips of several hundred miles each way. This seems to most commentators to be implausible, and indeed ineffective, since the vital parts of the enactment would take place hundreds of miles out of sight of the people the prophet was addressing. It is claimed that there was a village called Perath only a few miles from Anathoth. This would have served the purpose well. It would then represent the better-known Perath/Euphrates river for the purposes of the enactment. Earlier commentators got round the problem by suggesting that none of this actually happened, but took place in a dream.

If the purpose of prophetic enactments is dramatically to make a point, then we have to observe that this one seems hardly to be well designed. It is not one of the more compelling enactments which scripture records.

The meaning of the little drama is that Judah, like the loin cloth, is to be exiled to the country around the Euphrates. The thrust of the enactment is surprisingly negative. Elsewhere the book of Jeremiah speaks of exile in terms that imply, or explicitly predict, an eventual return. But the state of the recovered loin cloth, *ruined and no good for anything*, does not suggest much of a future for the restored nation.

Vv.10–11   are in all likelihood an explanatory comment on the enactment by a deuteronomic editor. The two verses contain several typically deuteronomic words and phrases.

13.12–14   Another little prose section, unrelated to the foregoing. It begins by quoting what might be a proverb: *wine jars should be filled with wine*. But if it is a proverb it is a very cryptic one and we do not know in what sense it was normally used. It might mean something like: 'Everything has its proper use.' It might be rendered: 'All wine jars will be filled …' and read as a complacent statement about their continuing prosperity. It might be a drinkers' mutual encouragement to drink up. The word translated 'wine jar' here can equally well mean 'wine skin'. The drinkers themselves might be the 'wine skins', telling each other the sooner they were filled the better. Or there might be a play on words intended. 'Wine jar/wine skin' (n-b-l) has the same spelling, though not the same pronunciation, as n-b-l, 'fool', 'boor'.

I shall fill all the inhabitants of this land with wine until they are drunk.
The prophet sobers their boozy jollity with a biting sentence. The
Lord will make them drink the cup of his wrath; an image very
common in the Old Testament, and used elsewhere by Jeremiah.

13.14   *I shall dash them one against the other.* This comment certainly understands the n-b-l-m not as skins but as pottery vessels. Some
commentators find the imagery of drunkenness and breaking wine
jars confusing. In fact, whatever may be said of the Hebrew, the
imagery works quite well in colloquial English, where people drinking to excess are often described as 'getting smashed'.

13.15–17   is a little poem, which manages to be very evocative
without it being very easy to say precisely what it means. It is
certainly a poem of doom. Some things we can definitely say. It is
getting dark. It will get darker. It ends with *the Lord's flock* being
carried off into captivity. So perhaps we are meant to visualize a
shepherd trying to get his flock home before darkness falls. It falls
prematurely and they stumble on the rough hillside.

The light you look for. Is the shepherd anticipating moonrise which
will allow him to complete his journey? If so, the stormcloud
obscures it and defeats his hopes. He and his flock never make it to
the fold.

The poem has a sense of urgency. The prophet is making a last
minute appeal. Some commentators suggest that a likely point for
this appeal would be just before 597 when the first attack and first
deportation were imminent.

13.18–19   A snatch of oracle in the form of a dirge or lament,
addressed to the royal family. When a country was overrun by a conqueror the eventual outcome for the poor was probably one of not
much change. In practical terms, a change of government may have
meant very little to them. The men who came to demand the taxes
would wear a different uniform, that's all. But for the ruling classes
the result would be utterly disastrous. If they were allowed to survive at all their change of status was catastrophic, their humiliation
total.

13.18   *The king and the queen mother.* In most ancient near eastern
societies the queen mother was a very important figure; much more
important than a queen. In a polygamous society queens were two a
penny. The king only had one mother. This explains, for example,
Bathsheba's anxiety to get her son Solomon on to the throne (I Kings
1.5–48). It is not only her son's, but her own status that is at stake.

If, as seems likely, this oracle comes from the period just before or just after the first fall of Jerusalem in 597 then it is addressed to the young king Jehoiakin, who was only eighteen and had just succeeded his father Jehoiakim. Jehoiakim had rebelled against the Babylonians and then had either died or been murdered, leaving his son to face the consequences. Jehoiakin did the sensible thing and capitulated, for which at least his life was spared. He had ruled only three months when the city fell in March of the year 597. His mother's name was Nehushta. She is given a certain prominence in the account of Jehoiakin's reign and downfall in II Kings 24.8–15.

13.19   *The towns in the Negeb are besieged.* The Negeb is the rather arid area in the south of Judah. It is odd to find its cities singled out here for mention. They were neither numerous nor specially important. Some scholars suggest that the word *Negeb* here is not a place name as it usually is, but a rarer word, of the same spelling, meaning 'store place'. The text would then mean, 'the store cities are besieged', implying that Jehoiakin's supplies were cut off and his fall therefore inevitable.

13.20–27   Interpreters disagree about whether these verses should be seen as a unit or not. The passage certainly does not hang together very well. Vv.23–24 present us with a sudden change of subject matter; but even if we leave these two verses aside, the imagery of the rest of the passage still looks incoherent.

What is not evident in English, but unambiguous in Hebrew, is that these verses are addressed to a feminine singular subject, except for vv.23 and 24, where the language suddenly switches to masculine plural. Not until v.27 is it made explicit that the addressee is the personified Jerusalem (nations and cities in Hebrew are commonly treated as feminine).

This prophecy may come from a rather earlier period than the two that immediately precede it in the text. It speaks of 'the enemy from the north' (v.20) in a way that Jeremiah seems to have done in the early phases of his career. It may have been placed here because the mention of *the flock* in v.20 acts as a catchword connecting it with vv.15–17.

The imagery of 13.20–22 is kaleidoscopic. In v.20 the woman addressed is in charge of a flock; *the flock that was entrusted to you, the sheep that were your pride.* In v.21 her reaction to their loss is to go into labour. In v.22 she is being disgraced as an adulteress is disgraced. The first half of v.21 is very obscure in the Hebrew. REB represents a 'best guess' as to the meaning.

13.22   (cf. v.26) *Your skirts are stripped off you, your limbs uncovered.*

There is a good deal of evidence that in Israel, as elsewhere in the ancient near east, one of the regular punishments for adultery by a woman was the horrible one of being stripped naked in public. Or it may be that the reference here is to the stripping of prisoners of war. The stripping of war prisoners was normal practice.

13.23   *Can a Nubian change his skin, or a leopard his spots?* Such images, conveying the indelibility of Israel's sin, are frequent in Jeremiah. *Nubian* represents the Hebrew 'Cushite'. It seems that anyone with a black or dark skin was called 'Cushite' regardless of where they actually came from. In fact, most of the 'Cushites' an Israelite of this period would encounter are likely to have emanated from southern Egypt, the Sudan or Ethiopia.

13.24   *I shall scatter you.* The Hebrew actually says, 'I shall scatter them'. This is further evidence of the lack of coherence in the passage.

13.27   *Your adulteries, your lustful neighing.* It is characteristic of Jeremiah to switch abruptly between human lust and animal lust.

13.27 *How long will you delay?* The REB translators make the best of a bad job here. The Hebrew, 'after when still' makes no sense at all.

Laments on the people's behalf

14.1–15.9

14.1–15.9   makes up a substantial unit which breaks up into four subunits. These are likely to have originated independently but the unit does have a unity of theme. It consists of two laments, effectively communal laments, but voiced by the prophet, each being followed by a prose expansion.

The first of the laments is explicitly connected with the occasion of a drought. Jeremiah is important because of his political message and because of his predictions of the fall of Jerusalem and his theological interpretation of that event. These passages remind us that as well as fulfilling his epoch-making role he probably did all the ordinary, bread-and-butter things that a prophet was expected to do. It is rather like Samuel in the story in I Sam. 9.1–10.16, who is consulted by the young Saul about some donkeys which his father has lost. Samuel takes the opportunity to designate Saul as the first king of Israel. This is not only important for Saul, it changes the entire constitution of the nation. But after this, before Saul leaves, Samuel says: 'Oh, and by the way: about those donkeys …' The donkeys are not too trivial a matter to engage the prophet's attention. It was probably by answering questions about lost donkeys that he made his living. How did Jeremiah make his?

A prophet would, as part of his normal duties, express the community's anxieties on an occasion such as a drought, and pray to God on his people's behalf. Some prophets, doubtless, had official positions at the temple and did all this in the context of formal worship. Whether Jeremiah did this we do not know. He may have exercized his prophetic functions outside the formal and institutional structures of the temple cult, or he may not.

14.2–6 describes the dire conditions which the drought has brought about. Vv.7–9 contain the prophet's appeal to God on the people's behalf. He uses the 'we' form throughout. This type of lament is found frequently in the psalms.

14.2 If we take the language of this verse literally it conveys the striking image of the drought-stricken land drooping and its cities and their gates shrivelling.

14.4 *Because the ground is cracked* ... This is REB's attempt to translate a very difficult text. It is as good a guess as any.

14.5 *Wild asses ... snuff the wind as wolves do.* Or perhaps better translated '... pant like jackals'. Whichever way we translate it the picture is of these very hardy animals reduced at last to gasping with thirst.

In vv.3 and 4 REB, like its predecessor NEB, translates *Uncover their heads*. Virtually all other translators render the same Hebrew word as 'cover their heads'.

14.7 *Though our sins testify against us* ... The communal lament frequently contains such admissions of sin. Presumably the assumption is that if God is inflicting disaster on them they must have done something to deserve it. Jeremiah, of course, is thoroughly convinced that they have done something to deserve it.

Vv.8–9 are saying: 'Don't be like a stranger to us, a casual visitor with no obligations to us. You belong here. *You are in our midst, Lord*, dwelling in the holy of holies in the temple, and we belong to you, *we bear your name*. This plaintive little verse is made use of in the traditional service of Compline. 'Thou, O Lord, art in the midst of us, and we are called by thy name. Leave us not, O Lord our God.'

14.10 is a tantalizing verse. Is it poetry or prose? And should we read it in connection with the verses that precede it, or the ones that follow?

If we read in connection with what precedes the verse is dramatic.

The prophet has voiced a communal lament on behalf of the people. If this were done as we think it normally would be, in the setting of temple worship, it would be followed by an oracle assuring the people of salvation. See, e.g., Pss 12.5, 16.6–8, 91.14–16. Here it is not. Instead of assurances of salvation we have the firm statement that *he remembers their guilt now, and punishes their sins.*

But we may read v.10 as introducing what follows, and as giving the reasons why in v.11 God forbids Jeremiah to make any further intercessions.

14.11–16   is in the form of a conversation between the prophet and the Lord. Prophecy is not just a matter of the prophet being given a message by God, which he then simply has to deliver. The prophet can answer back, and prophets frequently do. The prophet is a go-between, between God and humanity, and carries communications in both directions.

The conversation begins with God's prohibition of intercession (cf. 14.11, 15.1 and 7.16, and see the comments on the last-mentioned text.) God not only rejects the prophet's attempts to mollify him, but the people's own. The usual responses to disaster or difficulty were to fast, to pray and to offer sacrifices. God is refusing pleas made in such ways. *Though they fast, I shall not listen to their cry; though they sacrifice whole-offering and grain-offering, I shall not accept them.* He is determined to make an end of his people, *with sword, famine, and pestilence.* These are not independent afflictions, they commonly follow each other. War, by disrupting normal agricultural and economic processes, leads to famine, and malnutrition leads to disease. Note that in the prose section (14.10–16) the drought has been lost sight of. The disaster envisaged here is military defeat and its consequences. This suggests that the prose section and the preceding poetic lament were originally independent and related to different threats.

The prophet's reply in v.13 introduces a fresh element into the discussion. What does God make of the fact that all the other prophets, apart from Jeremiah, have a different message, namely, that there will be no war, and no famine, and that prosperity for the future is assured? The prophet may be offering this as an explanation for the people's lack of response; they are being misled by prophetic voices which they may be pardoned for trusting.

14.14   The Lord's answer is simple: the other prophets have got it wrong. V.14 is emphatic: the prophets are prophesying *sheqer*, 'lies', 'illusion'. The Lord did not send them. They are not prophesying in response to any orders he has given them. Their visions are *sheqer* and their predictions *worthless augury, and their own day-dreams*. This problem of false prophecy was an acute one for Jeremiah and we shall return to it. (Cf. 2.8, 4.9, 5.13, 6.13.) It was also a problem for the deuteronomists (Deut. 18.20–22, and cf. Jer. 23.14–16, chs 27–28 and 29.15–23). It was all very well for God to tell Jeremiah that the prophets were wrong, but that did not save Jeremiah from the pain of being in a minority of one, nor from the nastiness of those prophets whom he contradicted. To a member of the Judean public the credentials of these other prophets were as good as Jeremiah's, there were more of them, and their message was much more congenial than his.

One occasionally meets a Christian who thinks that because he is in a small minority, and saying uncongenial things, he must therefore be right. This does not necessarily follow.

14.15–16   The Lord's reply is in the form of a pronouncement of doom on the false prophets and on those who receive their message. If to be a false prophet is culpable, to listen to a false prophet is also culpable.

14.17–22   is the second lament. Initially this does not seem to relate to the drought either, but to a situation following (apparently immediately following) an enemy attack. But the drought problem is alluded to in the closing verse (v.22). Conceivably, what has happened is that oracles composed on the occasion of the drought have been supplemented by, and combined with, utterances delivered later, during one of the invasions. There is no absolute reason why the prophet himself might not have done this. Few of us can resist the opportunity to re-use good material, even in situations where it is not quite as appropriate as it was originally. But perhaps it is more likely that an editor or collector of the material was responsible for putting it together in this way.

The book of Joel, which is an extended prophetic liturgy for a time of disaster, makes it very difficult for the reader to decide just what sort of disaster it was designed to address. Was it famine? Locust plague? Military invasion? All seem to be reflected in the text. Perhaps the answer is that prophets built up all-purpose liturgies calculated to be applicable to any sort of calamity. Perhaps they offered a rent-a-lament service for times of trouble.

Liturgy by its nature cannot be too specific. It has to consist of general confession, general thanksgiving, general intercession, and its readings from scripture are commonly determined by lectionaries which are predetermined and can take no account of the actualities of particular times. It is the preacher's job to relate the generalities of the liturgy, as well as the readings of scripture, to the time and place at which the worship happens, to recontextualize. It is important to recognize that this process is already taking place within scripture itself. A prophet offers an oracle on one occasion. On a later occasion, we are suggesting, that oracle is re-issued, possibly rephrased, and reapplied to a different situation, either by the prophet himself or by a disciple or by an editor of his work. What preachers do to it, scripture is already doing to itself.

The second lament, 14.17–22, ignores the prohibition which forbids the prophet to intercede.

14.18   *Prophet and priest alike wander without rest in the land.* The Hebrew actually reads, bafflingly, 'prophet and priest alike go around to a land they do not know'. It is hard to make any satisfactory sense of this. Brueggemann in his commentary suggests that the point of v.18 is that the country is devastated, corpses litter the streets, but the religious authorities, prophets and priests, barely notice. For them it is just business as usual.

14.20   *We acknowledge our wickedness.* Whether many of the people really did acknowledge their wickedness, or whether the prophet is making confession on their behalf (putting words into their mouths) we do not know. If the historical context of this oracle is after the Babylonian attack then the conviction of sin may be real.

14.21   *Do not despise the place where your name dwells.* The deuteronomic-sounding phrase is not really there in the received Hebrew text, which reads, 'Do not despise (us) for the sake of your name.' The idea of Jerusalem as the place where God's Name dwells is very characteristically deuteronomic. Some commentators suggest that Jeremiah must have found such a way of speaking uncongenial and is unlikely to have made use of it.

Or bring contempt on your glorious throne. Literally, '… on the throne of your glory'. To describe the divine presence by the term 'glory' (*kabod*) is characteristic of the priestly writings and of Ezekiel, though it is found earlier. Sometimes (e.g. in I Sam 4.21–22) the 'glory' is virtually identified with the ark, or with the real presence of God in the sanctuary.

Remember your covenant with us is again an expression strongly reminiscent of deuteronomic thinking. But deuteronomic thinking was very much in the air towards the end of the sixth century, and there is no reason why Jeremiah should not have made use of such topical language. Such expressions may be due to an editor, but they do not have to be.

15.1–4   Like Jeremiah's earlier lamentation (14.2–9) this one in 14.17–22 is followed by a statement from God that intercession is useless. It is set out in different terms, however. Even *if Moses and Samuel*, the two great prophetic intercessors of the past, were to plead for the people, in these circumstances their pleas would be unsuccessful. For Moses' intercession see Ex. 32.30ff; for Samuel's see I Sam.7.9 and 12.19–25. Samuel says in I Sam.12.23, 'God forbid that I should sin against the Lord by ceasing to pray for you.' Yet this ceasing to pray, which Samuel regards as a sin, is exactly what the Lord directs Jeremiah to do.

The heart of this little section, 15.1–4, is the terse poem in v.2, much crisper in Hebrew than in any readily conceivable English translation.

15.4   *Because of the crimes committed in Jerusalem by Manasseh son of Hezekiah.* This reference to Manasseh is surely an addition by a deuteronomic editor. The deuteronomic historians, looking to explain why the reform of Josiah did not avert the disaster of exile, seize on Manasseh as the culprit. His crimes were so great that even the merits of Josiah's reform could not counterbalance them. See II Kings 24.3–4.

Four kinds of doom. These are not alternative fates, but successive ones. Those killed on the battlefield are dragged away by the dogs, and the carcases are eventually picked over by carrion birds and jackals. The implication is that their fate will be to lie unburied.

15.5–9   This was no doubt originally an oracle independent of what precedes, but it is placed here appropriately because it picks up the theme of land devastated by invasion. It was probably uttered originally on the occasion of the Babylonian attack in 597, though there are other possible settings. The speaker is the Lord; unless we regard Jeremiah as the speaker in v.5, with the Lord then taking up the theme. V.5 is metrically different from the rest, being in the rhythm proper to a lament. The destruction is described as if it has already taken place, but it is possible that the tenses only reflect the certainty of the prophet's anticipation.

15.5   *Who will turn aside* …? Jerusalem had been Israel's metropolis and great place of pilgrimage. The prophet envisages the roads by-passing her. She is no longer worth a detour.

15.6   *You yourselves cast me off* … *you turned your backs.*

Throughout vv.5 and 6 Jerusalem is being addressed in the feminine singular, a fact which REB obscures.

15.7   *I winnowed them* ... Abruptly the form of the poem switches. Instead of talking to Jerusalem, in the singular, the poem now talks about its inhabitants, in the plural. On the image of winnowing see the comments on 4.11f. In Ps.1.4 it is the wicked who are driven away like chaff. *I winnowed them in every town.* The Hebrew reads literally, '... in the gates of the land'. The open space around the city gates often doubled as the threshing floor. Cf. II Chron. 18.9.

15.9   *The mother of seven sons grew faint.* The Hebrew at this point says nothing about sons. It is *the mother of seven.* The tragedy referred to is the wiping out of whole families, leaving no one to inherit.

Two more 'confessions'

15.10–21

15.10–12 and 15.15–21 are counted among Jeremiah's 'confessions'. (For a full list see the comments on 11.18–23.) In each a complaint by the prophet is followed by a divine reply. From this pair of passages a picture emerges of a beleaguered Jeremiah, isolated and ostracized, *a man doomed to strife with the whole world against me.* There are people who seem to relish controversy and to thrive on contention, and who go out of their way to stir things up. Jeremiah is not one of them. Humanly speaking, he seems quite the wrong person for the job. If, as 1.5 asserts, Jeremiah was called and chosen before birth, one might have expected God to endow him with a personality better matched with the work he had to do.

15.10–12   The prophet's complaint is in v.10, the Lord's reply in vv.11–12. The complaint is clear, the reply unfortunately difficult to make sense of. Different translators produce very different renderings. Compare, for example, REB with its predecessor NEB. Interpretations are even more diverse than translations. It is not even clear whether the Lord's words are intended as a comfort or as a threat.

15.10   *Alas, my mother, that ever you gave birth to me.* Jeremiah's language in the 'confessions' is sometimes strongly reminiscent of that of Job. Cf. Job 3.3ff. *I have borrowed from no one, I have lent to no one.* The significance of this disclaimer is not entirely clear. Perhaps the idea is that getting involved in business is a common way of getting at cross purposes with people.

15.10   links up with the account of Jeremiah's call in 1.5. There it is said that God called him before he was born. Here he expresses his disillusion by saying that it is a pity he ever was born.

The echoes in this passage of the call account in ch.1 may give us some clues to the meaning of the obscurities. 15.11–12 might be intended to pick up the imagery of 1.18, where the Lord promises to make the prophet 'a fortified city, an iron pillar, a bronze wall'. The verb translated by REB as *utterly dismissed* is of extremely debatable meaning. One suggestion is that it means 'I have armoured you'. And whatever v.12 may originally have said, it reads now in the received Hebrew text: 'Can one break iron, iron from the north, and bronze?' which could readily be understood as an echo of 1.18. But even if these suggestions are correct, they remain no more than tantalizing leads to what the text may originally have said.

15.13–14   is virtually duplicated in 17.3–4. In v.10 we began with a personal complaint by the prophet. In v.11 the Lord answers him, appropriately, in individual terms. But with vv.13–14 the Lord's address suddenly switches into an address to the nation. It looks as if a defective record of the reply to Jeremiah has been finished off by incorporating words from a fairly routine prophecy against the people of Israel.

15.15–18   is Jeremiah's second complaint of the current pair, answered by the Lord in vv.19–21. The complaint consists of an impassioned protestation of innocence. Jeremiah claims that he has done his best to fulfil his commission and got nothing but trouble for his efforts. He does not deserve this. In v.18 he says quite roundly that God has let him down. *You are to me like a brook that fails, whose waters are not to be relied on.* These are very strong words. At the time of his call, according to 1.17–19, Jeremiah was promised by God total support. Here he is saying that the support has not materialized. We should not sidestep this, or explain it away by observing that even prophets are subject to bouts of spiritual depression. In religious circles we are used to hearing, and to making, statements about the dependability of God and the efficacy of faith. Our scriptures, our hymns, our liturgies are full of them.

> 'God never yet forsook at need
> The soul that trusted him indeed.'

Here we have a man of God, a person of profound faith, saying: 'That's not true. It does not match up with my experience.' This has to be faced. Sometimes believers discover that when they are really up against it, faith does not actually help.

15.19–21 *This was the Lord's answer.* It is in one respect an astonishing answer. The prophet has just protested his innocence, but here the Lord calls him to repent. The preacher of repentance, who appealed so powerfully to his people to turn back to the Lord, is himself called to turn back. The preacher has to be his own first convert. This answer of God's assumes some serious failure on Jeremiah's part which the text does not reveal to us. *If you can separate the precious from the base* implies some failure of discrimination by the prophet. Does he always know *sheqer*, 'falsehood', when he sees it? The Lord's criticism suggests not. There is no reason to believe the prophets were infallible. Even the 'true prophets', who got their words into the scriptures, did not necessarily get things right all the time. As for Jeremiah, if he can turn, then the people may turn to him.

God does end with reassurance, picking up the language of ch.1. See especially, 1.18–19.

Judgment on Judah – leading to 'confession' number five

16.1–17.27

In 16.1–4 Jeremiah is forbidden by God to marry. This instruction must have been given quite early in his career since all the indications are that Israelites of this period normally married at an age which we would consider very young. This fits in with the implication of 1.6f. that he was only a boy at the time of his call. In Jewish thinking marriage has traditionally been regarded as a religious duty. It is an act of obedience to the command of God in Gen. 1.28, 'Be fruitful and multiply …' And in the ancient world generally, people who did not marry were probably very rare.

Just as Hosea's marriage becomes an enacted prophecy, so Jeremiah's refraining from marriage is an enacted prophecy. Sometimes an enacted prophecy is a gesture, but these examples are far more than gestures. Hosea's marriage and Jeremiah's bachelorhood involve the prophet's whole life and profoundest being. There are hints in Jeremiah's prophecies that he feels his lack of a normal family life very keenly. Jeremiah accepts bachelorhood in order to demonstrate that he takes his own prophecies of destruction seriously. A family would be destined only for suffering and death. This is spelled out here in a quite dreadful way. Any children born to the people of Judah at this time will *die a horrible death; there must be no wailing for them and no burial; they will be dung spread over the ground. They will perish by sword or famine, and their corpses will be food for birds and beasts.*

16.5 *Do not enter a house where there is a funeral feast ...* Jeremiah is forbidden to take part in any funerary rites, just as Ezekiel, later, is forbidden to mourn the death of his wife (Ezek. 24.15–24). There are two possible approaches to the meaning here. First, it may be that the abstention from mourning expresses the acceptance of loss; it is an acknowledgment that the grief inflicted is the just judgment of God; cf. the behaviour of King David in II Sam, 12.15–23. Alternatively, the refusal to mourn the individual death is an indication that the particular and local grief is to be overtaken and overwhelmed by grief for the destruction of the nation.

A refusal on the prophet's part to observe the usual mourning customs would certainly be noticed, and would be regarded as shocking. No one would neglect such a social duty without some overpowering reason.

The exact details of Israel's mourning customs during the Old Testament period are not known to us, but some hints are dropped in various Old Testament texts. *Burial,* of course, was essential. Public *wailing* was expected. To *shave the head* and *to gash* oneself seem to have been common rituals. (Jer. 41.5, 47.5 Amos 8.10, Micah 1.16, Isa. 22.12, Ezek. 7.18) though Lev. 19.38 and Deut. 14.1 condemn them. The offering of food and drink to mourners, the *portion of bread to console him* and the *cup of consolation* are referred to elsewhere, but the significance of these actions remains obscure.

16.8–9 The prophet is likewise forbidden to share in celebrations. It is no time to celebrate when divine judgment hangs over the community.

Imagine, again, what a powerful isolating effect this must have had on the prophet. He is forbidden to share either the joy or sorrow of his family and friends. A call of God can mean different things in different circumstances. Paul in Rom. 12.15 summons Christians to share in the feelings of those around them: 'rejoice with those who rejoice, and weep with those who weep'. Jeremiah is bidden, as a sign to them, to sit apart and share nothing.

This whole section, 16.1–9, seems to be a kind of comment on the earlier statement in 15.17. The threat in 16.9 is in 33.10–11 both fulfilled and reversed.

16.10–13 A very deuteronomic-sounding section, explaining why the exile had to happen.

16.14–15 These verses also appear in 23.7–8, where they seem to fit the context rather better than here. This is a good example of the way prophetic oracles could 'float', and be used in more than one context (even in quite different books: see, e.g. Micah 4.1–3, Isa. 2.2–4).

The oracle seems to presuppose that the exile has already taken place. This suggestion that the return from exile is a kind of new exodus is a theme common in Isa. 40–55.

16.16–18 Continuing the theme of judgment, interrupted by the promise in vv.14–15.

I shall send for many fishermen ... Similar imagery occurs in Ezek. 12.13, 29.4–5, Amos 4.2 and Hab. 1.14–17.

... from every mountain and hill and from the crevices in the rocks. Palestine is a country full of caves, and in times of crisis, especially military attack, to flee to the countryside and live in caves was a regular procedure.

16.18 *I shall first make them pay double* ... This suggests that God is punishing them to excess. But to pay double in reparation for damage done is not going beyond the law; it is the minimum recompense which the law requires (Ex. 22.4) and it may indeed demand five fold or fourfold reparations (Ex. 22.1).

16.18 *... defiling the land.* The idea that serious offences somehow 'defile the land' is a not uncommon one in the ancient world. In Gen. 4 the ground itself is offended by Cain's act of bloodshed. In Jer. 3.1 (though REB translates otherwise) serious sexual irregularities also 'pollute the land'; cf. Deut. 24.4, where similar language is used of the same offence.

This conveys the idea that sin is not something which human beings can either shrug off, or simply take it on themselves to straighten out between them. It has repercussions which are beyond human competence to control.

16.18 *... their lifeless idols.* The Hebrew word here suggests 'corpses'. The dead defile. In the same way the corpse-like idols defile the Lord's land. Again, we may have an indicator here of how the editor's mind works, and his association of ideas. The command in Jeremiah not to go to funerals (16.1) may have recalled this oracle about idols/corpses.

16.19-21 A passage with some disconcerting changes both of tone and speaker. It begins with an individual, presumably the prophet, speaking, and opens in the style of a personal prayer. It quickly makes a transition to talking about the conversion of the nations and their recognition of their idolatrous errors. Suddenly, in v.21, the Lord himself is the speaker, promising (threatening?) to manifest his power unambiguously.

17.1–4   It is interesting that some translations (e.g. RSV, NRSV, NEB) print these verses as prose; others (e.g. REB, JB) understand them as poetry. This demonstrates how hard it sometimes is to be certain.

The sin of Judah is recorded with an iron stylus, engraved ... on the tablet of their hearts. In the ancient world (and indeed in our own) if anything was chiselled in stone it was (1) meant to last, and (2) meant to be public. (See also Job 19.24 for the same image.) For Jeremiah, Judah's wrongdoing is obvious, incontrovertible, on public display. It is also ineradicable. It cannot simply be wiped off. The kinds of inks that were used in the ancient world for writing on such materials as parchment or papyrus could fairly readily be washed off. In fact, they frequently were, so the high cost materials could be re-used. Judah's sin is not so easily got rid of. The people's own perspective on their society's shortcomings was quite different from the prophet's. They would doubtless have acknowledged that not everything was perfect, but they could not be persuaded that the situation was as serious as the prophet made it out to be. As Jeremiah saw it, they were in a lot more trouble than they knew.

There is an echo here of the ten commandments, written on tablets of stone. Judah's sin is written *on the tablet of their hearts.* This is an image which is taken up in 31.33.

17.1   *On the horns of their altars.* Not all altars had horns, but many did. The 'horns' were projections, one at each corner. The ones which archaeologists have dug up (and there are a good many) appear to be vestigial and not functional. They do not project enough for anything to be tied to them; though it may be that originally animals were tied down to them before being slaughtered.

17.2   On *sacred poles* see comments at 2.27

As has already been noted, 17.3–4 has already appeared at 15.13–14. This is another fragment of a 'floating oracle'. The Greek Jeremiah does not contain 17.1–4 at all.

The theme of the compulsive and the ineradicable nature of sin is one of Jeremiah's main themes, though he uses many different sorts of imagery in order to express it.

17.5-8   This is like a little 'wisdom' psalm, contrasting the lives of those who trust human resources with those who trust the resources of God.

17.6 ... *like a juniper*. The Hebrew word is a rare one and its meaning uncertain. The ancient translators, however, thought it referred to some kind of tree or bush, and they may have had information which we do not. If this is a correct understanding of the text the image is a powerful one. The occasional, isolated tree or bush which stands in the wilderness, instead of relieving the barrenness almost accentuates the feeling of desolation.

17.7–8   The description of the righteous as a tree whose roots have acccess to a permanent water supply is strongly reminiscent of Ps.1, though the similarities of language are not so strong as to suggest that either passage is dependent on the other. Looking at the landscape of Israel during the dry summer the only surviving green is the irrigated land, and the trees with roots deep enough to tap into permanent water.

17.9–11   Sayings on a related theme. They are probably placed here because of the catchword 'heart', which connects with 17.1 and 17.5.

The sentiments of v.9, *the heart is deceitful above any other thing, desperately sick* are very rare in the Bible, and especially in the Old Testament. These words have been understood as a statement of the doctrine of original sin, and if they are intended as a general statement about human nature that interpretation seems natural enough. But in all probability this is not what is intended. Jeremiah elsewhere makes it clear that he sees his own people as so far stained with sin that they can neither cleanse themselves, or even realize that they need cleansing. The words about the deceitful heart, or perhaps better, 'corrupt will', are best taken, therefore, as referring not to human nature as such, but to Jeremiah's Judaean contemporaries, to that particular people, at that particular time.

V.10 responds to the words about the unfathomable heart with the assertion that the Lord can fathom it, and can therefore judge and reward *conduct*. The Hebrew reads, literally, 'requiting each one for his way' or 'his ways', which may include not only overt behaviour but motives and intentions.

V. 11 moves on to a specific instance of reprehensible conduct, the acquiring of unjust wealth. The words about the partridge *sitting on a clutch of eggs which it has not laid* may refer to some piece of folklore about the partridge stealing other birds' eggs. But a broody bird will sit on any eggs it finds. Traditional poultry keepers routinely set birds on eggs of a different species. It is standard practice, for example, in rearing game birds to have them hatched by a domestic fowl. Such a brood of course outgrows its foster parent and reverts to a way of life natural to its species. If a hen has been employed to hatch ducklings its panic when the offspring insist on taking to the water is both distressing and amusing to watch. This is the heart of Jeremiah's little parable in 17.11. The riches amassed by the wicked man do not belong with him and will eventually leave him at a loss. This sort of reasoning is typical of the wisdom schools.

17.12–13   This pair of verses has little discernible connexion with its context. The content is also surprising. The *glorious throne* and *the site of our sanctuary* is Jerusalem with its temple. This 'glory' is often equated with the presence of the Lord in his sanctuary. (When the Philistines capture the ark in I Sam. 4 it is said that 'The glory has departed from Israel.' I Sam. 4.21). This is surprising because Jeremiah is elsewhere very negative about the temple. The phrasing of v.13 about rejecting *the source of living water* echoes the language of 2.13.

The saying in v.13, *Those who forsake you will be inscribed in the dust* may have been placed here because it picks up the vocabulary of 17.1. Judah's sin is inscribed ineffaceably on stone; but the future of those who forsake God is written in the sand.

17.14–18   Another of Jeremiah's 'Confessions', expressing the prophet's despair and confusion. One reason for his frustration is that his prophecies never seem to come true. His opponents can mock: *'Where is the word of the Lord? Let it come, if it can!'* The truth of a prophet's predictions was regarded as a simple test of whether he was genuinely inspired. Deut. 18.21–22 sets this out very plainly. By Deuteronomy's test, Jeremiah was a failure.

Of course, Jeremiah's prophecies eventually came true, but that was little comfort during the long wait for their fruition.

V.16   *It is not the prospect of disaster that makes me press after you.* Comparison with some other translations; see, e.g., NRSV, NIV, or JB; with their very different renderings, shows how obscure the opening of v.16 is in the Hebrew.

I did not desire this day of despair. The prophet is saying: 'I didn't ask for this.'

You know all that has passed my lips. God knows precisely what Jeremiah has said, and knows that it is no more and no less than he gave the prophet to say. So ... (remonstrates the prophet) *Do not become a terror to me* (v.17): don't get at me as if *I* were the one who has not come up to expectations. *You are my refuge on an evil day*: you are the one who is supposed to be looking after me. What about all that encouragement that God gave to the prophet in chapter 1? How do Jeremiah's experiences match up with the promises in 1.7–12, for example, and 1.17–19?

V.18 'It's my opponents', says the prophet, 'you should be getting at, not me.'

Why is this 'confession', or any of the other confessions, here at all? Why did the book's editor include it? Why did the prophet, or someone else on his behalf, ever put it on record? Is it just to satisfy the curiosity of readers about the inner thought processes of a prophet?

In all likelihood the motive of the editor, and the motive of whoever first recorded the words, had something to do with Jeremiah's claim to authority. The 'confessions' make it clear that the words Jeremiah speaks are not his own words. He does not choose to utter them. He does not like the things he is obliged to say. The responsibility for them is elsewhere. And if they are not quickly fulfilled, that proves nothing as to their genuineness, because the responsibility for their fulfilment lies elsewhere too.

For ourselves, however, the 'confessions' are important for other reasons. We could so easily get the impression from reading most of the prophets that inspiration was something effortless: God dictates, the prophet speaks. Inspiration is probably never, or at least rarely, effortless; and what the prophet says entails consequences for the prophet himself. There is always a cost. He has to bear the cost of opposition to his message: the unpopularity of what he has to say makes him unpopular.

Prophets often speak of God 'putting a word in their mouths', as if there was something almost mechanical about it; as if the prophet was a mere machine for vocalizing the message of another. Does this ring true? Does the prophet really bear as little responsibility for the content of the message, and its form, as that sort of language suggests?

17.19–27   Words about observing the sabbath, uttered at a gate of the temple, and addressed to the king and citizens of Judah.

The prophets in general have little to say about sabbath-keeping (though Amos has a reference to it in 8.5), and in spite of the appearance of the sabbath command in the decalogue there is little evidence that sabbath-keeping was much of an issue in pre-exilic Israel. The account in II Kings 22–23 of Josiah's reform says nothing about sabbath-keeping. Sabbath-keeping seems to become an important indicator for Jews of loyalty to the law only when we reach the post-exilic period, and Neh. 13.15–32 shows that in that period the insistence by religious rigorists on keeping the sabbath caused conflict with commercial interests.

The style of 17.19–27 is typical of the prose material of the book of Jeremiah. Some associate it with the 'Deuteronomic school'.

17.23 *They, however, did not obey or pay attention.* The evidence does not bear this out. The Old Testament's own evidence does not suggest any lack of enthusiasm about sabbath-keeping in the pre-exilic period. The sabbath is mentioned frequently in the penta-teuchal laws, and there are enough references to it in narrative texts to show that it was a living institution in the pre-exilic period: e.g., II Kings 4.23 and II Kings 11. Amos's one reference to it in 8.5 speaks of people who are impatient for the sabbath to be over so that they can get on with business. Isaiah has one reference, a disapproving one in 1.13, and Hosea has a rather similar one in 2.11. For Hosea, sabbath-keeping is one of the things that God is going to put a stop to. The few references we do have in the pre-exilic prophets to sabbath-keeping make it look as if for them sabbath-keeping meant something like 'holiday-making'. This would explain why sabbath-keeping is not an issue in the pre-exilic period. No one needs to exhort people to go on holiday. The different attitude to the sabbath encountered by Nehemiah almost certainly means that a more restrictive form of the institution was being introduced.

Of potters – leading to 'confession' number six

18.1–23

18.1–12   The Potter's 'House'. Even modern translations stick liter-alistically and quaintly to the phrase *the potter's house*. The Hebrew *beth* can apply to a building of almost any sort. What Jeremiah visited was of course the potter's workplace (though he may indeed have lived on the premises). The sensible modern translation would simply be 'the pottery'. Most communities of any size had their own local pottery. The basic techniques of pottery making have not changed substantially for nearly four thousand years, since the invention of the 'fast' wheel in the middle bronze age. The reader who watches a modern potter at work will see substantially what Jeremiah saw.

We are accustomed to the idea of 'enacted prophecies', in which a prophet, instead of merely speaking, acts out in some dramatic way what he wants to say. Jeremiah's manipulation of the loin cloth in ch. 13 is an example. What is described in 18.1–12 is not formally an enacted prophecy in quite that sense, because the prophet himself does not enact anything. The enactment is being done by somebody else. And the enactment (the making of pots) is not done in order to demonstrate the prophet's message. The potter is not concerned to illustrate anything at all, he is simply going about his trade. But the prophet effectively turns his activities into prophecy, whether the potter wishes it or not, by seeking him out and by his commentary on what the potter is doing.

But if the episode at the pottery relates closely to enacted prophecy, it also relates closely to prophetic 'visions'. The 'visions' in ch. 1, of an almond twig and of a boiling pan, are ordinary objects which the prophet (apparently) just happens to see. A potter at work is a similarly ordinary sight, though providing a less static image than the almond twig or the pot on the fire. In this case, however, the text is explicit that the prophet did not see it by chance, but actively sought out the place where the potter was working.

The account also relates to yet another species of communication. As we read the words, the prophet is telling a story about something that has already happened, his witnessing of the potter at work, and the account thus meets us as a parable.

Thus the formal categories of vision, parable and enacted prophecy blur into each other. In the New Testament Jesus' blasting of the fig tree (Mark 11.12–14, 11.20ff. and parallels) is in a similarly ambiguous category. But whether we describe Jer. 18.1–12 as parable, as enacted prophecy, or as vision, the prophet is doing something which we discussed earlier. He is acting as a 'significancer', seeing meaning in the ordinary.

Curiously, the story is introduced in the third person (vv.1–2) but from v.3 the story is told by Jeremiah himself, *I went down to the potter's*.

The message of the parable/prophecy hardly needs labouring. What impresses the prophet is the potter's complete control over his material. (Paul exploits this to make a different point in Rom. 9.21f.). He shapes it as he chooses. If he is not satisfied, a single movement of his hands collapses the partly-formed pot back into a lump, and he starts again.

18.5–10   spells out the interpretation. God's control over nations is as absolute as that. If he is not satisfied, he can as easily as the potter squash them up and start again. The moral of all this for Judah is made excruciatingly plain in the words of the Lord quoted in vv.11–12. The divine potter is about to squash them up.

V.12 is important. No repentance is expected. The people's own reaction is predicted to be: 'Things have gone too far; we must stick to the road we have chosen.' Though the message has been elaborated in very deuteronomic-sounding terms, there are plenty of indicators that it is the prophet's own. Vv.7 and 9 pick up the vocabulary of Jeremiah's call (1.10) with its talk of 'to pull down and destroy' and 'to build and to plant'. And the perception of the people as too far gone in wrongdoing to turn back is very characteristic of Jeremiah. The word put into the people's mouths in v.12 *'things are past hope'* (a single word in Hebrew) is the same word as that used in 2.25, where REB translates 'I am desperate', and where the image is of the people in the grip of a lust which they cannot control.

The episode at the pottery raises interesting questions about how we go about our interpretation. The interpretation offered above sees the image as being about judgment. The point is the potter's sovereignty over the clay. If he does not like the way the pot is turning out, he collapses it. The message: he will collapse Judah. Vv.11–12 interpret in the same way, except that they are conditional. God will do this if they do not mend their ways. They are not expected to mend their ways.

But the interpretation in vv.5–10 sees the heart of the image as being about making and remaking. The potter can change his mind about the clay, and make it into something different. He can collapse the half-made pot, but then he makes the clay into another and more satisfactory one. For the composer of vv.5–10 neither salvation nor doom are irrevocable. The potter can make, or destroy, or remake at will. A whole stream of interpreters has looked for this more hopeful message in the image.

Note that both interpretations, that of pure judgment and that of remaking, are already there in the text of the book of Jeremiah.

The Hebrew of v.11 contains a play on words which most English translations lose. REB translates *'I am framing disaster ...'* The Hebrew word rendered *'I am framing'* is *yotser*. This is the same as the word for 'potter' (literally 'former'). In v.11 we may well have the original punchline of the story. Jeremiah goes to watch the *yotser*, the 'former' at work. The message from God: 'I am forming disaster for you.' This would give us an account closely paralleling that of the vision in 1.11–12, when Jeremiah sees a *shaqed*. The message: 'I am *shoqed*, "on the watch", to carry out my threat'. If this reconstruction is correct, it would mean that the purely judgmental interpretation is the oldest.

18.13–17   In vv.13 and 14 we have a recurrent Jeremianic theme, the unnatural and perverse quality of Israel's behaviour. That behaviour is contrary to all that one could reasonably expect. In 2.10–13 and 8.7 Jeremiah uses different images but makes the same point. The translation here is not without problems, but the point seems to be that Israel's inconstant and unlooked-for behaviour is being contrasted with the constant and predictable course of nature. God's people have done the unthinkable: his (own) *people have forgotten* him, and worship idols. The word translated by REB as *idols* actually means 'worthless things', virtually 'nothings'. They leave the well-trodden, established routes, and give themselves the problem of negotiating the minor and unmaintained tracks. Who would be so stupid?

V.16 They so far make fools of themselves as to lay waste their own land, their chief asset, on which their livelihood depends.

V.17 The consequences.

18.18–23   A plot against the prophet, and the prophet's reaction to it. The passage begins abruptly: a literal tanslation is simply, 'And they said …' The editor may have placed the account of the plot here because he thought the oracle of 18.13–17 was typical of the things that upset Jeremiah's audience so much.

There will still be priests to guide us, still wise men to give counsel, still prophets to proclaim the word. The point may be that Jeremiah has been very critical of the leaders of the community, accusing them of leading the people astray. The plotters are affirming their faith in the established leadership and asserting, or at least implying, that it is Jeremiah who is wrong.

The listing of these three as the major categories of leaders is interesting. How did Israelites know what was the right thing for them and for their country? How did they know what God required of them? They had the priest, with his torah; the wise man, with his counsel, and the prophet, with his word. (REB's translation obscures the fact that the text places emphasis not simply on the three kinds of community leaders, but on the peculiar 'weapon' that each wielded.) The priestly torah gave access to the traditions of the past; the word of the prophet delivered the divine verdict on present circumstances; the counsel of the wise was the application of observation and intelligence and insight to the issues confronting society. These are sufficient, Jeremiah's opponents are saying, and justified by their results. No one needs somebody like Jeremiah to rock the boat. V.18 suggests that all the forces of the establishment are lining up against poor Jeremiah.

Let us invent some charges against him. Literally, 'Let us strike him with the tongue.' *Let us pay no heed to anything he says.* The Greek book of Jeremiah omits the negative. 'Let us pay attention to what he says.' The Greek may be correct here. If so, the adversaries are deciding to listen carefully to Jeremiah so that they can find something to accuse him of.

18.19–23 is another of the 'confessions', consisting almost entirely of prayers for vengeance on those who plot against him. In v.20 the prophet protests that he has previously made intercession for these people, his accusers, to persuade God to spare his wrath against them. If they are now so ungrateful he will offer other prayers.

Some readers find it hard to believe that a prophet of God could have prayed in these terms. But the passage is a warning to us not to idealize the prophets. Christian interpreters have often seen Jeremiah as someone almost christlike; and there are respects in which that may be a true judgment. But Jeremiah is not Christ. Like Christ he suffers the plots of those who seek to trip him up and eventually to bring charges against him to encompass his death. But he does not pray: 'Father, forgive ...'

Of pots and persecution

19.1–20.6

19.1–20.6   Cf. 7.30–34. This passage has three main components: (1) an enacted prophecy by Jeremiah in which he ceremonially, and in front of chosen witnesses, smashes a pot. (2) A 'sermon' or prophecy about Topheth in the valley of Hinnom (which is closely similar to the one at the end of ch.7). (3) An account of the action taken by the priest Passhur in response to Jeremiah's threats.

In 19.1–2 the prophet is instructed by the Lord to procure a *baqbuq*, which seems to have been a particular type of pot with a long neck, and to take along reputable witnesses, *Some of the elders of the people and some priests*, and ceremonially smash it at *the Gate of the Potsherds* (v.10). The words accompanying this action seem to be those recorded in v.11: *These are the words of the Lord of Hosts: Thus shall I smash this people and this city as an earthen vessel is smashed beyond all repair.* There is a clear contrast here with the image of the potter in ch.18. The potter may collapse the pot he is making, but the image inescapably leaves open the possibility of re-making. The shattering of the earthen vessel forecloses any such possibility.

The prophecy about Topheth seems to have been used editorially to expand the account of this simple action and its brief exposition. For comments on this prophecy see the notes at 7.30–34.

Ch.19 ends (vv.14–15) with a statement that Jeremiah returned to the temple court, which was on the opposite side of the city from the Hinnom valley, on the eastern hill, and there repeated the substance of his message, where he attracted the attention of *the priest Pashhur ... the chief officer in the house of the Lord.* Precisely how Pashhur's office is to be understood is not clear. The title 'high priest' was not in use at this period. It did not become current until after the exile. It is conceivable that Pashhur held a position analogous to the one that later carried the title of 'high priest', but far from certain that he did so. He may simply have been responsible for good order in the sanctuary precincts. His encounter with Jeremiah is strongly reminiscent of the encounter between Amos and Amaziah at the sanctuary at Bethel, described in Amos 7.10–17; though Amos seems to have got off more lightly than Jeremiah.

20.2   Jeremiah is flogged, and put in the stocks for twenty-four hours. He responds by prophesying doom on Pashhur personally (as Amos prophesied doom on Amaziah). Note once more that prophets are not averse to using their prophetic gifts against those who assault them personally. They would doubtless justify this by asserting that anyone who resists and offends the prophet resists and offends the God who sent him.

Jeremiah's lament – 'confession' number seven

20.7–18

20.7–18   This is perhaps the most powerful and thought-provoking of the 'confessions'. It may have been placed here because Jeremiah's treatment at the hands of Pashhur is an example of the persecution which he complains of in this prayer.

20.7   Jeremiah is a mirror image of his ancestor Jacob, 'the deceiver'. After a successful career of deception Jacob was brought at last to struggle with God and 'prevailed'. (The Hebrew word in Gen. 32 is the same as Jeremiah uses here.) Jeremiah is no deceiver, but has been, he asserts, deceived by God. He, too, has struggled with God, but in his case, God has prevailed.

You have duped me, Lord, and I have been your dupe. Jeremiah is accusing the Lord here of giving him a false message, predictions to make which do not come true and which therefore involve him in ridicule. The obvious solution, if he really does not trust his own message, is to keep quiet altogether, and simply refrain from prophesying. He has tried this (v.9) and it did not work. The *word became imprisoned within* him. He could not hold it in. The word burst out of him. The prophet here speaks of an extremely powerful sense of compulsion, such as few preachers experience (cf. Amos 3.8).

But how could a prophet seriously conceive the possibility that God had given him the wrong message? Although the possibility seems strange to ourselves, it is one which some Old Testament writers are quite prepared to envisage.

There are examples of prophets knowingly giving false messages; e.g. II Kings 8.10, and the extraordinary story in I Kings 13, see especially 13.18. But in I Kings 22 we have the revealing story of Micaiah. The kings of Israel and Judah are about to go to war, and 400 prophets prophesy success. Micaiah alone predicts defeat. How can this conflict of prophecies be explained? Our natural assumption is that the 400 were insincerely prophesying what the kings wanted to hear. Neither the narrator of I Kings 22 nor any of the characters in the story countenances this possibility. Micaiah assumes that his opponents are prophesying in good faith. His explanation is that God has, for his own purposes (i.e. to lure the kings to defeat) deliberately put 'a lying spirit in the mouths of all these prophets'. Unknown to themselves they are prophesying falsehood.

This sort of explanation raises, for a modern reader, far more problems than it solves, but I Kings 22 does demonstrate that in the Israelite prophetic tradition in which Jeremiah stood, such a possibility could be seriously contemplated.

We have spoken before about Jeremiah's struggle with *sheqer*, falsehood. *Sheqer* surrounds him. *Sheqer* has the nation, and all the great institutions of state, in its grip. But here, insidiously, the most terrible doubts assail him. What if God has given him a false message, and *sheqer* is, after all, within?

In 20.11–13 the prophet asserts, as the writers of the psalms of lament characteristically do, his faith in God; his confidence that God knows what is in his heart; his assurance that God will both rescue him and give him vengeance on his opponents. In 20.14–18, however, we are back in profound gloom, where the prophet, as in 15.10, regrets that he was ever born.

Warnings to kings and people
21.1–24.10

Chapters 21–24 form a fairly clearly defined unit, comprising, in the main, warnings to the nation's leaders.

Zedekiah formally consults the prophet
21.1–10

There is a very abrupt change of perspective between ch.20 and ch.21. In 20.7ff. the prophet complains that God has duped him: his prophecies of destruction do not come true and everybody mocks him. His treatment in 20.1–6 fits in with this low valuation of the man and his words. But in ch.21 his prophecies manifestly are coming true and his prestige is so high that the king is asking his advice. We can only assume that ch.20 comes from a period some years earlier than the reign of Zedekiah, to which 21.1–10 relates. The positioning of ch.21 may be due to nothing more substantial than that the collector of the material, having mentioned Pashhur in 20.1–6, had his memory jogged about the other Pashhur referred to in 21.1.

21.1–7, then, offers us a story about how Jeremiah was formally consulted by King Zedekiah during the siege of Jerusalem, the siege which finally led to the city's fall in 586. There are actually six passages which need to be considered together. All of them deal with events which are said to have taken place during that final siege of Jerusalem, and all relate to dealings between Jeremiah and the king. Conveniently, they fall into three pairs. In 27.12–15 and 34.1–7 the prophet delivers a message of doom to Zedekiah. In 27.12–15 he advocates submission to Babylon. In 34.1–7 he does not explicitly do this, but asserts that the fall of the city is certain. The accounts are alike in that the prophet's advice is not asked for; it is offered by the prophet on his own initiative.

In 21.1–7 and 37.1–10 the initiative is taken by the king, who formally consults the prophet, sending to him a deputation consisting of a priest and a government official. The priest is the same person in both accounts. The major difference between these two accounts is their chronological setting. The events of 21.1–7 appear to be placed during the early stages of Nebuchadnezzar's attack on Judah, whereas in 37.1–10 the consultation explicitly takes place some time later, at the point where the Babylonian siege was lifted in response to the approach of an Egyptian relief force.

In the third pair of passages, 37.17–21 and 38.14–28, the initiative is again, in both cases, taken by the king, but instead of formal and public consultations we have private ones, not to say clandestine. More will be said about some of these passages at the appropriate points in the commentary.

The story here in 21.1–7 (and the same is true of 37.1–10) is closely parallel to the one in II Kings 18.13–19.37. The crucial part of that account for our present purposes, the consultation with Isaiah, and what followed, is in II Kings 19.1–7 and 35–37. This recounts how, during Sennacherib's siege of Jerusalem in the previous century, King Hezekiah sent a deputation of senior government ministers and priests to consult Isaiah. They outline the military position to him and ask him (II Kings 19.4): 'Offer a prayer for those who still survive'. Isaiah sends an encouraging reply and promises the removal of the Assyrian army. 'That night the angel of the Lord went out and struck down a hundred and eighty-five thousand in the Assyrian camp' (II Kings 19.35). Sennacherib consequently withdrew. When Zedekiah's deputation goes to see Jeremiah their reported words *Perhaps the Lord will perform a miracle as he has done in times past* are a clear reference to those earlier events.

But Jeremiah's answer is the opposite of Isaiah's. God will not deliver them, but will ensure their defeat. He will go so far as to join their enemies, for he says (21.5) *I myself shall fight against you in burning rage and great fury.* He predicts that defeat will be thorough-going and uncompromising. 21.6 refers to *a great pestilence*, which will destroy the inhabitants of Jerusalem. This is an echo of the plague which destroyed the besieging army in II Kings 19.35, but a reversal of it, for it will not destroy the besiegers but the besieged.

For further exposition of the significance of this parallel between Sennacherib's siege and Nebuchadnezzar's see the commentary on 37.1–10.

21.8–9 goes on to say that the king and people have a choice of life or death. To stay in the city and try to maintain resistance against the enemy will mean death. Life is an option only for those who leave the city and surrender to the besiegers. The language here is strongly reminiscent of Deuteronomy. See, e.g., Deut. 30.15, 19. To make a pronouncement of this sort in the middle of a war could only have been extremely damaging to public morale. This was the sort of message which made Jeremiah deeply unpopular with the people and its leaders alike.

21.1 *Pashhur son of Malchiah* is a different Pashhur from the one encountered by Jeremiah in 20.1ff. This Pashhur appears again in 31.1–6 as one of a group of officials opposed to the prophet. *Zephaniah the priest* is also mentioned again, in 29.24–32 and 37.3–10.

Jer. 52.4–16, which purports to be an account of what actually happened when the Babylonians took Jerusalem, does not agree in its details with the prophecies of 21.3–10. 21.7 predicts that Zedekiah and his courtiers will be captured by Nebuchadnezzar, and that *he will put them to the sword and show no pity or mercy or compassion.* According to Jer. 52 Nebuchadnezzar certainly showed no pity, mercy or compassion, but he did not actually put Zedekiah to death. This prediction is in contrast with the much kinder (but also inaccurate) one in 34.4–5.

21.9 suggests that those who stay in the city will die, whereas everyone who surrenders to the Babylonians *will escape with his life.* According to 52.15 those who stayed in the city and those who surrendered were treated in exactly the same way. They were all deported. Given the discrepancies it is hardly likely that 21.1–10 was a prophecy after the event. Indeed, the fact that in its details it does not correspond with actuality (assuming that the ch.52 account is correct) suggests that it may reflect memories of a real prediction.

Condemnations of kings

21.11–22.30

The next large section, which runs from 21.11 through to the end of ch.22, is a collection of prophecies largely concerned with kings.

21.11–12 is an oracle against *the royal house of Judah.* It was one of the principal functions of a king to *dispense justice.* Failure to do so could bring disaster not merely on the king himself but on the whole community which he represented.

21.13–14 is an oracle having no discernible connection with what immediately precedes it, but possibly placed here because its ending is similar to the ending of the previous one. It opens by addressing someone in the feminine singular (a fact which English translations cannot make apparent). It is usually assumed that it is addressing Jerusalem, and therefore, more specifically, its inhabitants. But the descriptions: *You inhabitants of the valley, the rock in the plain,* do not fit Jerusalem's geographical situation at all, so it may be that originally the oracle was directed against some other city.

Who can come down upon us? The verb translated here as *come down* is ambiguous, but if its derivation from a verb 'to descend' is correct, then this would be another argument against identifying the city concerned as Jerusalem. From every direction except the north one must emphatically 'go up' to Jerusalem.

22.1–5   This passage is effectively a prose version of the little poem in 21.11–12, probably uttered during the days of Jehoiakim, who was a far from exemplary monarch and who did not live up to the reputation of his father Josiah. These verses appear to threaten the end of the royal house. This was a very large threat, since it was widely believed that the covenant with David guaranteed that his dynasty would last for ever. Some commentators point out that all that is actually being threatened is the destruction of the royal palace, but the destruction of the palace surely implies the end of its occupants. In any case, the Hebrew word used here is the ambivalent *bayith*, 'house'. In 22.5 REB must be correct in rendering it *palace*, because in the context it can only refer to a building, but the reader can hardly fail to notice that to prophesy the destruction of 'the royal house' can be understood in more ways than as a simple reference to demolition.

The same ambiguity carries through into the following oracle, vv.6–7. It is directed against 'the house of the king of Judah'. This is what the Hebrew literally says. Again, the 'house' might simply be the palace building, but this time REB takes the word in its other sense and offers us: *the royal house of Judah*. The translators' judgment is surely right again. Would it be natural to put into the mouth of God phrases like *You are dear to me as Gilead* if the subject were merely a building?

The phrase 'the house of the king of Judah' in v.6 is identical to the one at the beginning of v.1, and doubtless provides the catchword which linked the oracles.

22.4   virtually repeats 17.25.

22.8–9   reverts to the subject of the destruction of the *city*. The phrasing and sentiments are characteristically deuteronomic.

22.10–12   These verses sound very specific, and no doubt were understood as very specific at their point of utterance, but they are surprisingly ambiguous to the modern interpreter. They offer us a good example of the indirectness and deliberate vagueness typical of oracular speech (v.10). But even the prose explanation in vv.11–12 has ambiguities of its own, and fails to give us any certain elucidation. We need to discuss separately the meaning of the poetic oracle and that of the prose explanation in vv.11–12, since we cannot assume that the writer of the prose explanation himself correctly understood the poetry.

The poetic oracle (v.10) contrasts two people, one who has died and whose loss is not to be mourned, and 'one who is going'. REB's *who is going into exile*, though several translators and commentators would support it, is not what the Hebrew literally says. If we take this poetic oracle by itself there are two main possibilities: (1) the contrast is between the dead Josiah and his son and successor Jehoahaz, who was very briefly placed on the throne but almost immediately deposed by pharaoh Necho, who deported him to Egypt and replaced him by his brother Jehoiakim. In this case the reason for not mourning is not because the loss of Josiah was no cause for regret, but because (the prophet is saying) by contrast with his son, he was the lucky one.

Alternatively (2) the one not to be mourned is the dead Jehoiakim, who died just before the Babylonian advance on Jerusalem in 597. His successor and son, Jehoiakin, was deported by the conquerors to Babylon. The reason for not mourning in this case was that Jehoiakim in the prophet's view is no great loss.

The prose explanation in vv.11–12 may or may not derive from the prophet himself, or from his lifetime. In v.11 the 'one who goes' is identified as *Shallum son of Josiah*. If the word 'son' is to be taken absolutely literally, and if the words *who succeeded his father on the throne* mean 'who immediately succeeded ...' then Shallum must be Jehoahaz.

But 'son' is often used in the extended sense of 'descendant', and may readily be applied to a grandson. *Who succeeded ...* does not have to refer to an immediate successor, so our interpretation (2) above remains a possible one, even of vv.11–12.

Even if the writer of vv.11–12 does think the reference in v.10 is to Jehoahaz, if he is not a contemporary of the prophet, he might be wrong.

22.13–30 Whatever may be said of 22.10–12, the oracles that follow refer explicitly to Jehoiakim and Jehoiakin.

22.13–19 concerns Jehoiakim. The prophet takes a very low view of Jehoiakim. It is clear from this oracle that Jehoiakim had engaged in some grandiose building schemes and had made use of forced labour to carry them through. This was a common practice with kings of the ancient near east, but such use of forced labour was resisted in Israel. It was the issue, above all, which had precipitated the rebellion that led to the secession of the Northern Kingdom at the end of the reign of Solomon. I Kings 9.15–23 says that Solomon only put foreigners to forced labour, but 5.13–14, 11.28 and 12.1–16 reveal otherwise.

There are problems in sorting out the syntax of v.14, but the main thrust of the meaning is clear enough.

22.17   suggests that his use of forced labour was not the worst of Johaiakim's offences, for it accuses him of being interested only in making money (his *eyes and ... heart are set on naught but gain*), of shedding *innocent blood*, and of perpetrating *cruel acts of tyranny*.

22.15–16   offers a very laudatory judgment on King Josiah. It says that he *dealt justly and fairly* and *upheld the cause of the lowly and poor*. This agrees with the judgment on Josiah offered in the book of Kings. If the words really come from the prophet Jeremiah they have implications for our assessment of his attitude to Josiah's reform. He could hardly have spoken so highly of Josiah if he strongly disapproved of that king's major achievement.

22.15   *He ate and drank.* The implication is that he lived in kingly style, but he did not overdo things like Jehoiakim.

22.16   *Did not this show he knew me? says the Lord.* The Hebrew is more direct. 'Is not this to know me?' which suggests that 'knowledge of God' can actually be equated with the doing of justice and righteousness.

22.19   *He will be buried like a dead donkey*, i.e. not buried at all, but *dragged along and flung out beyond the gates*. The corpse of a donkey is merely rubbish to be disposed of. Jer. 36.30 repeats the prophecy that Jehoiakim's corpse will be unburied. There is no evidence that this prophecy was fulfilled, or that Jehoiakim's burial was anything other than normal.

22.20–23   It is curious to find this passage addressed to Jerusalem (Jerusalem is not named, but the verbs throughout are feminine singular) sandwiched between the oracle on Jehoiakim and that on Jehoiakin. Its position may indicate the editor's idea of where this oracle belongs chronologically, viz., in the period between the death of Jehoiakim and the fall of the city to the Babylonians, when Jehoiakin was taken away to Babylon.

Lebanon ... Bashan ... Abarim, are all mountainous regions on Israel's borders. The nation's distress is to be proclaimed from the heights so that all may hear.

22.22   *A wind will carry away all your friends.* The Hebrew is curiously ambiguous, as a comparison of translations will illustrate.

22.24–29   Prose oracles on Jehoiakin (Coniah). We may be unsure who Shallum was (22.1) but there is no doubt who Coniah was. 'Jeho-yakin' means 'the Lord (Yahu) will establish'. 'Con-yah' simply puts the two elements of the name the other way round, 'he establishes – i.e. Yahu (does)'. This sort of variation in the form of Hebrew names is not uncommon, though the English transliterations often obscure the connexion between the forms. E.g., Hananiah ('Hanan-yahu', i.e. 'He is gracious, i.e. Yahu (is)') is a reversed form of John, 'Yeho-hanan.'

This oracle against Jehoiakin is markedly lacking in blame. Jehoiakin was not on the throne long enough to prove himself, whether he would be a creditable ruler like his grandfather or a discreditable one like his father Jehoiakim. A king of only three months' standing and just eighteen years old, he is just unlucky. Jehoiakim provoked the Babylonian attack, and died, so the weight of imperial displeasure falls on his son.

Whatever God's assessment of him; however attached the Lord might be to this young king, even though he were *the signet on my right hand,* there would be no help for it, his fate is sealed by the events which have gone before; events for which he could hardly be held responsible.

This comparison of a ruler to a signet ring on the hand of God appears again in Haggai 2.23, where it is applied to Zerubbabel.

Jehoiakin was taken into exile in 597 at the first fall of Jerusalem, and kept under something like house arrest in Babylon, where he eventually died (See Jer. 52.31–34 and II Kings 24.8–25.30). At least he fared better than his successor Zedekiah, who was in charge when the city fell again for the second time in 586.

22.28   uses one or two words whose meaning is uncertain, but it looks as if Coniah is being compared to a broken, and therefore no longer useful, household utensil or piece of crockery. He is damaged goods, and fit only for the scrap heap.

22.30   *Write this man down as stripped of all honour.* The Hebrew word in other contexts means 'childless'. Some translators assert that it cannot have this meaning here since we know that Jehoiakin did in fact have children, as v.28 makes clear (Cf. I Chron 3.16–17). Babylonian records detailing his rations mention five sons of Jehoiakin. But this is to miss the point. To 'write him down' as childless means to count him as childless. Jehoiakin is described as 'childless' because he is effectively without descendants. None of his children will sit on his throne or inherit his royal dignity. If, however, the alternative interpretation of the word as *stripped* is preferred, what the oracle is saying is: 'Write this man off', as a person with no future, who will leave no mark on history.

During the exile there seems to have been a hope in some minds that Jehoiakin might eventually be restored to the throne, and the old promise to David be thus re-established. This oracle seems to be an attempt to combat that deluded optimism.

From a Christian point of view it is of interest that his name does appear (in the form Jeconiah) in Matthew's genealogy of Jesus (Matt. 1.12). Matthew does not *write this man down* as childless. As Jeremiah saw it, the promise of God came to a 'No!' with Jehoiakin; but Matthew has unearthed an unexpected and strange 'Yes!'

Bad and good shepherds
23.1–8

23.1–8   There are three distinct sayings here, making a transition from judgment to hope. 23.4 is a prose saying about the *shepherds* (i.e. rulers and leaders of the nation) who have failed to look after the flock, and about how God himself will step in and do the shepherding. *Woe betide the shepherds*, recalls the 'Woe!' introductions to the words about Jehoiakim in 22.13, 14. There are plays on words here that translation does not easily reproduce. REB tries in 23.2 with *You have not watched over them; but I am watching you*. An alternative might be: 'You have not attended to them (the flock); but I will attend to you'. The promise in v.3 that he will *gather the remnant of my sheep from all the lands to which I have dispersed them* presupposes a date after the exile has taken place.

The phrase *all the lands* reminds us that the exile did not just result in the deportation of people to Babylon, but that many fled to Egypt (as the book of Jeremiah itself makes clear) and that there was a scattering of Jewish refugees at this time into many of the neighbouring countries.

23.3   *And they will be fruitful and increase.* The same vocabulary as in Gen. 1.28. According to v.3 God himself will be shepherd; but in v.4 he will appoint other shepherds, better than the ineffective ones condemned in v.2.

This whole passage about the shepherds seems to have been the text for a much longer essay on the same theme in the book of Ezekiel (ch. 34) and Jer. 23.1–4 itself may represent reflection on the text of 10.21.

23.5–6 This poetic oracle about the restoration of the *righteous Branch*, a king *from David's line*, may have been placed here as a counterweight to the negative words about Jehoiakin at the end of ch. 22. Although (according to 22.24–30) there is no future for Jehoiakin, this does not mean that there is no future for the Davidic dynasty. (There is a very similar oracle at 33.15–16.)

There is a strong possibility that the phrase translated *righteous Branch* may mean 'legitimate branch'. Even if this is so, the double meaning may be intended and the moral sense of 'righteous' not excluded.

The *Branch* seems to have been a popular way of referring to the expected messiah. In Zech. 3.8 (and cf. 6.12) Zerubbabel, in whom the prophet apparently placed messianic hopes, is referred to (in God's name) as 'my servant the Branch'.

The idea of the kings of the Davidic dynasty as 'shoots' from the 'stock' or trunk, or tree of Jesse, goes back at least as far as Isaiah. See Isa. 11.1 (though the precise word which Jer. 23.5 uses does not appear in Isa. 11.1).

The idea of the 'tree of Jesse' became an important one in Christian iconography and appears frequently in mediaeval art and subsequently.

The Lord our Righteousness. If there is an implicit contrast between the new *Branch* and the dead wood, Jehoiakin, there is an explicit one here between the *Branch* and Jehoiakin's successor, Zedekiah. The prophet seems merely sorry for Jehoiakin, who was a victim of circumstances. But about Zedekiah he has little good to say. Zedekiah by his short-sighted foreign policy precipitated the final crisis. His name, *Tsidkiyyahu* in Hebrew, means 'the Lord (Yahu) is my righteousness'. The oracle in 23.6 predicts the advent of one who will genuinely deserve the name. *Tsedek* does not merely mean 'righteousness' but, in certain contexts, 'salvation' or 'victory'.

Whether these 'messianic' oracles come from Jeremiah himself is very much to be doubted. They probably reflect the hopes of a rather later period than his.

Christian tradition of course sees the fulfilment of these prophecies in Christ, who is at once the Good Shepherd (Jer. 23.4) and also the Branch from the stock of David.

23.7–8 duplicates 16.14–15. In the Greek book of Jeremiah the verses do not appear here but at the very end of ch.23. The literary tradition is clearly uncertain as to where they ought to stand.

Condemnations of prophets
23.9–40

The rest of ch.23, vv.9–40, consists of sayings related to false prophecy. The heading that stands at the beginning of v.9, *Of the prophets* (or more literally, 'to the prophets') may apply to the whole section, vv.9–40. The words are not an appropriate introduction to vv.9–12, taken by themselves.

23.9–12 In v.9 the speaker is the prophet; in vv.11–12 the speaker is clearly the Lord. What of v.10? REB reads v.10 as part of the speech of the prophet, but there is some obscurity in the Hebrew and other interpreters read it differently. V.9 is a powerful and emotional statement of the prophet's distress at the desperate state of society and the low level of morality. He is literally 'overcome' by it. The language is reminiscent of that of the confessions. V.10, whoever is the speaker, reverts to the image of adultery which has been expounded earlier in the book. It is not really a metaphor, but in some respects a literal description of the religious infidelity which the prophet observes. ... *because of them the earth lies parched.* These words seem to suggest that this oracle belongs in the period of the drought, which appears to have prompted so much of the prophet's early preaching. There is irony here. The sexual rites were supposed to ensure the fertility of the land. God's punishment on them ensures exactly the opposite.

In v.11 the argument moves on to put the blame on the nation's religious leaders, *prophet and priest.* V.12 pronounces doom specifically on the leaders. In 23.13–15 the spotlight focusses sharply on the prophets, of both halves of the nation, North and South.

The paragraphing of REB seems to associate vv.13 and 14 with the preceding section and to give v.15 separate status, but the commentators in general take vv.9–12 as one unit and vv.13–15 as another.

23.13 ... *a lack of sense.* The Hebrew word is a rare one. Some suggest that it means 'unseemliness', or 'something inappropriate'. The ancient translators took it to mean 'tasteless', 'lacking salt'. The prophets themselves, the salt of the nation, have 'lost their savour'. These unsavoury prophets *led my people ... astray,* whereas the prophets' job was precisely to keep them on the right track.

They prophesied in Baal's name; a total reversal of their function. The prophets were traditionally the champions of Yahweh against Baal. What the prophets are doing is completely at variance with what one expects of prophets.

23.14 *I see a thing most horrible.* The single Hebrew word which

121

translates *a thing most horrible* occurs nowhere in the Bible except in Jeremiah.

Adulterers and hypocrites. REB, like NEB, is paraphrasing here. More literally, 'they commit adultery, and walk in *sheqer* (falsehood)'. Their job is to condemn evildoing and to call people to repentance; but they actually *encourage evildoers so that no one* repents.

23.15   The condemnation. The threat to *give them wormwood to eat and bitter poison to drink* may be a reference to the judicial ordeal. See comment on 8.14, and cf. 9.15, 25.15–29, 48.26.

... *a godless spirit has spread.* The prophets are the source of an infection *which has spread to the whole country.*

23.16–22   Again the paragraphing of REB breaks up the passage in a manner not supported by most commentators. Vv. 16–22 could be regarded as spelling out what 23.14 means by 'walking in falsehood'.

The job of prophets is to perceive how things really are, notwithstanding appearances or wishful thinking, and notwithstanding fears. Again note the words of Elisha in II Kings 6.17. In II Kings 6 the city is besieged and surrounded by troops: but this is only the apparent situation. The reality is that the besiegers themselves are surrounded by a force beyond their imagining, for the mountain is full of 'horses of fire and chariots of fire'. The prophet is the one who sees beyond the illusion that human beings take for reality, and perceives the truly real. But the prophets of whom Jeremiah speaks do the reverse. While Jeremiah is appalled at his perception of the true condition of his people (23.9–10) these prophets of illusion *buoy* (them) *up with false hopes* and tell them everything is all right.

Their job is to speak the word of the Lord, but *it is not the Lord's words they speak* (23.16). *They give voice to their own fancies.*

Let us not be too smug about the false prophets. It is all too easy to be uncritical of the state of one's own society; not to see what is wrong in it. When things are close to home it is easy to take their imperfections uncritically for granted. Suddenly to see our familiar lives with the eye of an outsider can be a nasty shock. The true prophet is such an outsider, who, if we allow it, will shatter our complacency and our illusions about ourselves. Prophecy is about shifting our perspective, so that our complacency and self-satisfaction (be it individual or corporate) are challenged.

But these prophets, whom Jeremiah has in his sights, confirm the illusions and unrealistic attitudes of their fellow Israelites. *To those*

who spurn the word of the Lord they say '*Prosperity will be yours'; and to
all who follow their stubborn hearts they say 'No harm will befall you.'*

All that is said about these prophets adds up to a consistent
picture.

23.18 *For which of them had stood in the council of the Lord?* Cf. 23.22:
But if they had stood in my council, they would have proclaimed my words.
The implications of this are startling. For the background to it see
I Kings 22, especially vv. 19–23, the story of Micaiah ben Imlah.
Micaiah has a vision in which he sees what is going on in heaven. He
sees 'the Lord seated on his throne' (cf. Isa. 6.1) 'with all the host of
heaven in attendance'. (For other references to this divine council see
Ps. 82.1 and 89.6f.). More than that, he listens in to the deliberations of
that heavenly assembly and reports on them. Jeremiah's words in
23.18 and 22 reveal that this claim to be a witness of what goes on in
heaven is not a peculiarity of Micaiah's. Jeremiah assumes that any
prophet worthy of the name has access to a seat in the public gallery
of that heavenly parliament. Without such a seat, how could a
prophet know what to say? What credence could we place on the
reports of a parliamentary correspondent who had no access to
parliament?

23.19–20 Jeremiah knows what is going on, and what the Lord's
intentions are, and in these two verses he tells us what the Lord has
planned. (These verses appear again at 30.23–24.)

23.21 But his opponents do not know. They have no commission.
They behave as if they have; they rush about and say 'Thus says the
Lord'. But the Lord has given them no message.

23.22 *If they had stood in* (the Lord's) *council*, as any genuine
prophet was entitled to do, they would have had genuine words of
the Lord to speak to the people; and this would have been demonstrated by its results, for they would have *turned them from their evil
ways and their evil doings.*

23.23–24 The REB translation obscures the point of v.23. God is
both *near at hand*, and *far away.* i.e. in our theological language, he is
both immanent and transcendent. V.24 spells this out. There is
nowhere in the universe where we can hide from him or escape his
presence (Ps. 139). He fills the whole universe, its most intimate inter-
stices and its furthest spaces. The relevance of this to the subject of
false prophecy is not entirely clear.

23.25–32 is in prose. Some commentators regard the verses as
editorial, but there is no strong reason for doing so. It may be presumed that Jeremiah did know how to express himself in prose.

These verses give us the most detailed picture yet of the people whom Jeremiah regards as false prophets, and of the way they behave.

23.25–26   The God who knows everything is aware of the hypocrisy of the false prophets. By the time the book of Jeremiah was written it was of course obvious who the false prophets were. Those who had said 'Peace, peace', who had promised prosperity and had seen nothing wrong, had been proved wrong by events.

23.25   *'I have had a dream, I have had a dream!'* Whether there is an implied contrast here between 'dream' and 'word', the dream being thought of as an inferior form of communication, is not clear. Dreams are certainly not always thought of in scripture as a false or inferior form of revelation (see, e.g., the well known passage in Joel 2.28) and the man who says 'I have a dream' may be a true prophet of God.

23.26   The real criticism here of the false prophets is not that they appeal to an inferior medium of inspiration, but that what they say is *lies* and *their own inventions*.

23.28   contradicts my observation above, that the difference between true and false prophecy may be apparent only in retrospect. *Chaff and grain are quite distinct, says the Lord.* Chaff and grain may in fact, at a quick glance, be mistaken for one another, but anyone who takes care to look will readily perceive the difference. And anyone who picks up a bag of grain and a bag of chaff will know immediately which is which. What reveals all is the weight. There are Christian communities in our own day who indulge in what they are pleased to call 'prophecy'. Such 'prophecy' is almost invariably trivial in its content. It is readily recognizable as chaff.

23.29   The true word is not something flimsy that will blow away in the wind: it makes itself felt. It has substance. It has force. It is *like fire ... like a hammer that shatters rock*. One good test of any word or dream that purports to come from God is, 'Is there challenge in it? Does it make any demand? Does it call for change? Does it convert?'

23.30   The false prophets cannot even produce an original message; they take over other prophets' oracles. Moreover, *they concoct words of their own*. Note that these false prophets are therefore quite different from Micaiah's opponents in I Kings 22. Micaiah never accuses his opponents of inventing their message. He assumes that they are prophesying in good faith, but that God, for his own reasons, has given them a false message to speak.

23.32   Jeremiah's opponents are not wrong because they dream, but because they *deal in false dreams*, and deliberately *relate them to mislead*.

The final damning indictment of the false prophets is that God did not send them. They have no call and no commission.

23.33–40 The passage centres upon a word-play on the Hebrew word *massa*. The word basically means 'burden', something carried or lifted; but apparently it could also describe the 'message' of a prophet or other communicator.

Though there is no noun in English which has the same double meaning we could produce something like the Hebrew word-play by using a verb. It is idiomatic enough in English to speak of someone 'bearing' a message. When the prophet is asked, 'What message do you bear from the Lord?', he replies, 'The message I bear is that the Lord can't bear you.'

But having said this, there remains much that is obscure in the passage. It is not totally clear what point is being made by means of the word-play, or why the prophet resents (as he appears to do) being asked, *What is the burden of the Lord?* or why he tries to forbid his questioners the use of this particular form of words.

What is clear is that the only word the prophet can be prevailed on to deliver is a word of disapproval of the people who questioned him.

Several commentators regard v.33 as the kernel of the passage and see it as an original brief oracle by Jeremiah, with vv.34–40 as a later 'midrashic extension' (Holladay's phrase). Midrash is a style of traditional Jewish interpretation which extends the meaning of a text, often in fanciful directions.

Vision of the good and the bad figs

24.1–10

24.1–10 The two baskets of figs. The setting of this prophecy is specified clearly in v.1. Its delivery follows the first capture of Jerusalem by the Babylonians in 597 and the first deportation, when Jehoiakin (here called Jeconiah) was taken away captive and replaced by Zedekiah. (See II Kings 24.10–17.)

These events were, of course, traumatic. But one reaction seems to have been a feeling of relief on the part of those left behind in Judah that at least the worst fate, that of deportation, had fallen on others. There may have been an idea around that those who had been taken away must have been more deserving of divine retribution than those left behind, with whom God had dealt more kindly. Jeremiah's message about the figs contradicts any such view very firmly. Contrary to appearances, the 'good figs', the people whom God favours, are the exiles. The 'bad figs', so bad that they are rotten and useless, are those left in the homeland. Against all expectations, the future lies with those apparently despised and rejected.

This view of the matter quickly became that of the exiles themselves. They saw themselves as the ones in whom the true faith continued to burn. In exile they remade the religion of Israel, and eventually brought back from Babylon the law around which the people of God could be reconstituted.

That the exiles should have come to see themselves in this way is perhaps not totally surprising. What is surprising is that Jeremiah, a prophet who was not one of them, should see them in this way too, and that he should do so at such an apparently early stage.

This is so unexpected that some scholars have suggested that this is not a genuine prophecy of Jeremiah's at all, but one constructed in the exilic community at a later date, to express that community's own estimate of itself, and fathered on Jeremiah.

This is possible, but the style and nature of the prophecy is very typical of Jeremiah's utterances. See, e.g., the visions in ch.1. If it is an invention, it is a clever and convincing invention that successfully captures the prophet's 'voice'. Some commentators hear instead the voice of the Deuteronomists in this passage, but only if we dogmatically regard all prose in the book of Jeremiah as 'deuteronomistic' can this be maintained. It may conceivably have been subjected to deuteronomistic expansion. Even if the exilic community did not invent it, it would surely have been important to them.

The strongest argument for concluding that the prophecy is what it purports to be is that nothing in the entire chapter so much as hints at the experience of a second deportation. It is evident that whoever put this chapter together knew nothing of the events of 586. The statement in 24.1 that the setting is in the period after 597 but well before 586 is thus confirmed.

24.1   *I saw two baskets of figs.* Is what the prophet describes here a 'vision'? It depends on how we understand the word. It may be that he saw the baskets of figs in some dream or trance-like state – that the baskets of figs were only in his mind's eye. They are perhaps more likely to have been real baskets that his eye fell upon, since he indicates clearly where he saw them, *set out in front of the temple of the Lord.* They may thus have been part of the autumn harvest festival, the Feast of Tabernacles, and intended as offerings. But would anybody have offered rotten figs? Or they may have been on a market stall at the temple entrance. In ch. 1 the prophet similarly sees a divine message in mundane objects.

24.2 ... *like those that are first ripe*. Fig trees bear two crops each year. The first crop is borne on the old wood, and appears even before the new leaves sprout, in May/June. The second crop is borne on the new wood and ripens later. The first crop is known by a special name, the *bakkuroth*, and is highly prized.

24.6   The language of building and planting is reminiscent of chapter 1.

24.7   At the same time the words *They will be my people and I shall be their God* (which might be described as 'the covenant in a nutshell') recalls the language of 31.33. Likewise the emphasis in v.7 on 'knowing the Lord' finds an echo in 31.34 (but see also 7.23, 11.4, 30.22, 31.1 and 32.38).

I shall give them the wit to know me. The REB translation here is carried over from NEB. 'Wit', however, is hardly the right word. The Hebrew, literally, has 'I shall give them a heart to know me'. This does not so much suggest 'wit' as 'will'.

In 4.4 Jeremiah appealed to his people to 'circumcise their hearts', implying that they could do this for themselves. Here in 24.7 it is recognized that if there is to be any renewal of the heart, then God must do it for them. This accords with the language of v.5: *I count the exiles ...as good*. Whether there has been any real change of heart or not, God is crediting them with one. The verb used is the same as is used in the famous text of Gen. 15.6, where it says that Abraham's faith was 'counted as righteousness'. The exiles may still be no better than they should be, but Jeremiah sees them as 'justified by his grace, as a gift'.

... and to *those who have settled in Egypt*. Some commentators assert that this phrase is a later addition to the passage, others that its presence marks the entire vision of the figs as later than the time of Jehoiakin to which it ostensibly relates. They claim that it presupposes the story of the flight into Egypt in Jer. 43, which did not take place until some time after the second deportation. This argument is faulty. The Jews who fled to Egypt in Jer. 43 found Jewish communities already there (ch.44). Though we are nowhere told explicitly that some Jews fled to Egypt around the time of the first deportation it is wholly plausible that some did so. From 597 onwards, and possibly even earlier than that, there is evidence of a sizable Egyptian diaspora as well as a Babylonian one. There are reasons to believe that the community of Jews at Elephantine on the Nile, of whom we have evidence in the fifth century, had its roots in a movement of refugees who fled to Egypt in the eighth century, at the time of the Assyrian conquest of the Northern Kingdom. So a reference by Jeremiah to Jewish refugees in Egypt could have been made at any time during his career. 24.9 (though its authenticity has also been challenged) speaks of a Jewish diaspora spread through a number of countries.

Summary of the book so far

25.1–14

25.1–14   We are now about half way through the book of Jeremiah and these verses act as a kind of summary of what is in the first half. There can be little doubt that we owe these verses to an editor, who is explaining his own understanding of where we have arrived at. The passage is in prose, of a fairly typical deuteronomic sort, and it refers to Jeremiah in the third person. In the Greek Jeremiah the speaker throughout the passage is the Lord. In the Hebrew this is not consistently the case.

25.1   *In the fourth year of Jehoiakim;* i.e. 605/4. This year was some sort of landmark in the career of the prophet. It was the year in which, according to ch.36, Jeremiah dictated all his oracles to date to his scribe Baruch. It was also a momentous date in world history, the year in which the Babylonian victory at Carchemish over Egypt and Assyria confirmed her as the world's foremost power.

25.3   *... from the thirteenth year of Josiah.* This agrees with the date given in 1.2 for the beginning of Jeremiah's prophetic career.

25.4   As the editor sees it, Jeremiah is only one in a whole succession of prophets, and his experience typifies that of all the others: they were not listened to. On the deuteronomic interpretation, this is the pattern of the entire history of the kingdoms. God sent his prophets to keep his people faithful to himself, but they were at best ignored, at worst persecuted.

25.9   *... my servant King Nebuchadnezzar.* Strikingly, the pagan emperor is described in exactly the same terms as *my servants the prophets* in v.4. The same description is applied to Nebuchadnezzar in 27.6 and 43.10. On each occasion the Greek Jeremiah omits the phrase. But though the prophets and the pagan king share the same title, the word 'servant' does not have exactly the same meaning in the two cases. Both Nebuchadnezzar and the prophets are the Lord's 'servants' in the sense that they do what God wants of them, but Nebuchadnezzar is not 'called' by the Lord. (Though, interestingly, the pagan Cyrus is, according to Isa. 45.1–4.) He does not worship the Lord. He does the Lord's will as a tool in the hand does the will of the one who wields it. The prophets are called. They are not tools but fellow-workers; not insensible of God's purposes, but profoundly in sympathy with them.

25.10 ... *the voices of bridegroom and bride, and the sound of the hand-mill, the light of every lamp.* An evocative and regularly repeated formula in the book of Jeremiah, employed usually in threats, as here, (cf. 7.34 and 16.9) but in 33.11 in a prophecy of hope.

25.11 *For seventy years* ... The Israelites regarded seventy years as a round figure. It means 'a long time', well in excess of a generation. In fact, the exile did not last as long as this: it was more like sixty years, if we reckon from the first deportation in 597 to Cyrus's edict in 538, allowing the return. And it is barely fifty years if we reckon from the destruction of the temple and the second deportation. Those who are concerned to safeguard the literal accuracy of biblical statements argue that the seventy years is reckoned from the destruction of Solomon's temple in 586 to the completion of the second temple in 516.

25.12 *I shall punish the king of Babylon and his people* ... Isaiah said something very closely similar about Assyria. The Assyrians were doing God's work in punishing Israel. They are the stick with which he beats his people. But when they have served their turn they too will be punished and destroyed. See especially Isa. 10.5–12.

25.13 *All that is written in this scroll* ... These words must once have marked the end of a collection of Jeremiah traditions. Perhaps it contained much of what is now included in 1.1–25.12. At all events, it now marks the end of a major division of the book, for 1.1–25.13 is recognizable as one of the four primary sections into which our present book of Jeremiah falls.

At this point the Greek book of Jeremiah records the oracles against foreign nations, which in the Hebrew form of the book we do not reach until ch. 46.

Judgment on foreign nations

25.15–38

25.15–29 These verses appear in the Greek Jeremiah at the end of the oracle on Moab, which in the Hebrew is in ch. 48. In fact they make very good sense either as an introduction to the oracles against the nations or as a summary of them, so it is very likely that the Greek edition represents the more original ordering of the material. In its present location in the Hebrew 25.15–38 makes up a sort of mini-collection of oracles against foreign nations, anticipating the much lengthier collection in chs 46–51.

In 1.5 Jeremiah is said to have been appointed 'a prophet to the nations'. Up to this point in the book there is no real evidence of his having fulfilled, or attempted to fulfil, that part of his commission.

25.15 *Receive from my hand this cup of the wine of wrath* ... This image of the 'cup of wrath' that God makes his enemies drink is one that occurs elsewhere in the book of Jeremiah and elsewhere in scripture. See, e.g., Jer. 8.14, 9.15, 48.26; Ps. 75.8; Isa. 51.17; Lam. 4.21; Ezek. 23.32f.; Hab. 2.16; Rev. 14.10, 16.19, 18.6. See comment on 8.14.

25.16, cf. vv.27, 29. The introduction of *the sword* seems inappropriate, and not in accord with the imagery of the poisoned cup.

25.20 The location of *Uz* is unknown. Job lived there, according to Job 1.1. *Ashkelon, Gaza, Ekron and ... Ashdod* were all cities of the Philistines. There were originally five of them, but Gath, the one nearest to Israelite territory, seems to have disappeared from history before Jeremiah's time.

Egypt and its allies, who are mentioned first, are of course to the south. Philistia is on the coast, south-west of Judah. *Edom, Moab, and the Ammonites* are countries immediately to the east. North-west are *Tyre and Sidon*, cities of the Phoenicians. With *Dedan, Tema and Buz* we come full circle, back to the southern side; not the civilized and urban south (Egypt) but the desert south, the Arabian peninsula. With *Zimri ... Elam and ... the Medes* we move to the far north-east. *Last of all the king of Sheshak will have to drink.* 'Sheshak' is probably a coded form of the name 'Babylon'; coded, because during the period of Babylon's power it would have been unwise publicly and overtly to threaten its destruction.

The passage has something of the quality of enacted prophecy. Jeremiah does not, of course, actually enact the giving of the nations the cup to drink, but sees it in his mind's eye.

The offering of a drink has a certain symbolic force even in our own culture, but in that of the ancient near east evidently a much richer and profounder one. Cf. the use made of the image by Jesus in Gethsemane ('Let this cup pass from me') and in his reply to James and John ('Can you drink ...?') Mark 10.38 and parallels; cf. John 18.11. There is a cup of salvation as well as a cup of wrath and of suffering; e.g. Ps. 116.13 (cf. 23.5).

25.30–38   These verses are a kind of commentary on 25.15ff., spelling out something of what it means to make the nations drink 'the cup of the wine of wrath'. We are presented here with a kaleidoscope of shifting images. If anything holds the passage together it is the theme of shouting and tumult. Though it is not altogether impossible that Jeremiah should have prophesied against the nations in general, and in these terms, the tone of the passage and its theme of universal judgment are typical of the prophecy of a later period.

25.30   *The Lord roars from on high.* Cf. Amos 1.1 and Joel 4.16. The idea of God making a lot of noise may seem an odd one to us, but the picture is of the Lord as a warrior, a not uncommon one in the Old Testament. Warriors in ancient times did shout and make a lot of noise. It was all part of the process of intimidation. Isa. 63.1–6 offers us the same image of God the warrior, and makes the same transition as Jer. 25.30 to the image of the vintager, the treader of grapes. The shouting of the grape-treaders is probably a reference to the singing of work songs, which in the days before modern machinery tended to accompany any rhythmic activity. Isa. 16.9–10 also refers to the shouting of harvesters.

... *against all the inhabitants of the land.* The words could just as easily be translated '... all the inhabitants of the earth'. In view of the universal judgment of which the rest of the passage speaks, 'earth' is probably the better rendering.

25.31   *For the Lord brings a charge* ... The idea of the divine lawsuit, in which God brings a case against his people, or, as in this instance, against humanity in general, is a very widespread one in prophetic literature.

25.33   The scene here is that of a battlefield or of natural disaster, where the bodies lie thick on the ground.

25.34–38   We move next to another noisy scene, the 'shepherds', i.e. rulers, shouting in grief and dismay at the havoc which the Lord is wreaking.

25.34   *Sprinkle yourselves with ashes.* A sign of mourning.

Reports of the Prophet's Activities
26–45

Again the temple speech: the trial of Jeremiah
26.1–24

Chapter 26 is best interpreted in connection with ch.7. The notes on ch.7 discuss the relationship between the two and the reader should consult those before proceeding. This second telling of the story exemplifies the theme of 'rejection of the word' so prominent in the second part of the book.

The people we call the 'deuteronomic historians', who produced the history which comprises the books of Joshua, Judges, Samuel and Kings, were concerned above all to explain to their people why the catastrophe of the exile had taken place. Central to their presentation of the history is the series of prophets who tried repeatedly to recall Israel to her allegiance to her God. And central to their explanation of the exile is their contention that the prophets were consistently ignored and their word rejected. The deuteronomic influence on the book of Jeremiah is seen in the way this theme of the rejection of the word is given prominence. Just as in ch.36 there is an implied contrast between Jehoiakim's treatment of Jeremiah's scroll and Josiah's earlier reception of the Book of the Law, so ch.26 makes a contrast, this time with Hezekiah, asserting that in his time the prophetic word was treated with more respect. In this case the contrast is not merely implied, for 26.17–19 makes an explicit reference back to the reign of Hezekiah and the treatment of Micah.

Chapters 26 and 36 are in any case closely parallel. In ch.26 the prophet delivers his spoken word in the temple precincts. In ch.36 his written word is delivered on his behalf, again in the temple court. On both occasions the prophet, like Jesus of Nazareth after him, challenges the religious (and political) authorities of his people in their own stronghold.

Whatever reshaping the contents of ch.26 may have undergone, either at deuteronomic or any other hands, there is no good reason to doubt that a real historical event underlies this account. Some commentators treat the chapter as a piece of prophetic legend, but legendary material does not contain the amount of circumstantial detail (about procedures and movements and about the personnel involved) that we see in this passage.

26.1 *At the beginning of the reign of Jehoiakim.* It may have been the feast of Tabernacles, which counted as the beginning of the king's regnal year. This would be the year 609.

26.2 *Stand in the court of the Lord's house and speak to the inhabitants of all the towns of Judah who come to worship there.* All Israelites were expected to come to Jerusalem to worship on at least three occasions in the year, the great festivals of Tabernacles, Passover/Unleavened Bread and Weeks (later called Pentecost). A prophet who addressed the temple crowd on such an occasion would be heard by people from all over the country, *from all the towns of Judah.*

26.3 *Perhaps they may listen.* The way this is phrased does not suggest much optimism. Nevertheless, prophetic threats are always conditional. If they meet with the response of repentance, God will change his mind. The book of Jonah is an unusual commentary on this assumption. The book of Jonah does not argue *for* the conviction that God will have mercy on those who repent, but *from* the conviction that he will do so.

26.4 *If you do not live according to the law I have set before you ...* Appeals to the *law* are rare in prophetic literature before Jeremiah. It may be the voice of the deuteronomic editor we are hearing here.

26.5 Again this is likely to be the deuteronomic voice rather than the prophet's. This is a typical summary of the deuteronomists' reading of their people's history.

The idea eventually grew up that not only had Israel consistently rejected the prophetic word, but that the prophets themselves had regularly been persecuted and killed. This tradition is referred to in the New Testament in Acts 7.52 (and Matt. 5.12, 23.35, 23.37) and underlies the parable of the Wicked Husbandmen (Mark 12.1–12 and parallels). In fact, the Old Testament does not record many explicit examples of prophets being persecuted, apart from Jeremiah himself, and instances of prophets being killed are even fewer (though II Chron. 24.20–22 is one, which the New Testament refers to in Matt. 23.35).

26.6 *I shall do to this house as I did to Shiloh.* See the comments on 7.12. This was evidently the crux of Jeremiah's speech, or at least, the part of it which caused most offence. This is what, in 26.9, his

133

accusers seize on. But note that the prophet's threat has a double target. It is a threat against the temple and city.

26.7 *The priests, the prophets and all the people heard Jeremiah*. The audience was not only representative of all parts of the country (cf. v.2) but of the various social and religious classes. The list of hearers and accusers does not, however, include the *sarim*. This is the Hebrew word regularly translated as 'princes', though REB here renders as *chief officers*. Precisely what the status and function of the *sarim* was we do not know, but at this period the word seems to apply to people who held some sort of formal office and had judicial functions. In the present account they intervene and set up a formal hearing of the complaints.

In v.8 *all the people* join priests and prophets in threatening Jeremiah. In v.11 *all the people* together with the *officers* (i.e. *sarim*) hear the accusations made by *the priests and the prophets*. In v.16 *the officers and all the people* respond to the accusers. Some commentators find a difficulty here, alleging that the narrative is confused and that *all the people* appear on different sides at different points in the story. But the phrase *all the people* may not refer to precisely the same group throughout. In vv.7–8 they are the mob, incensed at what they hear the prophet saying. In vv.11 and 16 the phrase refers to people who are part of a properly constituted court, which is giving the prophet a judicial hearing. In v.24 *the people* from whom Jeremiah has to be saved are again the mob. The implication is that the court did not reach a verdict and that the proceedings threatened to break up in disorder.

26.10 The *sarim went up from the royal palace to the Lord's house*. This suggests that they were normally based in the palace, which was of course the seat of government. The palace and the temple were next door to each other on the top of the eastern hill, the palace being only a little lower than the summit.

They took their places. This is clearly a formally constituted court. In any other city the court would have been composed of the elders of the community, but it looks as if there were special arrangements for the administration of justice in the capital. According to the Chronicler (II Chron. 19.5–11) King Jehoshaphat set up a court consisting of priests, levites and lay elders. If this is correct, such a court may have been the ancestor of the court of the *sarim* mentioned here in Jer. 26.

26.11 It is *the priests and the prophets* who actually bring the charge. *All the people* now seem to join the *officers* as part of the court.

The presence of the public appears to have been essential to the constitution of a court in ancient Israel, and it is likely that their assent to the judgment was necessary.

The charge, as indicated in v.11, does not mention the threat to the temple, but complains only that Jeremiah *has prophesied against this city*. But the answer attributed to the prophet in v.12 picks up both halves of his original threat *against this house and this city*.

26.11 Jeremiah's fellow *prophets* are amongst his accusers. According to the book, Jeremiah was at odds with his prophetic colleagues throughout most of his career. He would expect no support from that quarter. It is the religious authorities, the prophets and the priests, who accuse Jeremiah and wish to have him suppressed, but the 'secular' court which insists on giving him a hearing, and the lay *elders of the land* (v.17) who are credited with citing the precedent of Micah in his defence.

26.12 There is no argument about the facts. Jeremiah freely admits that he has used the words complained of. His defence, which is implicit at this point rather than explicit, is that the words are privileged, because he has said them on divine authority.

26.13 reiterates that the doom predicted can be averted by repentance.

26.14–15 Because his words have divine authority Jeremiah cannot be held responsible for them, and if they punish him with death they *will be guilty of murdering an innocent man*.

26.16–23 What follows is an argument based on precedents. Two are presented, one in Jeremiah's favour, the other against. It is widely believed that the latter of these precedents cannot have been appealed to at any trial at the beginning of Jehoiakim's reign, and that vv.20–23, with their account of Uriah b. Shemaiah, must have been added later to the record of the trial. Some commentators indeed think that both precedents are later additions.

The case against vv.20–23 does seem strong. If the trial really took place at the very beginning of Jehoiakim's reign then the case of Uriah can hardly have been cited at the trial, since it is Jehoiakim who is said to have had him put to death. But the words of 26.1, *At the beginning of the reign of Jehoiakim* are not very precise. Even if the events happened at what was officially the beginning of the regnal year Jehoiakim could have been on the throne for some months, which would give time for the execution of Uriah to have taken place. The possibility should not be ruled out that both these precedents were indeed quoted.

One of the reasons for doubting whether either of the precedents was actually appealed to at the time is that some commentators interpret v.16 as the judgment of the court, and it is observed that there would be little point in citing precedents once the judgment had been delivered. But it is not necessary to understand v.16 as a judgment. It could just as readily be understood as part of the debate. Moreover, the whole account ends with the statement (v.24) that *Ahikam son of Shaphan used his influence on Jeremiah's behalf to save him from death at the hands of the people.* This would scarcely have been necessary if the court had pronounced in his favour. The account as it stands makes good sense if we take it that the court, faced with conflicting precedents, delivered no judgment, and Jeremiah had to be rescued by a powerful friend from the clutches of his dissatisfied accusers.

26.18–19   According to the first precedent the prophet Micah prophesied against city and temple in terms not dissimilar to Jeremiah's. The words here ascribed to Micah appear in the book of Micah at 3.12. Micah, it is argued, was not charged with any offence, but rather was listened to. This was under King Hezekiah.

26.20–23   The second precedent happened under Jehoiakim, and Jehoiakim's behaviour is explicitly contrasted with that of Hezekiah, just as in ch. 36 the behaviour of the same Jehoiakim is implicitly contrasted with that of Josiah. Hezekiah and Josiah are the only two kings of whom the deuteronomic historian says that they 'did what was right in the eyes of the Lord' (II Kings 18.3 and 22.2).

Uriah the son of Shemaiah is not mentioned elsewhere in the Bible. His words are not quoted, but the substance of them is said to be the same as that of Micah's and Jeremiah's oracles, in that *he prophesied against this city and this land.* Like them, too, he claimed divine authority. He *prophesied in the name of the Lord.* He was threatened with death and fled to Egypt, and from there he was extradited and executed.

26.24   *Ahikam son of Shaphan* is mentioned in II Kings 22.12 and 14 as having served earlier under Josiah. From much of the book of Jeremiah we get the impression that Jeremiah is a lone voice, 'crying in the wilderness'. But from this incident we learn that he is not by any means totally isolated. Other prophets, Micah (admittedly a hundred years earlier) and Uriah (his contemporary), bear a similar message, and Jeremiah is not without sympathizers among the ruling class, and has at least one friend in high places; cf. also ch. 36.

Jeremiah opposes false prophets
27.1–29.32

Chapters 27–28 continue exploring the theme of 'rejection of the word'. This time it is an enacted word as well as a spoken one. Ch. 27 begins with the prophet being directed to wear a wooden yoke, of the sort worn by draught cattle, and then addressing the ambassadors of foreign nations, who are visiting Jerusalem (vv.1–11), counselling them to submit to Babylon. This message is qualified by the promise that Babylonian sovereignty will not last for ever. The same message is then addressed to Zedekiah (vv.12–15). Ch. 27 anticipates ch. 28 by taking up the problem of false prophecy (vv.9–10, 14–18), and answers in particular the false predictions of an early return of the temple vessels which the Babylonians had taken away.

All this, to the end of ch. 27, is a first person account, the words being put into Jeremiah's own mouth. Some commentators find the chapter confused, and suggest that it has been elaborated and expanded. However that may be, the core of it is an account of an enacted prophecy, in which the prophet appears wearing a wooden yoke, indicating that the nations should accept Babylonian domination.

27.1 *At the beginning of the reign of Zedekiah.* The Hebrew actually reads: '… the reign of Jehoiakim'. This must be wrong. The story that follows relates to Zedekiah, and some of the prophecies in this and the following chapter are addressed to him. The events in ch. 28 follow closely on those of ch. 27 and are dated (28.1) 'at the beginning of the reign of Zedekiah'. It looks as if at some early stage in the text's transmission a scribe has erroneously repeated at the beginning of ch. 27 the opening words of ch. 26. The whole verse is in any case missing from the Greek version of the book.

27.1–11 concerns a message addressed by Jeremiah not to his own people but to diplomatic representatives of various foreign nations who have been visiting Zedekiah. This is one of the places where Jeremiah may fairly be said to fulfil his commission in 1.5 to be 'a prophet to the nations'. It is to be remembered that at the point at which this incident takes place Jerusalem has already fallen once to the Babylonians and the first deportation has already taken place. Zedekiah's kingdom is, perforce, part of the Babylonian empire, and Zedekiah reigns as the Babylonians' nominee. If he has received the ambassadors of *Edom, Moab, Ammon, Tyre and Sidon* it is virtually certain that the purpose of their meeting was to orchestrate resistance to Babylon. Jeremiah's message to the ambassadors, spelled out in words in 27.5–11, is that resistance to Babylon is useless, because God has willed to put the world (for the time being) into Babylon's power. On the phrase in 27.6, *my servant King Nebuchadnezzar*, see the note on 25.9.

27.6   *I have given him even the creatures of the wild to serve him.* This hyberbolic statement of the cosmic power exercized by Nebuchadnezzar is echoed in Dan. 4 in the vision of the great tree. It suggests that in some circles Nebuchadnezzar came to be regarded as an almost mythological figure. The statement is repeated in 28.14.

27.7   The precise understanding of 27.7 is debatable, but on any showing it is not an exact historical prediction. Its main thrust is to suggest that the nations will remain subject to Babylon for three generations. This agrees substantially with the prediction in 25.11 and 29.10 that the exile is to last seventy years. The whole verse is in any case missing from the Greek and may be a late addition to the book.

27.9–11   Just as the kings of Judah have their prophets (most of them false prophets, as ch. 28 will demonstrate) so the kings of the other nations have their occult advisers, *prophets, diviners, women dreamers, soothsayers and sorcerers.* Their comforting assertions that Babylon is not to be feared are lies. They, like Judah's own false prophets, are accused of *sheqer,* 'falsehood', 'dangerous illusion'. The only way to avoid deportation is to submit. All this is making explicit the message which is already there in the enacted prophecy with which the chapter began. The words are simply there to explain the action.

The text in 27.2 speaks of *the cords and crossbars of a yoke.* There is some obscurity in the words used, but ch. 28 makes it clear that it is a complete yoke that the prophet wears.

27.12–15   applies the same message to Zedekiah and to Judah. Zedekiah too, like the foreign kings, is supported by false prophets. But they are false, and no notice should be taken of them; cf. 34.1–7, and see the notes at 21.1–7. This is the second direct address by the prophet to Zedekiah, but unlike 21.1–7 it is not in the context of a formal consultation. It is the prophet's unsolicited advice.

27.16–22   delivers a like message to *the priests and all the people.* These verses give us more detail about what exactly the false prophets are saying. They predict an early end to the deportation that has already taken place. They also predict that the vessels taken by the Babylonians from the temple will soon be restored. 'Quite the reverse!' says the prophet. The vessels which the Babylonians did not take away in 597 will be taken at the next attack.

28.1 *That same year, at the beginning of the reign of king Zedekiah of Judah.* See the note on the date in 27.1.

In the fifth month of the first year. The Hebrew text actually reads, 'of the fourth year'. The translators of REB evidently felt the 'fourth year' to be incompatible with the statement (both in 27.1 and 28.1) that this was 'the beginning of the reign'. This is hardly a good enough reason for refusing to translate what the Hebrew says. 'Beginning' is not a precise term. The fourth year might still be seen as early enough in the reign to be regarded as the beginning. If we follow the Greek Jeremiah the problem (if it is a problem) in any case disappears, for it reads simply: 'Now in the fourth year of Zedekiah, king of Judah, in the fifth month ...'

The prophet from Gibeon. Gibeon is just a few miles north-west of Jerusalem. The way Hananiah is described as 'the prophet from Gibeon' suggests that he was a well-known figure. Gibeon is barely four miles from Jeremiah's own home village of Anathoth.

In 28.2–4 Hananiah delivers an oracle. He uses exactly the same formulae and turns of phrase as Jeremiah himself. There is nothing in the form of the oracles of the false prophets to distinguish them from those of the true ones. He is also described quite simply as 'a prophet', though the Greek (along with other ancient translations) is unhappy with this and calls him a 'pseudo-prophet'.

It is a neatly balanced oracle. Hananiah begins *I shall break the yoke of the king of Babylon.* He then specifies what this means: the sacred vessels taken by Nebuchadnezzar from the temple will be restored; the exiled King Jehoiakin will be brought back, and *all the Judaean exiles* who went with him will return. Finally, he repeats that *I shall break the yoke ...*

Jeremiah's reply at this point is very mild. He begins by saying (v.6), 'I hope you're right'. REB *May it be so!* The actual Hebrew word here is 'Amen!' But in vv.7–8 he raises a query. It was characteristic of the prophets of the past to deliver warnings of disaster. If a prophet claims to foresee salvation his words need special scrutiny, and should not be trusted until they demonstrably come true.

This severe test would call in question Jeremiah's own words that he uttered later in his ministry, and many of the oracles of the post-exilic prophets in general. The 'wait and see' test reminds us of Deut. 18.21–22.

28.10   Hananiah now dramatically counters Jeremiah's enacted prophecy by taking the yoke from him and breaking it, repeating the substance of the oracle as he does so. He adds a very specific message that *within two years* Babylon's domination *of all nations* will be ended.

Did Hananiah really break the yoke? It would have been a very considerable feat of strength.

Then the prophet Jeremiah went his way. Jeremiah neither displays anger nor attempts immediate rebuttal or retaliation. This is consistent with the behaviour ascribed to him in ch.42, where the question is put to him about whether to flee to Egypt. On that occasion he does not immediately venture an opinion. He is not being asked for an opinion: he is being asked for a word from the Lord, and he is prepared to say nothing until that word comes. In the event, he waits ten days. So here in the case of Hananiah, it is only when the word comes to him again that he responds.

28.13   Jeremiah asserts that the wooden yoke will be replaced by an iron one. Whether he actually did reappear wearing an iron yoke the text does not make clear. He may simply have announced it. We find not infrequently in the book of Jeremiah that the prophet is given an instruction by God to do something, and the significance of the act is explained, but we are never explicitly told that he did it. Presumably the reader is simply meant to assume that he did.

28.14   The word of the Lord that accompanies the instructions about the iron yoke asserts that, far from being broken, Nebuchadnezzar's power will be total. It will extend over creation. See the note on 27.6.

28.15   Having received his additional word from the Lord Jeremiah now knows for certain that Hananiah is a false prophet. Now Hananiah is personally condemned, because he has *led this nation to trust in false prophecies.* He is to die within the year. The REB's rendering: *The Lord never sent you* therefore *I shall remove you …* misses the word-play in the divine sentence. The Hebrew uses the same verb twice. 'The Lord never sent you, therefore now he is sending you – off the face of the earth.'

This is to happen because he has *preached rebellion against the Lord.* This seems harsh. All that Hananiah had done was to express a certain optimism about the political situation. How did this amount to serious *rebellion against the Lord*? The optimism in this case was a refusal to acknowledge the full rigour of the divine judgment on his people. It was a refusal to accept the Lord's declared will. This is rebellion. It is worth noting that Deut. 13.5 decrees the death penalty for any prophet who 'preaches rebellion against the Lord'. The sentence on Hananiah, in the form in which the Hebrew text records it, looks like a deliberate echo of the Deuteronomy passage. The Greek Jeremiah, however, does not include the crucial words and it may be that the allusion to Deuteronomy was not present in the earliest form of the story.

Some have doubted whether the saintly Jeremiah could have condemned an opponent in these terms: but a similar condemnation of Pashhur is ascribed to him in 20.4, and of Shemaiah at the end of ch.29. Amos 7.17 shows that such curses on their opponents were not unknown among prophets. We must beware of seeing Jeremiah as a Christ-figure and attributing to him a kind of saintliness grounded in nothing firmer than our own wishful thinking. On the evidence of the book, Jeremiah too was a violent Benjaminite.

Chapter 29 gives an account of correspondence which passed between Jerusalem and the community of exiles in Babylon. This is still in the reign of Zedekiah, in the period between the two deportations. There is little indication that prophets before Jeremiah's time communicated their message in writing. They did not need to. But once the first deportation has taken place, if Jeremiah wishes to prophesy to the exiles then to do it by letter is the only way open to him. The text of the letter begins in v.4 but it is not immediately obvious where it is to be regarded as ending. It is evident that a quite separate letter, specifically to one individual, Shemaiah, begins in v.24. Is everything up to v.23 therefore to be understood as part of the first letter? There are other points at which the letter might conceivably be seen to end, but in this case the 'non-letter' sections of the chapter would have to be interpreted as separate oracles, placed in this context because they are addressed to the exiles.

29.1 *To the elders ... to the priests, prophets and all the people.* It is interesting to speculate about the mechanics of the process by which the letter was to be communicated to this wide range of people. The exiles were not all in one place, but in different groups in different parts of the country. Nevertheless, as the book of Ezekiel shows, some structure of Jewish community life was created. Jeremiah's letter must have been read out, probably on several occasions and in several different places, to community gatherings of some sort, in a way similar to that in which, much later, Paul's letters were read out in the churches.

141

Vv.1–3 are not part of the letter itself. It would have been normal practice in sending such a letter to keep a copy. Vv.1–3 would in this case represent the annotation added to the copy to explain what it was. We are told who carried the letter. There is of course no public postal service. The carriers are official envoys sent by the king of Judah to the king of Babylon. In spite of their dignity they do not mind being used as the prophet's postmen.

The substance of the letter is that the exile is going to be a long-term affair, so the best way to deal with it is to recognize that fact and behave accordingly. The exiles may as well make long-term investments: build houses; plant orchards and gardens; marry and raise families.

Seek the welfare of any city to which I have exiled you. They should stop behaving like strangers in a strange place. Let them play any part in civic life which is open to them; behave as though they belonged. (In what respects should God's people behave as though they are at home in the world; and in what ways ought they to live as strangers?)

29.8–9   The reason why this chapter about the letter is placed where it is, is that, like ch.28, it focusses on the theme of prophetic conflict. There are others who offer a contrary, and in some ways more reassuring message than Jeremiah's. They are saying: 'It will be over by Christmas.' This, Jeremiah is telling them, is a false hope that will only make it harder for the exiles to come to terms with their situation.

These opposing voices are not just those of prophets, but of *diviners* and *women whom you set to dream dreams.*

29.10–14   There is hope of future restoration, but it is a restoration not a few years ahead but a few generations ahead. In a year or two from Jeremiah's writing of this letter there would be a generation of Jews who were born into exile; for whom 'home' was a place where they had never been.

29.10   *When a full seventy years have passed* ... See the note on 25.11.

29.12   *If you invoke me and come and pray to me, I shall listen to you.* A divine U-turn. In 7.16, 11.14 and 14.11 Jeremiah is instructed not to pray for the people, because God has made his mind up not to listen.

The greater part of v.14 is not in the Greek Jeremiah.

29.15   *You say that the Lord has raised up prophets for you in Babylon.* We know this was true, for one of these prophets was Ezekiel, who received his call to prophesy in Babylonia. The circumstances and nature of this call are described in some detail in his book. Ezekiel's message, however, was very different from that of the prophets with whom Jeremiah is taking issue. Indeed, at this point in history, between the two deportations, Ezekiel and Jeremiah were saying very similar things.

29.15–19 Unexpectedly and abruptly the text turns to address those Jews who had not gone into exile. That Jeremiah might, in a letter to the exiles, have something to say about the community still in the homeland, is not in itself surprising, but the terms in which the letter speaks of them suggest that this section may not have been part of the original correspondence. Suspicions are strengthened by the observation that vv.16–20 do not appear in the Greek version of the book.

29.16 *The king who sits on the throne of David*: a perhaps deliberately oblique way of referring to Zedekiah. Zedekiah's predecessor, Jehoiakin, was still alive in exile, and Zedekiah had been placed on the throne by the Babylonian conquerors. In the eyes of some Jews, therefore, maybe most, the legitimacy of his kingship was questionable.

29.17–18 Further disaster is predicted for the community still at home in Judah.

29.17 The phrase *making them like rotten figs, too bad to eat* is a clear reference back to the vision in ch.24, but a clumsy one. The image is the same, but the point it makes is quite different. In ch. 24 the rottenness of the figs is their culpable condition, of which the punishment by 'sword, famine and pestilence' is to be the result. But in 29.17 the rottenness, less plausibly, is the result of punishment.

29.19 A typical piece of deuteronomistic theologizing.

29.20 ... *all you exiles whom I have sent from Jerusalem to Babylon*. Nebuchadnezzar and the Babylonians might have thought they had something to do with this 'sending'. But no! Nebuchadnezzar and the Babylonians had exiled the Jews only in the sense in which the axe cuts down the trees or the brush sweeps up the dirt. The real agent is the one who wields the axe or the brush: the real exiler is the one who uses Nebuchadnezzar and his army.

29.20–23 Condemnation of two named individuals who are prophesying in Babylon. They are claimed to have prophesied falsely, and without divine authority, but we are not told what they said. Perhaps we are meant to understand that they are specific examples of the sort of prophets referred to in 29.8, who by implication have contradicted Jeremiah's prediction of a long exile. But such prophecies would hardly have been sufficient to prompt the

Babylonian authorities to put them to death, as v.22 asserts. It seems more likely that they had plotted an actual revolt or caused a political disturbance of some kind. It may be that the words, *whom the king of Babylon roasted* to death *in the fire* were added later by someone who knew their actual fate. It may be that the fate of these two prophets, fulfilling Jeremiah's curse on them, is seen as a proof that the word of the Lord, delivered by him, is effective over that great distance from Judah to Babylon. It thus acts as a warning to take his 'prophecy by letter' seriously.

29.24–28 begins as a separate communication addressed to Shemaiah the Nehelamite. There is some confusion and disorder in the way the content of these verses is presented. They speak of a letter written from exile, to the Jerusalem priesthood, complaining about Jeremiah. When was this letter written? 29.24–28 seems to be presented as part of Jeremiah's own letter to the exiles, but this cannot really be the case, because according to v.28 Shemaiah's letter quoted Jeremiah's and must therefore have been a response to it. What we must have here is a sample of correspondence subsequent to that letter of Jeremiah's which forms the main subject of this chapter. It appears, therefore, that one result of Jeremiah's initial letter was that complaints were sent back to the priestly authorities in Jerusalem suggesting that the prophet ought to be *restrained*. (On the claim of a priest to exercize such authority over a prophet compare Amos 7.10–17.) Shemaiah's initiative confirms that Jeremiah's advice to take the long view and settle down was very unwelcome to at least some of those in exile.

29.29–32   When Shemaiah's letter arrived in Jerusalem the priest communicated its contents to Jeremiah, which prompted him to deliver an oracle condemning Shemaiah personally. The phrase in v.31, *Send and tell all the exiles*, suggests that Jeremiah sent a further letter to the exilic community, following the former one.

Shemaiah takes his place in the line of prophetic opponents of Jeremiah. At home in Jerusalem there was Hananiah (ch. 28); and alongside him Pashhur the priest (ch. 20). In Babylon there were first of all Ahab and Zedekiah (29.21ff.), and now Shemaiah. In opposition to all of these, Jeremiah's is shown to be the true word.

It is interesting to note how the priest Zephaniah reacts. He does not automatically take Shemaiah's side. His behaviour contrasts strongly with that of Pashhur.

Promises of restoration for the people
30.1 – 33.26

Chapters 30–33 form a distinct section of the book, characterized by optimism and hope, which has traditionally been called 'The Book of Consolation'. It seems likely that the 'Book of Consolation' is composite. The view taken here is that it contains some oracles from Jeremiah's own time, some of which, at least, are likely to be by the prophet himself, and speaking mainly about hopes for the near future; hopes centring on return from exile and the restoration of the nation; but that the passage has been filled out by people who have added their own expectations, and these other contributors have mostly taken a longer view, and looked for a salvation further into the future.

30.1–11   may be treated as a unit, though the passage has been put together from smaller pieces. 30.1–3 forms an editor's preface to what follows.

30.2   *Write on a scroll.* Again the prophet is commanded to *write*; a theme that keeps recurring in the second half of the book. It may be that the editor thought of this scroll as containing the four chapters of consolation, though in the opinion of several commentators the scroll should be thought of as containing only the material of chs. 30–31.

30.3   sets out the keynote of what is in the scroll; it is about the restoration of the people of God. But who are the people of God? V.3 speaks of *Israel and Judah* (cf. v.4). It has been suggested that Jeremiah, early in his career, during the reign of Josiah, did prophesy about the restoration specifically of the North, and that what we have here in ch. 30 are some of these early prophecies, reissued and re-directed at Judah. Now it is quite clear that one of the political aims of Josiah's reform was the reunification of the country, North and South, and there is no reason at all why Jeremiah should not have shared Josiah's hope of re-establishing the ancient unity, and prophesied that when restoration took place, both halves of the nation would be included. Ezekiel, his contemporary, seems to have done so (See Ezek. 37.15–28). But though it would have made sense in that historical context to envisage the restoration of the fortunes of both North and South, it would not have been realistic to expect the return of the Northern exiles, who had been deported by the Assyrians over a century earlier, and Jeremiah's words should probably not be understood as predicting this. To speak of the return of the exiles of Judah was not unrealistic, as events ultimately proved.

30.4–7   A poetic oracle referring back to the time of terror when Judah was overrun and Jerusalem destroyed. The oracle uses a graphic image. Shock and fear of what is going to happen to them produces in the people of Judah a physical agony. Men, i.e. males, are writhing in pain as women do when giving birth. Yet the point of thus referring back is to insist that the experience was survivable. And the image is carefully chosen: with the pain of childbirth there is not only an end to it but an outcome to be thankful for.

30.8–9   A prose prediction picking up the language and imagery of chs. 27–28, the breaking of the yoke. The reference to *David their king* is unusual in the book of Jeremiah (elsewhere only 23.5–6, 33.14–26). The restoration of the royal house is not prominent in visions of the future as the book sets them out. Even here, the allusion is likely to be in the mind of an editor, not of the prophet.

30.10–11   These verses occur also at 46.27–28 (though not in the Greek Jeremiah). This little passage is strongly reminiscent of Deutero-Isaiah, and is likely to be from a later hand than Jeremiah's.

v.12 *For these are the words of the Lord* ... A fresh introduction, suggesting the beginning of a new oracle. It is a two-part oracle; vv.12b–15 set out the hopeless condition of the nation, with its incurable wounds, inflicted by God himself. Vv.16–17 insist, using the same language, that nevertheless there *is* hope, and the incurable may yet be cured.

What is actually being referred to here, under the image of the dreadful, unhealing wounds? It is hardly natural as a metaphor for exile. It is more likely a reference to the awful condition of the people resulting from Nebuchadnezzar's campaigns in the country which led eventually to Jerusalem's fall. Isa 1.5–9 uses very similar imagery in a description of the state of the land after the campaigns of Sennacherib and the Assyrians at the end of the eighth century.

Structurally, vv.12–17 are a beautifully balanced poem, in which everything asserted in the first half is reversed in the second. In the Bible, the imagery of healing is one of the great metaphors for conveying the meaning of God's saving work.

V.14   *Your lovers have forgotten you* looks like an abrupt change of metaphor. But perhaps not. Maybe the thought is that the once-attractive Judah, now disfigured by injury, is no longer desirable.

30.18–22   A rather more detailed picture of what restoration will involve, with its introductory formula, *These are the words of the Lord*, indicating yet another new beginning.

The archaeology of Palestininan cities reveals a repeated cycle of destruction and rebuilding, exactly as described here. After destruction by an enemy, sometimes after a considerable interval, the city would be *rebuilt on its own mound*. The mound itself (or 'tell') was created by the constant process of destruction and then rebuilding on top of the debris. These people had not yet invented the bulldozer, so ruined sites were not cleared. One episode of destruction could raise the height of the tell by several feet. Archaeology also demonstrates that very, very frequently the important buildings, the fortresses, the temples, the palaces, would be repeatedly rebuilt on the same spot, so that *every mansion* would *occupy its traditional site*.

V.19 *I shall increase them, they will not diminish.* Another consequence of natural disaster or military defeat, from which a community might take a very long time to recover, was a drastic reduction in the population. Jerusalem, having grown more or less steadily from the time of David up to the exile, and having spread westwards over on to the western hill, was after the Babylonian conquest very sharply reduced in extent, being cut back to a small settlement on the eastern hill (which is why, later, Nehemiah was able to rebuild the wall so quickly).

From them praise will be heard and sounds of merrymaking. A telling sign of recovery. At the time of writing I have just watched a television report on East Timor, which was brutally invaded and its population decimated by the Indonesians. The invasion began in the mid-seventies. Yet in the mid-nineties a reporter says: 'These people do not smile.'

V.21 *A ruler will appear ... a governor.* The significant word is the one that is not used. In contrast with v.9 this oracle says nothing of a 'king'. It is noteworthy that Ezekiel, too, when he describes the restored nation, is extremely reticent about using the language of royalty. He has a good deal to say about the functions and duties of the head of state in the restored community, but he describes him as 'the ruler'. During the period of exile itself it would probably have been very impolitic to predict the return of a king, with all the implications for national autonomy that such a title would suggest. A restored state, but one still within the empire, and controlled through a civil governor, would have been the most that could realistically have been expected. And this, when restoration did come, was precisely the form it took. In such a situation there was a significant

147

difference between a governor who was a foreigner, imposed by the imperial power, and one who, though appointed by the empire, was himself a Judaean national. Sheshbazzar, Zerubbabel, and, later, Nehemiah, all had this status.

V.22   *So you will be my people, and I shall be your God*. These are the terms of the covenant, set out in their briefest form. The covenant, implicitly set aside by the Lord when he allowed the destruction of Jerusalem, is to be re-established. The verse does not appear in the Greek Jeremiah and its abrupt change to the second person form of address is disconcerting.

30.23–24   appear also in 23.19–20, where they suit the context better.

31.1   voices a pre-occupation of the post-exilic period, the ingathering of *all the families of Israel*. 'Israel' in this context undoubtedly comprehends both North and South, but also in view here are the multitude of Jews scattered from their homeland.

The rest of ch. 31 consists of a mixture of short passages. Though these may not all be authentically Jeremianic, they do together illustrate one of Jeremiah's main themes, that beyond judgment there is hope for the nation. Oracles relating to both Northern Israel and Judah are found here.

31.2–6   An oracle of restoration. V.2a is an introduction to the oracle itself, vv.2b–6, which is in verse. It is significant that the oracle is addressed specifically to the North. It predicts the replanting of vineyards *on the hills of Samaria* (v.5). Its watchmen *cry out on Ephraim's hills*. Yet they are to go up and worship in *Zion*. The assumption is that the nation has been reunified.

The text is some respects problematic, but if REB's reading of it is correct, then vv.2–3 refer back to God's saving acts in the past. *Escaped the sword* probably alludes to escape from the pursuing Egyptians at the time of the exodus. The escapees found safety *in the wilderness*. After that, on Sinai/Horeb, the Lord *appeared to them*. All this provides grounds for trusting in God's continuing care. If these words go back to Jeremiah's own lifetime, then his hearers or readers would understand them as an assurance to themselves, in their own 'wilderness'.

V.4b   gives an indication of how Israelites generally enjoyed themselves, with dancing and the playing of tambourines. *You will provide yourself with tambourines*. The plain meaning of the Hebrew is 'You will decorate your tambourines'. Most commentators and translators make heavy weather of this, assuming the text cannot mean what it says. But in our own day tambourines are not infrequently decorated with ribbons, and there is no reason why ancient Israelites should not have done the same.

V.5b *Those who plant them will enjoy the fruit.* In the Hebrew this is a very compressed statement, but the meaning is clear enough. One of the greatest curses which the Old Testament writers could think of was to labour to plant a vineyard, and by reason of death or disaster never to enjoy the produce. Cf. Deut. 28.30, which uses the same vocabulary as here.

V.6 It is not clear who the *watchmen* are, or what they are watching for, or why they are summoning the people of the North to worship at Jerusalem.

31.7–9 and 31.10–14 are separate poems, but with a common theme. In style and language they are reminiscent of Deutero-Isaiah. They may have been placed together not only because of their common theme, but because they also share the verbal link of 'shouting'. V.7 *Break into shouts of joy* ... V.12 *They will come with shouts of joy to Zion's height.*

V.11 *For the Lord has delivered Jacob and redeemed him from a foe too strong for him.* Jacob, who in Gen. 32 had 'striven with God and with mortals, and ... prevailed', had at last met his match in the shape of the Babylonians, and had to be rescued. The word translated by REB as *delivered* is traditionally rendered 'ransomed'. It is a word characteristically used by the Deuteronomists of the exodus from Egypt. The word *redeemed* is even more characteristic of Deutero-Isaiah, in whose vocabulary it usually refers to the return from exile.

31.15–22 More prophecies concerning Ephraim and the reversal of his fortunes. *Ephraim* was strictly only half a tribe, though more numerous and powerful than most full tribes. Together Ephraim and Manasseh make up the tribe of Joseph, the principal tribe of the North. The name 'Ephraim' recurs several times in our present passage and acts as a link word holding the first half of ch.31 to-gether. 'Ephraim' is Hosea's favourite name for his people and the way it is used here in the book of Jeremiah is strongly reminiscent of Hosea's use of it.

Rachel (31.15) is the ancestress of Ephraim and Manasseh, and of Benjamin. The *lamentation ... and bitter weeping* which Rachel is said to make are related by some commentators to the exile of the northern tribes which took place in 722, well over a century before the exile of Judah. But this may not be the only loss that Rachel mourns. Rachel weeps *in Ramah*. 'Ramah' simply means 'height' and was a common place name, but 40.1 speaks of a Ramah which was used as a staging post for the collection of people who were being taken into exile in 586. Perhaps this is what the prophet had in mind. Or perhaps we need not look for any occasion so specific. Famine, military conquest, and other disasters, brought about their refugee problems in ancient times as they do today. Genocidal war was as regrettably familiar then as now. A man of Benjamin, reflecting on Benjamin's violent history, could have identified occasions in almost any generation when Rachel had cause to weep for her children.

Of course, the difference between ancient times and ours is that then there were no international relief agencies to offer even partial amelioration, and no television to bring a catastrophe to global notice.

Vv.16–17 promise a return of the refugees. But is this not too facile a promise for Rachel, who has watched her children die, with flies gathering round their mouths and eyes?

31.18ff.   Echoes of Hosea are especially strong in this passage. V.20 in particular is reminiscent of Hos. 11.1 and 11.8f. The sentiments are similar, and so is the imagery, though the language is by no means identical. Hosea not only speaks of sonship (Ephraim the child of God) as Jeremiah does here, but also uses the image of the heifer. Compare Jer. 31.18 with Hos. 4.16 and 10.11.

31.18–19   is an expression of penitence put into Ephraim's mouth, which Ephraim in Hosea 11 never makes. Hos. 11 expresses God, the father's, exasperation with Ephraim; his intense reluctance to mete out the punishment that Ephraim so well deserves. But nothing in Hosea's chapter speaks of any response on Ephraim's part. Jer. 31.18–19 articulates the response which Hosea despaired of eliciting.

31.19   *I beat my breast.* The Hebrew says nothing of breast-beating. It reads: '… I slapped my thigh.' Perhaps a legitimate piece of translator's licence. And perhaps not.

31.21   reaffirms the promise of return of the refugees. The imagery abruptly changes gender. This is more obvious and emphatic in the Hebrew than in English translation. Instead of the once recalcitrant, now repentant Ephraim, we have the prodigal daughter, the *virgin Israel.*

31.22   *How long will you waver?* The uncertainties and dangers of such a return journey might well make anyone waver, who had attained even a modicum of security in an adopted foreign land.

A woman will play a man's part. The translation at this point is problematic, and the interpretation of the statement even more so. No commentator has yet come up with a convincing explanation of what it means.

31.23–26 The centre of this little passage, vv.23b–25, is a poetic oracle relating to the restoration of Jerusalem and Judah, the Southern Kingdom.

v.26 is very enigmatic. There is again no agreement among commentators as to its significance.

31.27–28 Another little prophecy of restoration. It picks up the language of Jeremiah's commission in ch. 1. It speaks of God 'watching over' his word to see that it is fulfilled, as is done in the vision of the almond twig in 1.11. And it uses the same words about pulling down and uprooting, demolishing and destroying, building and planting as in 1.10. The present passage is saying that the first part of the commission, the destructive part, has already been accomplished; the building and planting are now to come.

31.27 *I shall sow Israel and Judah* ... Similar imagery is used by Hosea in 2.23, where he is playing on the name 'Jezreel' ('God sows'). For the ancient Israelite fertility, whether of plants, animals or human beings, is all of a piece, and the same language, of the sowing of seed/semen is seen as appropriate to all three.

31.29–30 Another brief oracle, this time one which has a close parallel in Ezekiel. Both Jeremiah and Ezekiel quote the same proverb (Ezek. 18.2; cf. also Lam. 5.7) which confirms that it genuinely was a popular saying of the early exilic period. We can see why this should be so. It is an understandable response to the prophets' and the deuteronomists' own interpretation of events. Both the prophets and the deuteronomic school explained the terrible catastrophe of the exile by saying that it was punishment for a long history of national unfaithfulness. It was natural for people at the time to respond by saying: 'So we are suffering for the sins of previous generations.' Lam. 5.7 puts it in exactly this way. 'Our forefathers sinned; now they are no more, and we must bear the burden of their guilt.' The unexpressed, and dangerous corollary to this is: 'So what is the point of our repenting?' Ezekiel in ch. 18 deals with this question in detail and at length, which shows how important the issue was for the exiles among whom he was living. Jeremiah here deals with it more peremptorily, but if this is a genuine saying of his, it shows that he was aware that it was also an issue in his own Palestinian milieu as it was for Ezekiel in his Babylonian one.

The more one examines the prophetic literature of the Old

Testament the more one becomes aware of the multitude of links, links of thought, language and imagery, between one prophetic book and another. There is a sense in which, if we are to get the best out of the prophetic literature, we need to study the corpus as an inter-dependent whole. To study any one prophet in isolation is to risk missing a good deal. Some of the echoes and inter-connections are likely to be due to the fact that the prophets were familiar with the work of their predecessors, and were influenced by it, and either sub-consciously or deliberately introduced reminiscences of it into their own work. This is almost certainly true, for instance, of the relation between Jeremiah and Hosea, and certainly true of that between Ezekiel and Jeremiah. Ezekiel very frequently seems deliberately to be picking up and developing ideas and images which Jeremiah introduces quite briefly or in passing.

But it is likely that some of the echoes and inter-connections were introduced, or emphasized, at some stage in the editing of the prophetic books. It looks as if there was a stage at which the prophetic literature was edited as a whole. In spite of the enormous variety of the prophetic literature, and the great differences between the prophets themselves, there is a coherence about the whole corpus. It is not a very tidy coherence, but there are both broad themes and images that hold the corpus together, and also a multitude of tiny crosslinks that knit it together into a whole.

31.31–34 is one of the Old Testament's most famous passages, and is apparently picked up by the New Testament writers at the crucial point at which they describe the institution of the Lord's Supper. I say 'apparently', since the New Testament manuscripts disagree with each other and it seems likely that the echo of Jer. 31.31 was less evident in the earliest copies of the gospels than later Christian tradition has made it. The best evidence seems to suggest that only Luke and Paul included the word 'new' in the words of institution. Mark and Matthew seem to have written simply: 'This is my blood of the covenant', which would be more readily taken as an echo of Ex. 24.8 than of Jer. 31.31.

Nevertheless, that this passage did influence some New Testament writers' interpretations of the last supper, and by extension their interpretations of the work of Christ in general, is hardly to be disputed. In addition to Luke and Paul, the writer to the Hebrews, in non-eucharistic contexts, picks up the idea of Christ as the mediator of a new or 'better' covenant.

But leaving aside, for the time being, New Testament and other

Christian uses of the new covenant idea, what did the idea convey, or was it intended to convey, to its original readers?

The Old Testament, of course, speaks of a number of earlier covenants between God and his people. There is the covenant made with Noah (and through him with all humanity). This appears only in the work of the Priestly writer, which means that it had probably not emerged by Jeremiah's time. But the covenant with Abraham, renewed with the other patriarchs, was certainly known. Yet the work of the deuteronomic school ignores this and concentrates exclusively on the covenant made on Sinai. This is what Jeremiah appears to do too. The only earlier covenant referred to in the present passage is *the covenant I made with their forefathers when I took them by the hand to lead them out of Egypt* (v.32). This Sinai covenant was emphatically a conditional covenant (unlike that with the patriarchs). It remained in force only so long as Israel met its demands. As the deuteronomists saw it (and the book of Jeremiah assumes the same perspective), Israel had, during her history, repeatedly failed to meet its demands. In spite of great forbearance, the Lord had eventually been obliged to let the covenant lapse: the Babylonian exile and the near-destruction of Israel was the consequence.

There is at this point a void in the relationship between God and his people. It had been based on the covenant. That covenant is now gone. If the relationship is to continue, or be restored, a new basis must be found for it; i.e., a new covenant.

But it is no good simply re-instituting the previous covenant. The previous covenant had failed. It was broken. This is the one feature of the old covenant which our present text picks out: it is *a covenant they broke*. The only hope for the future must be a covenant which cannot be broken, and this is what the book promises. The promise of the new covenant therefore fits perfectly into the historical context in which the book of Jeremiah places it.

It has frequently been claimed that the new covenant is new in that it is made with individuals, whereas the old covenant was a covenant with the nation. It is difficult to see how this claim could ever have been made, in view of the plain words of the text: *I shall establish a new covenant with the people of Israel and Judah*. The Hebrew, literally rendered, has: 'with the house of Israel and with the house of Judah'. 'House' is an undeniably corporate word. There is nothing here about a covenant with individuals. There is certainly no suggestion that individuals will be allowed to opt out or to opt in.

The effects of this covenant will be exactly the same as before: *I will be their God, and they will be my people.* These are exactly the terms in which the old covenant is regularly summarized.

The basis for the new covenant is law, which is precisely the same as the basis of the old one. There is no suggestion here that any new law is to be set forward. It is referred to, by God, simply as *my law*, the assumption being that the basis of the new covenant is the law with which his people are already familiar. The only difference between the new covenant and the old is that this law is to be *set ... within them*, written *on their hearts*. What is meant by this?

Earlier in this century it was assumed by some interpreters that the emphasis was on something called 'inwardness', and implied a rejection of 'external religion', viz., sacrifice and other forms of ritual. That Jeremiah did take a low view of the value of sacrifice is clear from what is said elsewhere in the book, but nothing in the passage suggests that this is the point at issue here.

The word 'heart' is a deceptive one. For the English speaker 'heart' suggests the emotions, and to speak of God's law as written *on their hearts* seems to imply an emotional dimension to the people's allegiance which had previously been lacking. It is all the easier to read the text in this way since such an understanding is extremely congenial to some traditions of Christian spirituality. But in the Hebrew tradition the heart does not generally represent the emotions. If an Old Testament writer wishes to speak of strong emotion he refers not to the heart but to the bowels. Interestingly, in this very chapter, in v.20, where REB has 'Therefore my heart yearns for him', the Authorized Version, literally translating the Hebrew, reads, 'Therefore my bowels are troubled for him.' For the Hebrew writer or speaker the heart is the organ of thought and of will. The Old Testament frequently uses the phrase, 'the thoughts of the heart'. So to write God's law *on their hearts* is to give them a mind to obey: it is, as it were, to re-programme the will.

The implied contrast is with the former law written on tablets of stone. Almost the first thing that happened to the original tablets, according to the account in Exodus, was that they were broken, which was symbolic of what was to happen repeatedly to the laws themselves. Jeremiah has used the same imagery in 17.1 where he spoke of 'the tablet of their hearts'. In 17.1 it is Judah's sin which is engraved there. The point is its indelibility. But here indelible sin is to be replaced by indelible obedience.

The image of the 'tablet of the heart' is not unique to Jeremiah. It occurs also in Prov. 3.3 and 7.3 where it is the instruction of the wise teacher that is to be written there. What is inscribed on the tablet of the heart is presumed to control all thought and behaviour.

The result is illustrated in v.34. There will be no more need for the Lord's people to teach or instruct one another about the things of God. The knowledge will be there already, built into them, so that they cannot but act as God requires. When this happens the past will be written off, *for I shall forgive their wrongdoing, and their sin I shall call to mind no more.*

The problem which the concept of the new covenant is designed to address is the problem of obedience. Israel has not obeyed the terms of the covenant. Most of the prophets before Jeremiah seem to assume that this is simply a question of will. Israel could obey perfectly well, if she made up her mind to it. The book of Jeremiah, however, raises the profounder question of whether obedience for Israel is possible. There is, it seems to be suggesting, some fundamental flaw in Israel's nature that fouls up her response to God. Israel is called by the prophets, including Jeremiah, to repent. But can she repent? Repentance involves change. Is she capable of change? Like the Ethiopian, claims Jeremiah, she cannot change her skin. Like the leopard, she cannot change her spots (13.23).

Many of the images of the first part of the book carry this same message. Judah's sin is written with an iron stylus, a point of diamond (17.1). It is indelible, ingrained, not to be washed away with the strongest cleansing agents known (2.22). It is like lust, compulsive, controlling, not to be denied; something which drives her even against her better judgment, if better judgment she has (2.23–25; 3.2).

The book does not consistently present the problem of sin in this light; it does often appeal in the old, simplistic way for repentance, as if the matter were easy. But at a multitude of points the picture of sin as a dominating, masterful force comes out strongly. If this really is Judah's condition, then calling for a fresh start does not answer the case. Even if she were capable of a fresh start, she would inevitably, sooner or later, be off down the same old road. The only possible answer to her condition, miraculous as it would need to be, is a remaking of the will. This is what the passage before us actually promises. Thus the idea of the new covenant not only fits perfectly into the circumstances of Jeremiah's time, it fits exactly the context of Jeremiah's theology as the book presents it to us. It answers the dilemma which much of the rest of the book sets up.

Is Jeremiah himself responsible for this passage? Some commentators argue that he is not. They find it salted with all kinds of deuteronomic phrases and deuteronomic ideas. But its main contention and principle insight, the inadequacy of the old covenant and the need for a new heart and will, cannot be paralleled in deuteronomic writings. Though admittedly Deut. 30.6–8, with its talk of a circumcision of the heart, comes close to the thinking of Jer. 31, Deut. 30.11–14 actually takes a line quite contrary to Jeremiah in insisting that it is not beyond his people's capacity to keep God's law as it stands.

Hos. 2.20 does not use the word 'covenant', but it does speak of a fresh betrothal of God and his bride Israel. This uses different language from Jer. 31 but it does envisage not merely a restoration of fortunes but a renewal of a relationship. And Ezekiel (18.31) speaks of the new heart in terms very similar to Jeremiah's, but here, of course, it is likely that Ezekiel is actually dependent on Jeremiah and following his train of thought.

We have to remember that if the dates given in the book are even approximately correct Jeremiah had in fact lived through a momentous attempt to remake the covenant, or at least to reassert it. In that heroic attempt the law had not been written on the hearts of the people; it had been written in a book, the Book of the Law. But the authors of that book had appealed to their readers to commit it to their hearts (Deut. 6.6–7). Whatever Jeremiah thought of Josiah's reform, it had not prevented the exile happening. The New Covenant passage in ch.31 expresses the prophet's conviction that something more radical was needed than his people had yet seen.

Jeremiah's understanding of the sin that overmasters has something in common with ideas about sin which we find in Paul, though the two are by no means identical. Although the New Testament does take up the phrase 'new covenant' the idea is not really integral to the thinking of the New Testament writers. It does not function for them as it does for Jeremiah, as an answer to the problem of the 'sin in the members'. The New Testament's answer to this problem is in its doctrine of the Holy Spirit. It is the Holy Spirit that enables believers to overcome what is otherwise the overwhelming power of their own sinful natures.

31.35–37 A strong reassertion that in spite of everything the relationship between God and his people is unshakable. The structure of the universe itself is not more firmly founded. Whether these verses represent Jeremiah's thinking or have been added by another hand is difficult to be sure of.

V.35 is strongly reminiscent of the so-called 'doxologies' which are scattered through the book of Amos (e.g. 4.13 and 5.8f.), though the phrase *who cleft the sea and its waves roared* is also found in Isa. 51.15. The imagery of v.35 is creation imagery, so the cleaving of the sea probably refers primarily to the dividing of the waters at creation rather than to the crossing of the sea at the time of the exodus.

31.38–40 Concerning the rebuilding of Jerusalem. The rebuilding of Jerusalem was of course a very important aspect of the restoration after the exile. In the book of Ezekiel the vision of the reconstructed Jerusalem occupies nine chapters.

Christians, whose hopes for the future tend to be expressed in terms of a person, the messiah, often fail to appreciate that for Jews the future hope has far more frequently been expressed in terms of a place, the restored Jerusalem. And whereas for Christians the image of the New Jerusalem was from early times spiritualized into that of a heavenly city, for Jews, hope has remained more firmly attached to a physical locality. In Jewish eschatological literature the messiah has rarely had more than a walk-on part in the drama of the last times. The real heroine in the drama is Zion.

The precise location of the landmarks mentioned here is in most cases uncertain, but for the writer and his intended readers they are clearly very specific. The prophet can tell us exactly what street corners mark the extremities of the holy ground. Many commentators take these verses as coming not from the time of Jeremiah but from that of Nehemiah, when the rebuilding of the city became a real possibility.

There is a kind of incarnational theology in the Old Testament, which sees God manifest, not in a person but in places. An Israelite could find God by going along David Street, right at the T-junction, first left, and then straight on. And there he was, in his temple, in the midst of his people, in the midst of their city, his city, among the shops and the banks and the building societies and the hairdressers. The tabernacle of God was with men. He dwelt with them and they were his people. And God himself was with them and was their God.

Jeremiah, of course, was one of the people who saw dangers in locating God in quite this precise way, and did not encourage some aspects of this kind of thinking; yet at this point, in 31.38–40, the book does recognize the importance of the holy city in expectations of the future. Whether in doing so it reflects the mind of Jeremiah himself may be questioned.

32.1–44 begins with a story about Jeremiah, set during the Babylonian siege of 586, which contains an enacted prophecy of hope. This is in vv.1–15. It is followed in vv.16–44 by some reflections on the story. Some of the oracles speaking of future hope which we have seen in the last two chapters may not be by Jeremiah, and look as if they might be later material, tacked on to the book. But the story of ch. 32, which, if anything is, is surely the record of an authentic enacted prophecy of Jeremiah's, demonstrates that he *was*, genuinely, a prophet of hope, and that he was prepared to assert that hope at the very point where things looked blackest.

Prophets are disconcerting characters. The prophets of the Old Testament constantly delivered criticism and announced judgment in circumstances where most of their hearers could see nothing wrong. But by the same token, they are capable of proclaiming a glorious future in situations where most of their contemporaries could see little reason for optimism.

32.1–5   sets the scene carefully. (This is not Jeremiah speaking, but someone else telling us the story about him.) The date is carefully given, according to the regnal year not just of Zedekiah but of Nebuchadnezzar. Jeremiah is in prison, allegedly because he has prophesied defeat, though ch. 37, which seems to be describing the same events, places them in slightly different perspective. See, too, 38.7–13, which also seems to relate to the same sequence of events.

Vv.3b–5 contain Jeremiah's prophecy of defeat, which predicts not only the fate of the city but that of the king (though what actually happened to the king was a good deal more horrid than Jeremiah's prediction here suggests. See II Kings 25.1–7.) The phrase in 32.5, in NRSV, 'until I attend to him', neatly preserves the ambiguity of the Hebrew, which could be understood as either promise or threat.

32.8   Jeremiah foresees that his cousin Hanamel will visit him and invite him to buy a piece of land at the family home at Anathoth. This is an instance of the operation of the law of redemption. This law is set out in Lev. 25.25–32. The incident here in the book of Jeremiah is evidence that the law of redemption was not just a piece of legal idealism, but that it did really operate. The theory was that land in Israel was inalienable. It belonged not to any individual but to the family. If an individual fell on hard times and became bankrupt, the hope was the someone within the family would be found to take the land over. Jeremiah is appealed to as next of kin, or 'redeemer', to fulfil this duty; which he is willing to do.

In times of peace this would not have been an extraordinary thing to do, but in the circumstances described here it would have seemed, to say the least, foolhardy. Not only is the country in the middle of a war, but the invading army is already overrunning the land, and Jeremiah himself has predicted his people's imminent defeat. Occupying powers normally redistributed land as they saw fit, rewarding their own troops and supporters, and paying little respect to existing titles of ownership. Jeremiah is being invited to buy land in circumstances in which his tenure of it would be extremely insecure. His solicitor would certainly have advised against proceeding with the transaction.

Jeremiah does buy the land, as a gesture of confidence in the future; confidence that Israelites will not be deprived of their land forever. In view of all his prophecies of doom, at the time this must have been a very unexpected assertion. It is not a cheap gesture. The price, seventeen shekels, would have represented the greater part of a year's income for a Palestinian peasant of the period.

Vv.9–15 set out in some detail the actual procedure of the sale. A deed of purchase is prepared, so there is a written record of the transaction. In ancient near eastern practice as we know it from Mesopotamia and elsewhere there were normally two copies of such a deed, one sealed and the other unsealed (v.11). The unsealed copy could be checked at any time, but was in principle open to being tampered with. To safeguard against this the sealed copy was preserved, and in case of later accusations of tampering, it was there to be appealed to.

32.10 *I … weighed the money on the scales.* Coinage had not yet been invented. In money transactions silver or gold had to be weighed out.

32.12 Not only is there a written record of the sale (the documents being committed for safe keeping to a professional scribe) but there are living witnesses who can testify to it, some of whose names are recorded in the documents, others of whom are simply reputable citizens who just happened to be there.

The scribe in this case is Baruch ben Neriah, Jeremiah's friend and colleague, here mentioned in the book for the first time. Interestingly, there is a seventh-century seal impression, now in the Israel Museum, which is inscribed as 'Belonging to Berechyahu ben Neriahu the scribe'. Most scholars assert that Berechyahu and Baruch are alternative forms of the same name, and claim confidently that this is the seal of the biblical Baruch.

From earlier periods we have similar accounts of business transactions, Gen. 23, recording Abraham's important purchase from Ephron the Hittite, and Ruth 4, which gives the account of how Boaz redeemed the property of Naomi.

The documents are to be kept *in an earthenware jar*; a standard method of preservation, well illustrated by the preservation of the Dead Sea Scrolls.

There is nothing to indicate on what materials the documents were written. It could have been potsherds (pieces of broken pottery; a commonly used material at the time), or specially manufactured clay tablets (common in Mesopotamia but rare in Palestine). Or it might have been papyrus, which would certainly have needed to be kept in a sealed container if it was not eventually to rot. Other materials were sometimes used: leather (very expensive), and in one case from around New Testament times, thin slats of wood taped together rather like a Venetian blind. Of all these, only baked clay tablets or inscribed potsherds would last indefinitely. The Lachish letters, written at precisely the period of the Babylonian attack on Judah, are still readily legible.

Half way through v.8 there is an abrupt shift. Up to this point we have been listening to another voice, telling Jeremiah's story. Suddenly it is Jeremiah's voice, telling his own story.

32.16–25   recounts a prayer which Jeremiah makes to God, and vv.26–44 convey God's reply. Both prayer and reply are full of characteristically deuteronomic phrasing and language. The prayer and its reply are probably the deuteronomic editors' comments on the enacted prophecy recounted in vv.1–15, setting it in what the deuteronomists saw as its broad historical context.

32.35   On *the valley of Ben-hinnom* see the notes on 7.30–34, and cf. 19.4–5, where similar words occur.

It is interesting to note the way in which this story of the buying of Hanamel's field is told. We might expect that Jeremiah had arrived at his conviction of hope (which is, after all, implicit in his commission at the beginning of the book) and then hit on buying the field as a dramatic way of expressing it. But this is not how the book tells it. According to the book, God first warns Jeremiah that Hanamel will come with his offer; then he directs the prophet to accept it and make the purchase. Jeremiah does this in simple obedience to God's command and then asks him, in great puzzlement: 'Why did you tell me to do that?' He then arrives at his message of hope by making a deduction from what God has instructed him to do. The psychology of all this is not at all what most modern readers would expect.

If the events of ch. 32 really are correctly set in the time when *the prophet Jeremiah was imprisoned in the court of the guard-house attached to the royal palace* (32.2) then the prophet's imprisonment can hardly have been one of close confinement. Whatever the restrictions on him he must have had considerable freedom of association as well as of action and speech.

Chapter 33 completes the so-called Book of Consolation. 33.1–13 is set, chronologically, at much the same period as the story of the redemption of the field in ch. 32. Jeremiah is said to be *still imprisoned in the court of the guardhouse*. If this is the correct setting it must be a little later in the siege, as the passage speaks of destruction which has already taken place in the city. The houses and the royal palaces *are razed to the ground*, and *the houses are full of corpses*. In fact, in the Hebrew the last part of v.4 and beginning of v.5, here quoted, make no sense as they stand. One way of understanding the words is reflected in the translation of NRSV, which implies that the houses and palaces had been pulled down to provide materials for building barricades against the attackers. This is a plausible guess, but no more than a guess. REB's translation leaves the interpretation more open. V.10 seems to envisage an even later stage in the conflict, when the city *lies in ruins, without people or animals throughout the towns of Judah and the streets of Jerusalem*; and v.12 similarly. Vv.11–13 assert confidently in the midst of this desolation that the desolation will not last for ever.

If we take the text at its face value, therefore, we have the prophet promising, in the very midst of the destruction, and at the very moment when his direst threats were being fulfilled, forgiveness and restoration (vv.8–9), and even *lasting peace and security*. Such promises, made in such a context, might have had a hollow ring in the ears of his hearers. But the transition to the message of hope at v.6 is extremely abrupt, and we really have to wonder whether the promises genuinely belong chronologically in this setting.

The restoration of *the sounds of joy and gladness, the voices of bridegroom and bride* (v.11) is an exact reversal of the threats recorded in 7.34, 16.9 and 25.10.

33.14–26 is a collection of oracles which may be broadly described as 'messianic'. This passage exists in the Hebrew Jeremiah only: the Greek Jeremiah does not contain it. Most scholars conclude that it has been inserted into the book at a late stage in its compilation, certainly later than Jeremiah's time.

Messianic expectation is not prominent in the book of Jeremiah. Such expectations seem not to have been part, or at any rate not a vital part, of the prophet's vision of the future.

When reading any biblical book it is always worthwhile noticing what is not there, as well as what is there. The silences of the biblical writers can be as significant as the things they say. For example, to read alongside each other the hopeful and future-directed prophecies of Ezekiel and those of Jeremiah makes the reader aware of an interesting pattern. For Ezekiel's future hope the expectation of a restored temple and restored sacrificial worship is of overwhelming importance. In the book of Jeremiah such things hardly figure at all. To do the same exercize with Jeremiah and Isaiah reveals that whereas the figure of the coming messiah is a vital element in the Isaianic tradition it is of little or no significance in the Jeremianic.

The incautious reader tends to assume in one prophet the ideas of the others, and thus to reduce these highly individual thinkers to a sort of uniformity. This process seems to have begun within the biblical period itself, with the addition of 'messianic' passages to the books of Jeremiah and Ezekiel.

33.15–16   is closely similar to 23.5–6. See the comments on 23.5–6, where this oracle relates much more closely to its context.

33.15   *A righteous Branch.* REB rightly here gives the word 'Branch' a capital letter. It is a recognized messianic title. Cf. especially Zech. 3.8 and 6.12, and see Isa. 11.1 (though the word used there for 'branch' is a different one.)

33.16   *This will be the name given to him.* The Hebrew in fact reads: '... given to her', i.e. to Judah (or Jerusalem). REB's rendering brings the text into line with 23.6.

There is a good deal of circumstantial evidence to suggest that in pre-Israelite times Jerusalem was a centre for the worship of a god called *tsedeq*. The word may be translated 'righteousness', or, in some contexts, 'salvation' or 'victory'. That a god whose very name was 'Righteousness' could have been absorbed by Israel by identifying him with Israel's own God, Yahweh, is perhaps not particularly surprising. However that may be, the name *Tsedeq* continues to have a special association with Zion and Jerusalem throughout the biblical period.

33.17   *David will never lack a successor on the throne of Israel.* This is a formula which appears several times in scripture in connection with the covenant with David. See, e.g., I Kings 2.4, 8.25, and 9.5 (and parallel passages in Chronicles). The covenant with David is announced first by Nathan in II Sam. 7 (though this particular formula does not appear there). According to this covenant God guarantees the permanence of David's dynasty. It promises that there will always be a descendant of his on Israel's throne. After 586 this was no longer true, and the covenant with David was called in question.

33.18 *A levitical priest.* The phrase used is again a characteristically deuteronomic one. Nowhere else in the book of Jeremiah is there any evidence that the continuation of the levitical priestly order and their sacrificial office was in the forefront of Jeremiah's mind. What we see expressed in this passage, both in its interest in the Davidic house and in the restoration of the priestly line, are the preoccupations of a rather later time than Jeremiah's, probably towards the end of the exile, when the return looked more like a realistic possibility. 33.19–22 firmly reasserts the validity of the covenant with David, and the status of the priestly order, in terms not dissimilar to those which are used in 31.35–37 of the permanence of the covenant of Sinai. 33.23–26 repeats the assertion, this time linking the two themes of the permanence of God's relationship with the nation and that of his choice of their Davidic rulers.

The Book of Consolation has taken us into the period of the final siege and destruction of Jerusalem by the Babylonians, and some of the materials in it, as we have seen, are likely to be later still, beyond the lifetime of the prophet himself. Chronologically the next few chapters take us back again, earlier in the siege, earlier in the career of Zedekiah, and in some cases back into the reign of his predecessor Jehoiakim.

Events under Jehoiakim and Zedekiah
34.1–39.18

Address to Zedekiah: release of slaves
34.1–22

34.1–7 contains a prediction by Jeremiah, delivered to the king, Zedekiah, that Jerusalem would fall to the Babylonians and the king himself be captured. According to 34.1 the prediction was first made when the Babylonian attack on Judah was well under way; and according to 34.6–7 it was repeated later, at the point when Jerusalem, Lachish and Azekah were the only cities still holding out. As in 27.12–15 (but unlike 21.1–7) the prophet is not asked by the king for this advice, he proffers it on his own initiative. (The passages in which Jeremiah addresses himself directly to Zedekiah are considered together in the notes on 21.1–7.)

It was presumably for uttering this sort of prediction that Jeremiah was locked up. 32.3–5 seems to be referring to a similar prophecy. To predict defeat for one's own side during a war is of course a desperately unpopular thing to do. It is also a very dangerous thing to do, because it is likely to damage morale and may therefore contribute to its own fulfilment. The prediction of the fate of Zedekiah himself is problematic in that it does not correspond to what the book tells us actually happened. The statement in 34.3, that Zedekiah will be captured, and taken to meet Nebuchadnezzar in person, is apparently accurate enough, as far as it goes, but the promise in 34.5: *You will die a peaceful death,* and the following prediction of an honourable funeral, are contradicted by the information given in 39.4–7, 52.7–11, and II Kings 25.4–7, and are also totally at variance with the prediction credited to Jeremiah in 21.7.

One possible way of reconciling this prediction with the narrative accounts of Zedekiah's end is to assume that there is an unexpressed condition in the prophecy, and to conclude that the king is being promised an easier ride *if* he capitulates to the Babylonians as Jeremiah is advising him to do. In support of this is the observation that another version of the prophecy appears in 38.17–18 in which this condition is clearly spelled out.

34.5   *They will kindle funeral fires in your honour.* This custom is not otherwise attested in ancient Israel, so we cannot be sure just what it meant. It is certainly not a reference to cremation, which the Israelites do not seem to have practised.

34.7   *Lachish and Azekah.* In the ruins of Lachish archaeologists found a file of correspondence, written on ostraca, i.e. pieces of broken pottery. The letters derive from this very point in history, while the Babylonian attack on Judah was going on, and they seem to confirm that Jerusalem, Lachish and Azekah were the last three cities to resist capture. One of the letters reports: 'We can no longer see the signals of Azekah.' Both cities were roughly south-west of Jerusalem, Lachish at about twenty-three miles and Azekah at about eleven miles.

34.8–22   describes a dirty deed. The facts are fairly straightforward, though the explanation of them is a little less so.

During the siege of Jerusalem by the Babylonians an agreement was made by the wealthier people of the city, the slave-owning classes, to give their slaves freedom. The king, Zedekiah, was directly involved in this arrangement, and it may be that such a general amnesty for slaves in any case required royal authorization. REB says that the king and people *entered into an agreement*. The actual word used in the Hebrew is the one usually translated 'covenant'. So this was a solemn undertaking, invoking divine sanctions.

This general release of slaves was not a disinterested act of charity, as indeed the sequel proved. The siege had evidently been going on for some time, supplies would be running short, and householders who released their slaves were freeing themselves of the obligation to feed them. (According to II Kings 25.3–4 it was famine that eventually brought about the capitulation of the city.) In such circumstances a freed slave would undoubtedly be very much at risk, with little means of support. It has been suggested that the slaves were freed in order to be armed, to take part in the defence of the city. But nothing in the text hints at this, and if the statement in vv.10 and 16 is correct, that female slaves as well as males were released, that makes the suggested explanation less likely.

At one point in the siege the Babylonian armies, hearing of the approach of an Egyptian relief force, lifted the siege in order to meet the Egyptians in battle. At this point the former slave-owners reneged on the agreement and reclaimed their slaves, demonstrating the hypocrisy of their original act of release. That the Egyptian intervention marked the point at which the re-enslavement took place is not only inherently plausible, it seems to be confirmed by the final words of 34.21. The account of this temporary raising of the siege is given in 37.5. The Egyptian intervention in fact came to nothing and the siege was re-imposed.

Up to this point the story is entirely clear and comprehensible. Scholarly argument, however, has been aroused by 34.12–14, which connects the episode with the law of slave-release which appears in our Bibles in Ex. 21.2–6 and Deut. 15.12–17 (Cf. the rather different provision of Lev. 25.39–55.) This law (i.e. the Exodus and Deuteronomy versions of it) set a six-year limit to the term a debt slave may normally serve. At the end of six years every such slave is entitled to freedom, if he wishes it. (Ex. 21.4–6 envisages the possibility that he might not wish it.)

Some scholars argue that the mention of this law in Jer. 34.12–14 is a red herring. The laws of Ex. 21 and Deut. 15 do not relate to general amnesties, but provide for the release of each individual slave six years after initial enslavement; they thus have nothing to do with the present case. Moreover, it is argued, the laws of Ex. 21 and Deut. 15 relate specifically to debt slaves, whereas nothing in Jer. 34 suggests that Zedekiah and his people were freeing only debt slaves.

With regard to this last point it should be noted that 34.9 speaks of *everyone who had Hebrew slaves, male or female*. This looks like a clear echo of the language of Deut. 15.12. (Ex. 21.2 is similar but, unlike Deut. 15.12, refers only to male slaves.) The precise meaning of the phrase *Hebrew slaves* is debated, but, at least in the context of Ex. 21 and Deut. 15, it seems to refer specifically to debt slaves. So if Jer. 34.9 and 10 genuinely reflect the language of the actual covenant which Zedekiah and his people made, then it did relate primarily to debt slaves. But it is possible that the editor of the book is responsible for the wording of vv.9 and 10, and that the connection between the incident and the laws of Ex. 21 and Deut. 15 is in his mind, not that of Zedekiah etc.. They may have thought of it simply as a general amnesty, of a sort that did occasionally happen in the ancient near east. We have some evidence of such amnesties from neighbouring countries, though none, outside the present passage, from Israel.

But whether or not the organizers of the amnesty saw it as connected with the Ex. 21 and Deut. 15 laws of slave release, whoever was responsible for the present form of the text of Jer. 34 certainly did. Whoever is telling the story seems to assume that the six-year rule had been generally ignored or neglected and sees Zedekiah's amnesty as a belated (and cynical) freeing of those whose release was in legal terms long overdue.

Perhaps more importantly, the prophetic condemnation in 34.12–22 emphatically connects Zedekiah's act with the existing laws of slave release. Indeed, it makes a rather more complicated, and rhetorically effective, set of connections than that. It seizes on the notion of covenant with which the story begins. The behaviour of Zedekiah and his people is full of the deepest ironies. Well might they make a covenant! They already had a covenant, made at Sinai, and with that covenant slavery had rather a lot to do. It was made when the Lord *brought them out of Egypt, out of the land of slavery* (34.13). The covenant celebrated *their* release. And it bound them to keep the law, which included the law of slave release after six years (34.14). So the existing covenant, which had stood since they first became a nation, already obliged them to do this. They had not kept it until now. Now, at last, they had done so, and had made an additional covenant binding themselves. So the re-possession of the slaves is not merely a double-crossing of the slaves, it is a double act of covenant breaking, and covenant-breaking in the near east was regarded, not just in Israel, as a extremely serious crime. The breaking of a covenant was an offence against the deity who was the witness and guarantor of the agreement. Zedekiah and his people, therefore, have settled their own doom.

34.17 contains a vicious *double entendre* on the technical word 'deliver', i.e. 'release from slavery'. Because you did not honour the terms of deliverance from slavery of your fellow countrymen – God is saying – I will deliver you. I will deliver you to the *sword, pestilence, and famine*. There are other word plays in the passage, some of which are difficult to reproduce in translation.

34.18 *I shall treat you like the calf that was cut in two*. This is a reference to a covenant-making ritual otherwise known to us in the Bible only from Gen. 15.6–18, though there are non-biblical parallels. There is no reason to believe that all covenants were initiated by this particular ritual. Perhaps it was used only for specially solemn ones. It is easy to guess that the meaning of the ritual is that the participants invoked on themselves the same fate as that of the calf if they broke the agreement, and Jer. 34.18 seems to confirm this. If God had already decided to hand over the city to the Babylonians then this act of hypocrisy has made him all the more determined to do so, and will make the fate of Zedekiah and the nation's other leaders all the more certain, and all the more horrific.

34.22 *I shall give the command ... and bring them back to this city*. The lifting of the siege is only temporary; it will be re-imposed. As we noted above, this indeed happened. Again we have word play: as they have 'brought back' the slaves (v.16) the Lord will bring back the Babylonians.

The Rechabites

35.1–19

Chapter 35 takes us back in time a step further even than ch.34. In ch.34 we were in the reign of Zedekiah, during the second Babylonian attack on Jerusalem, awaiting that city's second, and final, fall. Here we are back in the reign of Jehoiakim, and the context is that of an earlier Babylonian attack, that of 597. It is late in Jehoiakim's reign, because the attack which led to the first fall of the city has evidently already begun. The chapter concerns itself with another enacted prophecy.

The enactment involves the Rechabites, a group of people about whom we are not well informed. Much of the information we do have comes from this very chapter. I Chron. 2.55 connects them with the Kenites, a group which had associations with Israel during the period of wandering in the wilderness. They seem to have been an ultra-conservative group, who attempted to preserve the way of life of Israel's pastoralist ancestors, and had never accepted settled life. This fits with the statement in 35.7–10 that they lived in tents and did not cultivate the vine. Pastoralists will sometimes stay long enough in one place to grow grain (See, e.g., Gen. 26.12) but they can never remain long enough to plant vines; so the rejection of the vine and its products signifies the rejection of settled life.

The Rechabites were also said to have been involved in the revolution engineered by Jehu in the ninth century, about two hundred and fifty years before the events of which we are reading (II Kings 10.15–17). The Jonadab mentioned in the story of Jehu's revolt is claimed here as the founder of the Rechabite order.

The Rechabites have something in common with the Nazirites, who also rejected any produce of the vine (Num. 6; especially vv.3–4). But whereas the Rechabites were evidently an hereditary group, Nazirite vows were undertaken by anyone who chose to do so, and usually for a temporary period.

In 35.3 Jeremiah issues an invitation to a considerable number of Rechabites, though the exact figure is not specified. They are summoned to a particular room in the temple precincts. 35.4 is surprisingly precise and detailed about the location of the room. The Rechabites' reaction when they arrive is not described, but we can only imagine the amazement of these dedicated teetotalers on discovering that what they have been invited to is something like a cocktail party.

35.6–7   describes the peculiar lifestyle to which they are committed, and it goes well beyond merely refraining from alcohol. They are forbidden to *build houses or sow seed or plant vineyards*. They are to be permanent *tent-dwellers*. The implications of all this seem to be clear, that they are attempting to maintain the ancestral way of life of the pre-settlement Israelites. What kind of religious or ideological conservatism went along with this cultural conservatism we can only guess.

Such cultural conservatism is by no means without parallels. The Masai of East Africa, for example, are very rigorous in preserving their pastoralist way of life. They do not engage in any form of agriculture, and the men are firmly forbidden by custom to 'pierce the soil', a rule which they regard as absolute.

35.7   *The soil where you are sojourners* is a striking phrase. It emphasizes the nomadic nature of the group. Even in the land given by God they do not belong: they are only passing through.

35.8–10 The group claim that they have always rigidly adhered to the rules which their founder laid down.

35.11 explains why these people, who must normally have inhabited marginal rural land, are in a city environment at all. They are there for protection from the invading army. Jeremiah has evidently seized this rare opportunity when they are available, in order to make his point. The point being made is not dissimilar to that in 8.7 (and cf. Isa. 1.3). The Rechabites' obedience is exemplary. They feel themselves bound by rules laid down by a mere human ancestor. How much more should Israel feel bound by the rules laid down by God!

The commentary on this episode which we have in 35.12–17, the message which Jeremiah is represented as drawing from it, contains a good deal of deuteronomic phrasing, but there is little doubt that the message is in broad terms correctly stated.

35.12 expresses a view which runs right through the deuteronomic interpretation of events, and which underlies the editing of the entire prophetic corpus, that the warnings of the prophets provide the backbone of Israel's history. If their threats had been heeded the disaster of the exile would never have happened.

35.18–19 Having spelled out his public message, the prophet turns back to the Rechabites themselves, promising them a reward for their faithfulness.

The writing of the scroll

36.1–32

Up to the time of Jeremiah prophets have presented themselves to us primarily as speakers, conveying their message by word of mouth. Almost nothing is said, before this time, of prophets writing anything. The exception, in Isa. 8.1–4, rather proves the rule, for it is clear from the story there that Isaiah's action is unusual, and also that what he writes is extremely brief – hardly even a sentence – and is intended to stand as a witness for a short time only, a period of months, not to be a record for posterity.

Yet the prophets' words, or some of them, were recorded for posterity. We know this because they are there in our Bibles. How and why did this happen? Jer. 36 gives us some clues about how, in one prophet's case, it did begin to happen. And see also Jer. 30.2.

The incident described in the previous chapter, ch. 35, must have happened late in Jehoiakim's reign. The episode in ch. 36 takes us back seven or eight years earlier, to his *fourth year*. This would be 605 or 604. In 605 the Babylonians comprehensively defeated a combined army of Assyrians and Egyptians at the battle of Carchemish. In terms of world history this was an immensely important battle, though it gets no explicit mention in the Old Testament. It established the Babylonians as the up and coming 'great power' of the period. It would only be a matter of time before they made their grip firm on the western asiatic states, of which Judah was one.

There is no doubt that whoever put this chapter into its present form expected readers to be familiar with the story of the finding of the 'Book of the Law' in King Josiah's reign, and of the king's reaction to it. That story stands in our Bibles in II Kings 22–23. We are meant to appreciate the similarities in the two situations, the facing of a king with the word of the Lord in written form; and the contrasts, between Josiah who hears the word, respects it and responds to it, and Jehoiakim who treats the word with contempt. Whatever the historical facts may have been, the story in Jer. 36 is told not only very dramatically, but in such a way as to heighten the parallels with that of Josiah.

36.2 *Take a scroll.* Almost certainly this would be of papyrus. It was the least expensive writing material for writing long communications. Even so, papyrus reeds do not grow in Israel, and it all had to be imported from Egypt.

36.2 *Write on it all the words* ... This implies, first, that the prophet's oracles had not previously been written down; but second, that all his oracles, covering a period of more than twenty years (assuming the accuracy of the dates given in the book) were in the prophet's memory.

36.3 *Perhaps the house of Judah will be warned* ... Expressing the hope that publication of Jeremiah's collected oracles will give them an impact which they had not previously had. Perhaps there is a little naive optimism here.

36.4 *On Baruch the son of Neriah* see comments on 32.12.

36.5 *I am debarred from going to the Lord's house.* We are not told the reason why he was thus debarred. Perhaps there was no sinister reason: the prophet may simply have been ritually unclean. It is conceivable, however, that the authorities might have placed restrictions on his movements. As we have already seen, they certainly did this later, during Zedekiah's reign. As things turned out, Jeremiah and Baruch apparently waited several months before the scroll was actually read. Any ritual uncleanness would be likely to have expired by that time.

36.6 *On a fast-day.* We do not know what regular public fasts, if any, there may have been at this period. After the exile we know of at least one such regular fast, the Day of Atonement, and it is possible that there were pre-exilic equivalents. But we do know that special public fasts were proclaimed at times of national crisis. See, e.g., Joel 1.13–14. Perhaps in Jeremiah's time there were no regular fasts at all. According to 36.9 it seems that Jeremiah and Baruch waited over twelve months before one occurred. The instruction to Baruch to read the scroll *on a fast-day* would ensure a large audience, and a national one, *of all those who come in from the towns of Judah*, not just the Jerusalem crowd.

36.7 is perhaps suggesting another reason for reading the scroll on a fast-day. The prophet hopes to find the people already in a serious and receptive mood.

36.9 The actual reading did not take place until *the ninth month of the fifth year of the reign of Jehoiakim.* This is some considerable time after Jeremiah received the original instruction in the king's fourth year. It must be something of the order of twelve months. This was the point in time at which the Babylonian armies were taking over the Philistine cities in the coastal plain on Judah's very borders. If this caused enough alarm in Judah to provoke a national fast we need not be surprised. The Greek edition of the book of Jeremiah reads not *fifth year* but 'eighth year', which would make the chronological gap between the writing of the scroll and the public reading of it even longer.

36.10 *Gemariah, son of the adjutant-general Shaphan.* Shaphan was prominent in the carrying through of Josiah's reform, and there is evidence that his family (another son of his is mentioned in Jer. 26.24) were sympathetic to Jeremiah. A seal impression of Gemariah b. Shaphan has been found by archaeologists. *Micaiah son of Gemariah* (and therefore Shaphan's grandson) hears the scroll read and reports the matter to the *sarim* (REB *officers*), who were apparently meeting in conclave in the palace next door. (The temple and the palace stood next to each other on the temple mount, with only a wall between; the palace being on a slightly lower level.) The meeting includes *Elnathan son of Akbor.* Akbor, like Shaphan, had been involved in the reform of Josiah.

There is no suggestion in the text that either Micaiah or the *sarim* intend any harm to Baruch or Jeremiah (indeed, in 36.19 they are said to take precautions for their safety) but they take the scroll seriously and decide that it is important enough to bring it to the king's attention.

The parallels between this account and the account of Josiah's reform extend not only to the personnel involved but to their behaviour. The fathers of at least two of the *sarim* mentioned in Jer. 36 had been among those apprised of the finding of the Book of the Law in the house of the Lord, and who had reported it to the king (Josiah). On the present occasion, their sons are among those told of the reading of a book of prophecy in the house of the Lord and they act in a precisely similar way.

36.14–15   The *sarim* send for Baruch and hear the book for themselves. They react with alarm (36.16). They then check with Baruch the book's provenance and credentials (36.17–18). In II Kings 22, Shaphan, having been told of the Book of the Law, reads it for himself, reports to the king, and is among a small group sent to check the book's authenticity with the prophetess Huldah.

In the present case, however, the *sarim* are much less confident of the king's reactions. In v.19 they take steps to safeguard Baruch and Jeremiah. In v.20 they take care of the scroll. Only then do they report to the king.

36.21   The king demands to see the scroll and has it read to him. He is surrounded by his courtiers, also called *sarim*. The storyteller evidently sees the group to whom the reading of the scroll was first reported, and the group attendant on the king, as distinct parties, not at all in harmony as to their opinions and attitudes. But all of them, both groups, are courtiers and government officials, and the use of the same label, '*sarim*', to describe them indicates that they are of similar rank.

36.22   *It was the ninth month*; i.e. about December, a time of year when it can be distinctly chilly at the altitude of Jerusalem. This circumstantial detail is inserted in order to explain why there was a fire handy.

36.23   *Every time Jehudi read three or four columns of the scroll, the king cut them off with a penknife and threw them into the fire.* The king's gesture, in destroying the scroll piece by piece, expresses contempt. Unlike the *sarim* to whom the scroll was first reported, the king and the courtiers surrounding him do not show alarm. Neither do they tear their clothes, a gesture of distress and grief. There is an explicit contrast here with II Kings 22.11 and 19, which tells how Josiah did exactly that in response to the Book of the Law.

36.25 *Elnathan, Delaiah, and Gemariah begged the king not to burn the scroll.* The narrator is here making very clear which side the original group of *sarim* are on.

36.26 The precaution of sending Jeremiah and Baruch into hiding is shown to have been justified. *Jerahmeel, a royal prince.* A seal impression with the words: 'Belonging to Jerahmeel the king's son' has been unearthed by archaeologists.

Jehoiakim's action in destroying the scroll is not merely a practical one, it signifies his intention to deny, negate and destroy the word. The rewriting of the scroll in 36.27–32 is also not merely practical. It is not simply that Jeremiah wishes the record to be preserved, in spite of the king's attempt to destroy it. The fact that he could dictate again the oracles at will means that they were already available, preserved in his memory. But the word, having been challenged, must be reasserted. In spite of Jehoiakim's action, it still stands. The re-writing is itself a kind of enacted prophecy. Jehoiakim thinks that he has shown that the word is fragile and ephemeral. He will learn that it is not. Jeremiah's oracles are not paper threats. Holladay in his commentary writes: 'The king could not doom the word. The word doomed the king.'

This re-writing of the scroll is also bound to make us think of Moses, whose original copy of the law was destroyed in wrath at the worship of the golden calf, and which had to be re-written (Ex. 34).

As well as close parallels between this chapter and II Kings 22–23 there are parallels between this chapter and Jer. 26. In both of them Jeremiah's words are proclaimed in the temple court. In both they arouse opposition and Jeremiah is placed in danger. Jer. 26 ends with Jeremiah being rescued due to the influence of a son of Shaphan, one of the family who appear to take his part in ch. 36.

36.29–31 Part of Jeremiah's response is to deliver an oracle against the king himself, and his courtiers. *He will have no descendant to succeed him on the throne of David.* This was not quite true; Jehoiakim's son Jehoiakin did succeed him very briefly. *His dead body will be exposed* ... There is no evidence that Jehoiakim had anything other than a normal burial. A similar threat is made against Jehoiakin in 22.30.

36.31 The response, or lack of it, of the king and his courtiers to the prophet's words involves in destruction the whole nation which they represent.

36.32 ... and much else was added. It is generally assumed that the contents of the re-written scroll have found their way into our present book of Jeremiah. But precisely which parts of the present book were included in the two scrolls it is impossible to say, though this has not prevented some scholars from speculating at length. Any oracles which can firmly be dated before 605 are candidates for inclusion, but this criterion is not sufficient to allow us to reconstruct very much of the contents of the scroll. The story implies that the original scroll was not particularly lengthy. It was apparently read three times in the course of the day, to the general public; to the *sarim* and finally to the king.

Chapters 37–45 are very different in nature from most of what has gone before. They are narratives, covering the history of the last years of Judah. In content they are parallel to II Kings 24.18–25.26, but offer us much more detail than the Kings account. The account of this period in II Kings does not mention Jeremiah specifically, whereas Jer. 37–45 focusses very much on him.

It is often suggested that this narrative material emanates from Baruch, who seems to have been with Jeremiah throughout this period. This is a possibility, but we have no way of being sure.

The theme of these chapters continues to be that of the rejection of the word, but they take up the hint offered in the account of Jeremiah's call and confirmed in ch. 26, that rejection of the word also involves the rejection of the one who speaks it, and entails threats and suffering for him.

During the final siege of Jerusalem: consultations between king and prophet

37.1–38.28

The narrative of ch. 37 takes us forward again to the reign of Zedekiah, and to events which took place during the final siege of Jerusalem by Nebuchadnezzar's forces.

37.1   Zedekiah son of Josiah was set on the throne ... i.e. in 597, after Jerusalem's first fall to the Babylonians. *In place of Coniah,* i.e. Jehoiakin, who briefly succeeded his father only months before the fall of the city. So Zedekiah was the Babylonians' own nominee. At precisely what point he rebelled against his imperial masters is not certain, but he seems to have been encouraged to do so by the Egyptians, whose promise of support was never effectively honoured.

37.2 Zedekiah and his supporters did not heed *the words which the Lord spoke through the prophet Jeremiah*. i.e. the advice that they should remain loyal to Babylon.

37.3 In spite of this disinclination to follow Jeremiah's advice the king is represented as respecting Jeremiah sufficiently to hope for his support.

Chapters 36 and 37 may have been placed together in order to point up the contrast between the two kings, or maybe even the three kings. Josiah was prepared to listen wholeheartedly to the word of the Lord. Jehoiakim treated it with contempt. Zedekiah has neither the confidence to act on the word or to dismiss it. He is clearly worried by what Jeremiah says, but not worried enough to obey. In Zedekiah the word does not produce faith, only fear.

Some commentators find it incredible that Zedekiah should have consulted Jeremiah at all. They assert that Jeremiah's opposition to Zedekiah's policies was so well known that the king must have realized that no comfort for him would be forthcoming from that quarter. But do we know enough about the situation and about the personalities concerned to make this sort of judgment? The way the book of Jeremiah portrays the character of Zedekiah may or may not be historically accurate, but it is consistent and believable. He is pictured as a rather weak man, placed in an unenviable position and having to make some very hard choices on his people's behalf. Having been put on the throne by the Babylonians he has opted for, or been persuaded into, rebellion against Babylonian authority. The Babylonians call him to account, and are at his gates. Even a strong man would be unsure of himself in such a situation. If he casts around for support in any direction in which there might be the remotest hope of finding it, this is not to be wondered at. As the book tells it, he has enough courage to turn for advice to someone he knows will not say what he wants to hear; but not enough courage to act on the advice offered.

We cannot consider the present passage properly without raising the question of its relation to 21.1–7. (See the note at 21.1–7 on the whole subject of Jeremiah's encounters with Zedekiah.) 21.1–7 tells a closely similar story; the only serious difference being that the events of 21.1–7 are placed near the beginning of the Babylonian attack on Judah, while 37.1–10 puts its very similar events somewhat later, at the point where the siege has been lifted because of the reported approach of an Egyptian army. The accounts are so similar that they surely must be alternative versions of the same story. The clue to the story's significance lies in its parallels with the one in II Kings 18.13–19.37. These parallels are pointed out in the notes on 21.1–7. The account here in ch. 37 makes no explicit reference to the story of Sennacherib's attack, but 21.1–7 does, in very specific terms.

The reader is meant to see a very sharp contrast between the two sets of events. In Hezekiah's time when Jerusalem is besieged by an invading army the king officially consults a prophet, Isaiah, who promises deliverance. This promise is immediately, and apparently miraculously, fulfilled. Under Zedekiah, in similar circumstances, the king consults a prophet, Jeremiah, but hears not a promise of salvation but an announcement of doom. That this parallel is present to the mind of the book's editor is not in doubt. The way he tells the two versions of the story, especially that in 21.1–7, makes this clear. But was Zedekiah himself thinking along the same lines? If he did consult Jeremiah during the siege, could it not have been in the hope, however remote a hope it seemed to him, that in some manner history might repeat itself? We can be sure that the legend of the delivery of Jerusalem from Sennacherib exercized a powerful hold on the imagination of seventh century Judæans, and probably helped them to convince themselves that Jerusalem could not fall to a foreign conqueror, and that doom-sayers like Jeremiah must be wrong. The author of 21.1–7 and 37.1–10 is facing this argument head on, and asserting that whatever happened in the time of Sennacherib constitutes no precedent, and provides no guarantee at all of protection for the holy city. The words ascribed to the prophet make it clear that though there may have been miracles yesterday, and might be miracles tomorrow, it is best not to count on miracles today.

If the consultation did take place, and if the motive for it really was the hope of a repetition of the events of Hezekiah's reign, then the chronological setting given it in 37.5 makes a good deal of sense. The rumoured approach of an Egyptian force, and the lifting of the siege by the Babylonians, must have looked like a very encouraging sign. If at such a point the king had sent to Jeremiah asking: 'Does this mean what I hope it means?' the picture would be quite a credible one.

37.4   notes that at this point Jeremiah had not been placed under arrest.

37.5   The departure of Nebuchadnezzar's troops at the approach of the Egyptians was bound to recall the withdrawal of Sennacherib's over a century before. But, no! The language of 37.7 echoes that of

II Kings 19.7 in a way that can hardly be accidental. In II Kings 19.7 the prophet predicts that the besieging army will 'return to its own land'. In Jer. 37.7 the prophet asserts that it is the relief force which is already on its way home.

37.11–12 seems to be referring to the incident described in ch. 32, the redemption of the field, but if these verses do relate to the same incident there is a discrepancy, for in ch. 32 when the transaction takes place Jeremiah is already confined to the guardhouse, whereas in ch. 37 he is only put in confinement because of his attempt to leave the city to take possession of his property, if indeed that is what the text means. The Hebrew of 37.12 is obscure, and REB's rendering, *to take possession of his holding* is only one possible way of understanding the text, though it is a very plausible way. It is possible that the transaction was not regarded as having been completed until the purchaser had physically visited the property and set foot on it. An alternative interpretation is that Jeremiah was taking the opportunity of the siege being lifted to go to his family home and get fresh supplies of food.

37.13 *Irijah ... arrested the prophet, accusing him of defecting to the Chaldaeans* (i.e. the Babylonians). In view of Jeremiah's public support for the Babylonians the suspicion may be thought entirely reasonable.

37.15 *The officers* in these verses are again the *sarim*, who concern themselves so much with Jeremiah and his prophecies. Jeremiah is shut up *in the house of Jonathan the scribe*. If this house had been converted into a prison for the occasion it might suggest that Jeremiah was not the only person giving trouble. But this could be reading more into the text than is warranted. It may simply be that Jonathan happened to have a convenient cellar.

The Hebrew of 37.16 is again obscure, but it seems clear enough that the prophet's prison was some sort of subterranean place. 'Cellar' is probably a reasonably accurate translation.

The impression given by the passage is that the king and the *sarim* do not entirely see eye to eye on the subject of Jeremiah, that he is imprisoned on the *sarim*'s authority, but that the king himself has not written Jeremiah off and is prepared to consult him privately. Jeremiah briefly repeats his prophecy that the king will fall into the hands of the Babylonians, but then seizes the opportunity to make representations on his own behalf.

37.19 *Where are your prophets ...?* It is ironic that Jeremiah, whose predictions have now been confirmed by events, should be in prison, whereas the prophets who predicted that the Babylonian threat would not materialize are still at large.

37.20   *Do not send me back ... or I shall die there.* Jeremiah's plea for the amelioration of his conditions implies that they were very bad, to the point of being life-threatening. If, as we shall consider shortly, chs 37 and 38 are actually variant accounts of the same events, then the description of the prophet's predicament in ch.38 would certainly substantiate the fears expressed here. Even if this suggestion is discounted, *the court of the guardhouse* would assuredly be preferable to Jonathan's cellar.

It is difficult to be sure how the events described in ch. 38 relate to those of the previous chapter. In several respects the two stories are parallel. In both, Jeremiah is arrested and imprisoned in a very unpleasant, subterranean place, by some of the *sarim,* though the king himself appears to have a sneaking regard for him. In both stories the prophet is eventually rescued, not to be freed, however, but to be less uncomfortably confined in the court of the guardhouse. Both accounts seem to assume that this was the one spell of confinement which Jeremiah experienced and that he remained in the guardhouse until the fall of the city. 38.37 states this clearly.

Are we faced here, therefore, with two alternative versions of the same event? If that is what they are, then the discrepancies between them are considerable. If it is not what they are, then one of these two episodes must have ended with the prophet's release, only to be succeeded by a second confinement.

38.1ff.   The implication at the beginning of the story is that Jeremiah is free, and free to deliver his discouraging message.

38.2   is virtually identical with 21.9. Possibly it does not belong here but has been inserted from ch.21.

38.4   Some of the *sarim* regard Jeremiah's prophecies as tantamount to treason and therefore as deserving death. They apply to the king, who does not resist them (38.5). Nevertheless, there is apparently no formal trial or sentence; cf. ch.26, where there was a formal trial, but no conviction was obtained. The actions of the *sarim* in 38.6 seem to be designed to secure the prophet's death by letting him die in confinement.

The picture we are offered of Zedekiah, both in ch.38 and in ch.37, is of an ineffectual king who is not in control of some of his principal officers of state, the *sarim.* As far as the treatment of Jeremiah is concerned he seems to be bullied by them into acquiescing in decisions which he is later persuaded to regret. Whether this is a historically accurate portrayal of Zedekiah's character we do not know, but it is plausible enough. The story-teller in both chapters puts most of the blame for Jeremiah's treatment firmly on the *sarim*.

38.6 The place of confinement is underground, as in 37.15, but it is not in 'the house of Jonathan' but in the court of the guardhouse. In 38.6 the Hebrew actually reads: 'They put him into the cistern of Malchiah, the king's son, which was in the court of the guardhouse.' This makes it sound like quite a different place from the 'cellar' in which the prophet was kept in ch.37. It was certainly more unpleasant than a cellar. It is described as a *cistern*. Such cisterns were common, being used for storage of water. This one was more or less empty, suggesting that the time of year is well into the summer.

38.7–9 Zedekiah has just given the *sarim* permission to do what they like to Jeremiah, yet when Ebed-melech takes it on himself to appeal on Jeremiah's behalf the king responds very promptly. This suggests that he has no fixed policy but is guided by whoever he has spoken to most recently.

38.7 *The Cushite.* On the description 'Cushite' see the note on 13.23. *A eunuch.* Though it was not normal in Israel, in several other ancient near eastern countries many high officials in government administration were eunuchs. It appears to have been a condition of employment in such posts. So it is not surprising to find this foreigner described as a eunuch. Some have doubted whether a foreigner would have been influential enough to approach the king in the way Ebed-melech is said to have done, but it is hard to see the basis for such scepticism. We simply do not know what Ebed-melech's status was. For all we know he may have been a person of very high rank at the Jerusalem court.

38.10–13 gives us some colourful, and convincing, circumstantial details about how the rescue of Jeremiah was accomplished.

38.10 *Take three men* ... The Hebrew actually says 'thirty men', but most commentators argue that thirty is excessive and that 'three' must be meant.

38.14–23 As in ch.37, the release of Jeremiah from his incarceration underground is followed by a personal interview with the king, though the account of the conversation here is much longer and more detailed than that in ch.37.

38.14 *The third entrance of the Lord's house* is a unique phrase in scripture. There were several entrances to the temple area and we do not know which of them is meant.

38.16 As in the conversation reported in 37.17–20 Jeremiah is as much concerned to secure the king's promises for his own safety as he is to answer the king's questions. Zedekiah's *promise on oath* to the prophet in 38.16 is in strong contrast to his willingness in 38.5 to abandon him to the *sarim*. Some commentators see this inconsistency as evidence that the story is not giving us information about real historical events. They find it not credible that the king should act so. But our newspapers and current affairs programmes can provide examples any week of the year of politicians and persons in power acting with as much vacillation and indecisiveness.

38.17–18   In 37.17, in answer to the king's enquiry Jeremiah contents himself with an extremely terse statement that Zedekiah himself would be taken by the enemy. Here in ch.38 he offers a more nuanced message. The threat is basically the same, but it is conditional. The city will fall and be burnt down, and Zedekiah himself be captured unless he surrenders now. If the city is surrendered it will not be burnt, and Zedekiah and his family will escape with their lives. After the king replies that what he is really afraid of is not the Babylonians themselves, but the renegade Judaeans who have already joined them, Jeremiah repeats his conditional threat and promise, playing on the king's feelings by stressing what defeat will mean to the women of his family. Zedekiah, however, is not reassured. We shall never know, of course, whether Jeremiah was right.

Zedekiah rather pathetically appeals to Jeremiah to keep the content of their conversation secret from the *sarim*. This, and his words to the *sarim* in 38.5 show that he was afraid of them. Zedekiah is supposed to be in charge. The narrator paints him as a man in charge of nothing, least of all of his own destiny.

38.26   curiously refers to Jeremiah not returning to *the house of Jonathan*. In the story as we have it in ch.38 he was never *in* the house of Jonathan. This confusion between the two stories strengthens suspicion that they are different versions of the same story.

The fall of the city
   39.1–18

Chapter 39 records the actual capture of Jerusalem by the Babylonians in 586. This was one of the most important events in the country's history. 39.1–10 is in substance, though not in detail, the same as Jer. 52.4–16 and II Kings 25.1–12. The dreadful climax came *in the fourth month of the eleventh year of Zedekiah*. There is some dispute as to whether this makes the year 587 or 586. Whichever year it was, the city fell in July.

39.3   is not represented in either of the parallel passages, i.e. in Jer. 52 or II Kings 25. As the Hebrew text stands, it looks as if this meeting of *all the officers of the king of Babylon* is misplaced. We would expect it to happen rather later in the story. But in the Greek Jeremiah it reads quite naturally since the Greek contains no equivalent of vv.4–13. This connects the release of Jeremiah in v.14 directly with the meeting of the Babylonian officers reported in v.3, giving the impression that the release of the prophet was the chief business of these dignitaries' deliberations. But that a meeting of the officers in this manner did take place at some point we need not doubt. It seems to have been standard practice for the conquerors of a city to hold court (and the city gate was an obvious place to do it) and make their dispositions for its future and that of its inhabitants.

39.3   The titles and functions of the various officials are not all well understood, but this hardly affects our understanding of the main import of the passage. Nebuchadnezzar himself was not at the meeting. The siege was master-minded by his generals. In v.5 we find the Babylonian king in Syria.

39.4   Zedekiah *and all his armed escort ... made their escape towards the Arabah*, i.e. in the direction of the Jordan valley. They got as far as the region of Jericho, about twenty miles from Jerusalem.

39.5   *At Riblah* (in Syria) *... sentence was passed on him.* The language used is judicial. The Babylonians would certainly have thought of it as a judicial process, the charge being that Zedekiah had broken his oath of allegiance. Zedekiah's treatment is certainly harsh, and may be contrasted with the honourable retirement offered to Jehoiakin after 597. But Jehoiakin had done what Jeremiah advised Zedekiah to do, surrender his city without a struggle.

39.9   The Hebrew in this verse is somewhat confused. What REB offers us here is substantially what appears in the parallel account at 52.15. This represents the Babylonian deportation as very comprehensive. The *nobles of Judah* had, according to v.7, all been executed along with Zedekiah's sons. Of those of lower social rank the population of Jerusalem seems to have been deported wholesale. Those who had already defected to the Babylonians got no special consideration. The *artisans*, i.e. people with any useful skills, all went. Apart from the new governor, Gedaliah, and his court, the country is depleted of all its leaders. The Babylonians (v.10) *left behind only the poorest class of people*, redistributing to them the agricultural land.

The account of Jeremiah's release given in 39.11–14 is difficult to reconcile with the course of events described in 40.1–6. The problem will be considered in the notes on ch.40. What is claimed here in ch.39 is that Nebuchadnezzar, the emperor himself, sent orders, presumably all the way from Syria, specially concerning Jeremiah. *Nebuzaradan captain of the guard* is told to *do for him whatever he asks.* This suggests that Jeremiah is to be given some choice in what happens to him. In fact he appears to be given none, but at this point is sent to *Gedaliah son of Ahikam*, the newly-appointed civil governor.

Gedaliah was a grandson of the same Shaphan who had been involved in Josiah's reform, and whose family seem to have been consistently sympathetic to Jeremiah. That the Babylonians knew, or found out, about Jeremiah's pro-Babylonian stance is confirmed in 40.1–6. That he should be regarded, therefore, as a useful person to send to support and advise Gedaliah is not surprising. It may be that the Babylonians had learnt some lessons from their previous dealings with Judah in 597. At that time they had placed Zedekiah on the throne but seem to have left him surrounded by advisers who pushed him in the direction of anti-Babylonian policies. It may be that they had deported in 597 some people who from their own point of view would have been better left behind.

39.15–18 The chapter ends, unexpectedly, with an oracle concerning Ebed-melech, Jeremiah's African rescuer, promising him safety among all the turmoil of the fall of the city. At first sight the oracle looks out of place here. We might have expected it to follow directly on the story of Jeremiah's rescue from the cistern in 38.7–13. But though that is the setting in which the prophecy about Ebed-melech is said to have been uttered, it is probably placed here because this is where it is fulfilled.

When Jerusalem had fallen to the Babylonians before, in 597, the nation had been treated much more leniently. She had still been governed by a king, of the house of David, even though not one of her own choosing. The exiled king, Jehoiakin, though deported, was given the consideration due to his royal rank. The temple had not been destroyed. The city's defences had been left intact. This time, in addition to the crueller treatment of the king and his nobles, the temple is destroyed and looted, and the city's walls razed so that it is left defenceless. The king is not replaced, except by a provincial governor.

After the capture of Jerusalem
40.1–45.5

40.1–6 looks like an alternative account of what happened to Jeremiah, which partly confirms but is partly at variance with the one in 39.11–14. In 39.11–14 Jeremiah has already been sent to Gedaliah; in 40.1 he is being taken in chains to Ramah, which seems to have been used as a clearing station on the road into exile (cf. 31.15). Some commentators have suggested that Jeremiah was released from the court of the guardhouse, as ch. 39 states, but that he was later re-arrested by mistake and had to be again set free. This seems implausible. It is simpler to regard 40.1–6 and 39.11–14 as alternative, but not entirely reconcilable, accounts of the same events. The account in ch. 39 has been written by someone who assumed that the Babylonians knew all about Jeremiah and made his release one of their first priorities. The one in ch. 40 implies rather that they only found out something about him and the part he had played when they sorted out their prisoners. In this respect ch. 40 is likely to be closer to the truth.

40.1 in REB reads: *The word which came from the Lord about Jeremiah.* The Hebrew actually says: 'The word which came from the Lord *to* Jeremiah.' This is problematic because one naturally expects it to be followed by a prophetic oracle, which it is not. REB's reading does not really solve the problem. Whether the word of the Lord came to Jeremiah or was about Jeremiah the text still gives us no indication of what the word was. The puzzle remains.

A second curiosity of the passage is Nebuzaradan's speech to Jeremiah in vv.2–3, in which he, Nebuzaradan, puts in a nutshell Jeremiah's (and the deuteronomists') theological understanding of the fall of Jerusalem. Doubtless high Babylonian officials were men who were quick on the uptake, but we need not suppose that we are here being presented with historical fact. Rather, the storyteller is making a homiletical point. Jeremiah had laboured for the best part of a lifetime to get across to his countrymen this very message, and had failed to do so. This officer of a gentile empire grasps it immediately. Jeremiah's reaction is not recorded, but the point is not lost: he had not found such great faith; no, not in Israel.

40.4 Again, as in ch. 39, there is ambiguity about whether the prophet's own wishes are being taken into account. Nebuzaradan ostensibly gives him the choice about what is to happen to him but in fact seems to take the decision himself to send him to Gedaliah.

183

40.6   *Jeremiah went to Mizpah*, which was to be the new provincial capital. It is a few miles north of Jerusalem. The prophet remained at Gedaliah's court.

40.7–12   implies that Gedaliah established his control over the country sufficiently well for many of those who had previously fled to rally to him. The *armed bands* were presumably militias which were remnants of the Judaean army. Gedaliah convinces them that there can be security for them under Babylonian rule. He persuades them (40.10) to settle down to harvest what there is to be harvested. At this time of year (since the city fell in July it will by now be late summer) there will be grapes, olives and other fruits to be picked and stored. The earlier harvests, of grain, might or might not have been successfully gathered, given the presence of Babylonian troops. We are given no information on this point. But to bring in what harvest was available was essential, if the community was to avoid starvation in the winter.

40.13–16   Gedaliah is warned of an attempt to be made on his life. Tragically, he does not take the threat seriously. It is said to have been instigated by the *king of the Ammonites*, though the proposed assassin is a man of Judah. The Ammonites inhabited the area we now know as Jordan. The modern Jordanian capital Amman is the biblical Rabbath Ammon.

No motive for the assassination is suggested, and it is indeed difficult to imagine what the motive could have been, unless the Ammonite king was interested in keeping Judah unstable so that he could seize territory. It has been guessed that, whatever policies may have moved the Ammonites, Ishmael himself, the actual assassin, may have been prompted by personal jealousy. As a member of the royal family he may have felt that he had a better right than Gedaliah to head the government. Whatever political motives Ishmael and his Ammonite master may have had, they are not hinted at in the text. As the story is told, it has the characteristics of a mindless terrorist attack.

41.1   *In the seventh month*, i.e. September/October. The reader's natural assumption is that this is the same year, and therefore only a few months later than the fall of the city, but for various reasons some scholars doubt this and suggest that Gedaliah remained as governor for at least a year, and possibly for as long as five years, and conclude that the account of his period in office has been compressed.

41.1   *Ishmael ... a member of the royal house.* We are not told precisely what Ishmael's position was in the royal family, but given that kings were usually polygamous the royal family must normally have been quite extensive.

While they were eating together there ... Ishmael was a guest, who had accepted Gedaliah's hospitality. His act was therefore not only murder, but a violation of the most powerful social rules, and an especially despicable crime.

41.3   Ishmael and his ten men not only murder Gedaliah, but the Babylonian *soldiers stationed there* and the rest of Gedaliah's administration. This does not suggest a very large houshold. The statement that *Ishmael also murdered all the Judaeans who were with Gedaliah in Mizpah* has to be interpreted in the light of verse 10. Ishmael evidently assassinated Gedaliah, the garrison and the governor's immediate entourage, but v.10 implies that the slaughter was less comprehensive than the words of v.3, taken at their face value, suggest.

There is no suggestion that Ishmael was planning to take over Gedaliah's role. After completing his work he simply heads for the safety of Ammonite territory. It looks as if he was merely intent on doing as much damage as possible.

41.4–10   But Ishmael is not finished yet.

41.5   Eighty men from the North arrive, ignorant of what has happened. *They were carrying grain offerings and frankincense to present to the house of the Lord*. This is interesting on a number of counts. First, the temple had apparently been totally destroyed, yet the story implies that worship was still going on at the site. Secondly, these would-be worshippers were Northerners, yet the sanctuary at Jerusalem still has for them, even in its destroyed state, sufficient prestige to induce them to make quite long journeys to worship there. In spite of the fact that Israel and Judah had been politically separate states since the time of Rehoboam, i.e. for nearly three and a half centuries, it still functioned as a national shrine for both. Now it is possible, of course, that the narrator here is making a polemical point. The men, he tells us, came *from Shechem, Shiloh and Samaria*. Shechem and Shiloh were two of the North's most prestigious and ancient sanctuaries. Samaria was, before its fall to the Assyrians, the North's political capital.

Since this was the seventh month we may presume that the men were coming to Jerusalem to celebrate the feast of Tabernacles, which would normally have been a very festive occasion. The ruined state of the temple turns it into an occasion for grief.

41.5   *They had shaved off their beards, torn their clothes, and gashed their bodies.* All of these are signs of mourning. On the gashing of bodies cf. 47.5. Self-mutilation as a mourning rite was widely practised in the ancient near east. It is in fact expressly forbidden in Old Testament law (Deut. 14.1, Lev. 19.28 and 21.5).

Some commentators have seen the visit of the eighty men not merely as a pilgrimage to the temple site but as a recognition of Gedaliah's governorship, but nothing in the text so much as hints at any such motive. The narrator's assumption seems to be that they called at Mizpah because it happened to be on their route.

41.7–8   Ishmael and his ten supporters manage to kill seventy of the pilgrims, though it is implied that he used some subterfuge in order to get the better of them. The ten who survive do so by offering bribes. The murder of the pilgrims appears to be quite gratuitous, though the motive could conceivably have been theft.

41.9   *The cistern … which king Asa had made.* See I Kings 15.16–24.

The rest of the occupants of Mizpah *he rounded up* and set off with them for Ammon. Again one wonders how Ishmael and his ten supporters kept control of what was presumably a body of people considerably larger than his own. On any showing, a sizable group of prisoners must have been something of a liability. Why did he take them? They may have been intended as hostages, or, some have suggested, they were being taken as slaves.

41.10   Only here is it revealed that some of *the king's daughters* were among those not taken into exile but left in Gedaliah's care.

41.11ff   The militias hear about the murders in time, and come to the rescue. *They came up with him by the great pool in Gibeon.* So Ishmael had not, in fact, got very far. This 'great pool' is part of the very large scale water system at Gibeon. It is a huge pit, over eighty feet deep and thirty feet wide, with steps leading down into the water-bearing strata. The nasty events described in II Sam. 2.12–16 took place there.

There is some doubt about the site of Mizpah in that there are two possible identifications for it. If it is to be identified with Nabi Samwil, an impressive hill just north of Jerusalem, then Ishmael had not travelled more than a mile and a half from the scene of his crime. If Mizpah is to be identified with Tell en Nasbeh, just south of Ram'alah, the distance is still only a few miles, but Ishmael would be going the wrong way. Gibeon would not be on his direct route to the Transjordan. Ishmael escapes with eight of his original band intact, but the prisoners are rescued without further harm.

41.17–18   The survivors head immediately for Egypt, fearing that they might in some way be held responsible and anticipating Babylonian reprisals. From the Babylonian point of view, their governor and some of their troops had been murdered, and they would readily interpret such events as a rebellion. Jer. 52.30 mentions a third deportation, a small one, in the year 582. This is by many interpreters seen as an act of reprisal for the murder of Gedaliah and the garrison of Mizpah.

The party break their journey near Bethlehem, barely a day's journey from their starting point, and there consult Jeremiah about whether they are doing the right thing. The implication must be that he was among the prisoners taken by Ishmael.

41.17 ... *at Kimham's holding.* How *Kimham's holding* came to be there is at least partly explained in II Sam. 19.31–40.

Throughout ch.41 Jeremiah has not been mentioned, and some commentators have questioned why we are told the story at all, since the prophet has no part in it. But the story is surely necessary as an explanation of why the survivors of Gedaliah's administration fled to Egypt. Jeremiah is intimately involved in this decision; it is a theologically significant one for the compiler of the book, and it explains why the last phase of the prophet's career was spent in Egypt.

In ch.42 the fugitives consult Jeremiah about what to do. They ask him, first of all, to *intercede with the Lord your God on our behalf,* which earlier in the book he has been forbidden to do (11.14, 14.11). But they also ask him to appeal to the Lord to *tell us which way we are to take and what we ought to do* (v.3). It is evident that the issue is whether to continue with the flight into Egypt or to remain in Judah. In vv.5–6 the people swear to do whatever Jeremiah says, whether it is to their liking or not.

42.7 Jeremiah waits ten days before a word comes to him from the Lord. This is a very significant delay, and a surprisingly long one. The text is not telling us that Jeremiah took a long time to make up his mind. Making up his mind is not what he is about. This feature of the story is showing us that when the prophet speaks he is not giving advice on the basis of how things look to him. The word comes not from himself or from his own opinions, but from beyond. The prophet cannot decide what the word will be, or determine when it will be made known to him. All he can do is wait.

42.8ff. The prophet has been formally consulted: he gives the reply equally formally, summoning the leaders of the community and delivering the Lord's word. The terms in which he delivers it almost presuppose that he expects the word to be rejected. He is certainly credited with strong language in describing the fate which will overtake the community if they insist on going to Egypt. It is possible that this strong language has been elaborated and emphasized as the story has been handed on.

42.14 By contrast, the people's own expectations of life in Egypt are painted in rosy colours. *We shall see no sign of war ... and suffer no lack of food.* In the light of the insecurity of life in Judah since the Babylonian invasion, and the uncertainty of their future, life in a settled country such as Egypt no doubt looked very attractive. They would be encouraged by the knowledge that there were several Jewish communities in Egypt already, some of them long-established, where they might expect some sort of welcome and assistance. Some of these communities could have been established nearly one hundred and fifty years previously by refugees who fled from Northern Israel after the Assyrians' sack of Samaria.

The main purpose of the story is to demonstrate that to the very end the people of Judah learnt nothing. Even after all that has happened, because of their ancestors' and their own continued and repeated rejection of the word, they still reject the word.

The wording of the passage repays close study. *The entire people, high and low* (v.1) approach the prophet and pose their question. Yet this *entire people* is, so to speak, the remnant of a remnant (v.2). They promise to be a faithful remnant. They seem to want to be a faithful remnant (vv.4–6). Yet when it comes to the crunch, they act true to type. They do not recognize the truth when they hear it (43.2). They cannot bring themselves to obey the word of the Lord even though they have committed themselves to doing so.

In other words, they confirm all that Jeremiah has said about his people up to this point: the leopard has not changed his spots; the wild ass on heat has still no option but to obey her lusts. Covenant-breakers they have been since the beginning, and covenant-breakers they remain; and the law is still not written on their hearts.

If they had obeyed, they would have inherited the promise that goes all the way back to 1.10: they would be built up, and not pulled down; planted, and not uprooted (42.10). But they would not. (Cf. Luke. 13.34f and Matt. 23.37–39).

Other details of the wording are also significant. Twice, (in v.2 and again in v.3) the people ask the prophet to pray *to the Lord your God.* Jeremiah's answer, in v.4, pointedly promises: *I shall pray to the Lord your God as you ask.* In v.5 they commit themselves to *act exactly as the*

Lord your God sends you to tell us. Not until v.6 do they take Jeremiah's point and acknowledge that it is *the Lord our God* who requires their obedience.

42.10   *I grieve for the disaster which I have inflicted on you.* The precise meaning of the verb *I grieve* in this context has been much debated by commentators. It can hardly mean that God now thinks that his bringing about of the exile had been a mistake. It is not that he regrets doing it: he regrets having to do it.

42.11   *Do not be afraid ... for I am with you, to save you and deliver you* ... Yet another echo of chapter 1 (cf.1.19). The promises that God at his call made to Jeremiah he here passes on to the remnant of his people.

42.17–18   *All who insist on going to settle in Egypt will die by sword, famine, or pestilence* ... Though this is not a quotation it is strongly reminiscent of the language of Deut. 28.15–68. Those horrifying curses of Deut. 28 could be read as a commentary on this present passage of Jeremiah.

This episode of Jer. 42 also reminds us of Hos. 8.13 and 9.3. This is the ultimate irony. The story of God's dealings with his people began with their deliverance from Egypt. This was where the covenant began. But history has now been put into reverse; not by God's decision, but by theirs. The covenant is unmade. The history of salvation has gone for nothing. The people return to Egypt, and by choice!

43.1–7   Jeremiah's word from the Lord is categorically rejected. The text emphasizes by repetition what is seen as the crux of the story. In v.4 *All the people refused to obey the Lord's command*, and in v.7 they acted *in defiance of the Lord's command*.

43.2   *You are lying.* The Hebrew reads, literally, 'You are speaking *sheqer* ...' Jeremiah has struggled with *sheqer* throughout his career. He has accused others of *sheqer*; worried that *sheqer* might indeed have infected even his own life. It is ironic that he should be accused of speaking *sheqer* here at the end, when events have already done so much to prove that he is a true prophet of the Lord.

The Lord our God has not sent you. Jeremiah used almost identical words in condemning the false prophet Hananiah in 28.15 (cf. 29.9).

43.3   *It is Baruch the son of Neriah who is inciting you.* Elsewhere in the book we might get the impression that Baruch is simply Jeremiah's copyist, but we have a hint here that he may have played a much more potent role. In the perception of his contemporaries, it seems, Baruch is the moving spirit, and they are prepared to contemplate the possibility that Jeremiah is no more than his stooge.

43.6–7   To add injury to insult, the party not only go to Egypt themselves, but insist on taking Jeremiah, and Baruch, with them. Presumably they thought Jeremiah's advice might be useful on some future occasion. All this has happened 'near Bethlehem' (41.17), and from Bethlehem the flight into Egypt begins.

According to 43.8–13 Jeremiah continues prophesying, even in Egypt (as Ezekiel prophesied in Babylon). This is yet another enacted prophecy. The details of what the prophet does are obscure, mainly because we are unsure of the meanings of some crucial words, but the main thrust of the prophecy is not in doubt. The prophet apparently lays some sort of pavement, and predicts that the king of Babylon will set his throne upon it. Even in Egypt the refugees from Judah will not be safe from Babylonian rule.

43.9   *Set them in cement* ... The Hebrew is not easy to understand. REB's solution is only one of several possibilities.

... *at the entrance to Pharaoh's palace in Tahpanhes.* Tahpanhes was not the capital city, simply a town on the Egyptian frontier. It is doubtful whether it possessed any royal residence as grandiose as the word 'palace' suggests. The Hebrew actually says 'Pharaoh's house', which probably means simply an Egyptian government building.

43.10   The phrase *my servant King Nebuchadnezzar* is a striking one (though the Greek Jeremiah does not include it). It occurs also in the Hebrew at 27.6. It recalls the way in which Deutero-Isaiah, at a somewhat later date, speaks of the Persian Cyrus. See. e.g., Isa. 45.1ff, though Deutero-Isaiah seems to reserve the title 'servant' for Israel, and gives Cyrus the more prestigious one of 'my anointed'.

43.12 ... *carrying the gods into captivity.* This was standard practice for a conqueror. Nothing could better demonstrate his victory than to seize and exhibit as trophies the images of his defeated enemies' gods. Isa. 46.1–2 is a reference to the same practice.

He will scour the land ... The meaning of the Hebrew verb here is debatable. The two main possibilities are (1) the one favoured by REB, 'to delouse'. But in what sense can the behaviour of a conqueror be compared to that of a shepherd delousing his clothes? And if the image is of someone delousing his clothes, why does it have to be a shepherd? (2) The meaning may be 'to wrap up or roll up'. In this case the picture would be of the conqueror bundling up the spoils of conquest as a nomadic shepherd bundles up his possessions in his cloak as he breaks camp and moves on.

43.13   *Bethshemesh in Egypt.* There was at least one town called

Bethshemesh in Israel itself, but *Bethshemesh in Egypt* is presumably the Hebrew translation of 'Heliopolis'. 'Heliopolis' means 'Sun city', 'Bethshemesh' 'House of the sun'.

Though Nebuchadnezzar certainly did attack Egypt, he did not conquer it, and it does not appear that the prophecy recorded here was ever fulfilled. There was, however, a more substantial assault on Egypt in 525 BCE by the Persian emperor Cambyses, who did succeed in imposing his rule. Some suggest that the prophecy in 43.8–13, or at least the details in vv.12–13, reflects knowledge of Cambyses' conquest of Egypt, and must therefore have been inserted into the text of the book at some point after 525.

Chapter 44 gives a wordy and turgid impression. It is likely that it was elaborated and added to at later stages in the handing on of the material. But there are clearly discernible threads and themes that tie the chapter together. It is placed here, immediately after the account of the flight of the survivors of Gedaliah's court, because it consists of prophecies ostensibly delivered to the Judaean communities in Egypt. It condemns them for idolatry, warns them that they have learned nothing from the fate of their fellow-countrymen in Palestine, and threatens them that the destruction which overtook the Judaeans in the homeland will catch up with those in Egypt.

The prophecies are directed largely, though not exclusively, at women, and concern types of idolatrous worship in which women were apparently especially prominent.

Those addressed do not meekly accept the prophet's strictures or his arguments. They advance a theological interpretation of recent history which challenges his.

The overall message of the chapter is that there is no future for the Judaean communities in Egypt. They are to be wiped out.

Disasters such as those of 597 and 586 always displace populations and produce refugees, often in quite large numbers. Some of the displaced Judaeans, as we are well aware, were taken under duress to Babylon. But there must have been many others who became refugees, and about whom we are less well informed. Most of these would have fled elsewhere, and Egypt was without doubt the destination of many of them. Now we know that in the years that followed the exile the community in Babylon came to see itself as the true people of God, preserving and carrying on the authentic traditions of the nation, eventually to restore them in the homeland. In the book, Jeremiah, though himself not a member of the community in Babylon, is said to offer encouragement to this view, with his letter to the exiles (ch.29) and with his prophecy about the good and bad figs (ch.24). The Judaean community in Egypt was almost certainly large enough to consider itself a credible alternative for the role of the true people. Chapter 44 enlists the authority of Jeremiah to combat any such pretensions. It tells us that the Egyptian based communities are idolators all, and therefore under the same judgment as befell their compatriots at home. The real message of the chapter lies in what is not said. Its silence on the subject of the other exiles, the ones in Babylon, leaves open at least the hope that for them, having passed through the refining judgment, there is now therefore no condemnation.

We may presume that some genuine prophecy or prophecies of Jeremiah underlie all this, but they are difficult to identify, having been so overlaid and filled out at a later stage by persons for whom the supremacy of the Babylonian exiles was an important issue.

44.1 speaks of *the word that came ... for all the Judaeans living in Egypt*. The phrasing suggests that the numbers were considerable, and the verse lists what are apparently several distinct communities living in different parts of the country. *Migdol* and *Tahpanhes* are both in 'lower Egypt', i.e. the northern area (called 'lower' because it is further down the Nile). *Noph* is the Hebrew name for Memphis, which is further south (about a dozen miles south of Cairo, and *the district of Pathros* means upper (i.e. southern) Egypt in general.

How are we to envisage the prophet actually addressing these several groups? Did he write to them? Visit them all? Or did he simply trust that his prophecies would be passed by word of mouth from one settlement to another? We are not told. Has the composer of the passage actually thought of this problem, or is there some lack of realism on his part? Some commentators have postulated the holding of a great convocation representing all the Jews in Egypt. The text gives no support to this suggestion, and it is in any case not believable. It is not likely that we are here dealing with an account of historical events, but with a literary construction.

The prophecies here attributed to Jeremiah embody the standard deuteronomic interpretation of history. Israel's ancestors sinned repeatedly by worshipping gods other than their own. God sent a long series of prophets to convince them of their error. The people ignored them, so disaster had to happen and the nation was destroyed. According to 44.7–14, though the people to whom the prophet is speaking have escaped the destruction of Jerusalem and the other cities of the homeland, they are behaving no better in Egypt than they did there. God's destruction will therefore pursue them even in Egypt.

Those who reply in 44.15–19 are said to be Judæans *who lived in Pathros*. They argue for a completely different interpretation of Judah's experience. According to them, the facts contradict the picture they are being offered. When they worshipped idols, and especially the queen of heaven, they prospered. It was only when they were persuaded to abandon this worship that things began to go wrong. They are doubtless referring here to Josiah's reform. Since that reform there had first of all been the death of Josiah himself, and after that, endless trouble with the Babylonians, culminating in the double fall of Jerusalem and the two deportations. This is salutary. It shows that arguments from history are rarely watertight, and the data are nearly always capable of being read in different ways. Conclusions that seem compelling to the believer may look quite uncompelling to the unbeliever.

Nothing in this chapter answers, or attempts to answer, the argument in vv.15–19.

Worship of *the queen of heaven* is mentioned earlier in the book at 7.17–18. The title probably refers to the Canaanite goddess Astarte, or conceivably the Babylonian Ishtar.

From v.20 onwards the chapter becomes rather repetitive. It is noteworthy that though the women take the lead in the worship of *the queen of heaven* this is not said with any intention of exonerating the men: they knew what their wives were doing and approved it (v.19).

44.27 *I am on the watch* ... An echo of 1.12.

44.29–30 The Judaeans are offered a 'sign' that the prophet's words are true. This offering of a sign, though we meet it elsewhere in the Old Testament, notably in Isaiah (e.g. 7.10–17), is actually quite uncharacteristic of Jeremiah. The sign in this case is that the pharaoh Hophra will be handed over to his enemies in the same way as King Zedekiah of Judah was handed over. Hophra did in fact lose his life following a military coup. It is possible, indeed likely, that the prophecy here is a 'prophecy after the event' by someone who knew of Hophra's end.

There is no record of the Jewish communities in Egypt suffering disaster on the scale predicted in Jeremiah ch. 44.

Chapter 45 is a curious and personal little chapter. Prophets in the Old Testament most frequently transmit the word of the Lord to the nation. Where they address it to individuals it is most often to individuals in their representative capacity, especially kings. Just occasionally they offer a more directly personal word. When that does happen, it is usually a word of condemnation against someone who has especially angered the prophet. E.g., Amos curses Amaziah (Amos 7.17), and Jeremiah condemns Pashhur (Jer. 20.6) and Hananiah (28.15–17).

But in ch.45 the personal word is one of consolation, though it is a rather minimalist sort of consolation (cf. the oracle on Ebed Melech in 39.15–18).

45.1 ... *when Baruch wrote these words in a scroll ... ... in the fourth year of Jehoiakim.* As the text stands, this is a clear reference back to the events and to the time of ch. 36. It is commonplace to assume that Baruch had a part not only in recording at least some of Jeremiah's oracles, which the text plainly tells us he did, but also that he had a role in the writing down of some of the stories about the prophet, the third person accounts of what he did. Some scholars, indeed, attribute to him a very substantial responsibility for the collection, handing on and organization of the material of the book of Jeremiah. The present author's opinion, for what it is worth, is that the evidence available to us is simply insufficient to allow us to judge accurately how large a hand Baruch may have taken. Chapter 36 is evidence that, at least at one point in the prophet's ministry, Baruch's scribal role was an important one. That is the fairly firm ground: beyond it, all is the bog of uncertainty.

But ch. 45 seems to imply (and there are bits and pieces of evidence elsewhere in the book to support this view) that Baruch was more than a secretary; he was an active supporter of Jeremiah's work. 43.3, as we have seen, suggests that in some people's minds Baruch was the man with the policies and Jeremiah the prophetic voice who supported him and gave those policies religious backing and authority.

45.3 ... *the Lord has added grief to my trials. I have worn myself out with my labours and have had no respite.* Such words would occasion no surprise in the mouth of the prophet himself. They are only a hint, but a powerful hint, that Baruch knew the cost of discipleship, and shared the sufferings of his master. It will be recalled that after the scroll is written, Jeremiah and Baruch are both sent into hiding for fear of the king's reaction (36.19 and 26).

45.5 *You seek great things for yourself* ... suggests that amid all the turbulence of the times Baruch did have ambitions. But it is not the time for ambitions. Simple faithfulness is enough. And the most that can be expected by way of reward is survival.

Why is ch. 45 placed here? Would it not come more logically at the end of ch. 36?

We have just been told, at length, the story of the unfaithful remnant; of the people who escaped exile by the skin of their teeth, and who had not learnt, even by that experience, the lesson of obedience. After failure to listen to the word of the Lord had led to the destruction of their nation and the loss of everything, they still could not bring themselves to listen to the word; to be faithful in the one small thing of not fleeing to Egypt.

And now, by contrast, we are pointed to Baruch, the remnant of a remnant of a remnant; the one faithful witness; the watchman; in Hebrew the *baruch*, 'the blessed one'.

Some commentators suggest that 45.1 did not originally refer back to the events of ch. 36, the writing of the scroll, but was intended as a claim that Baruch was the author of the substance of the entire book. This is often combined with the suggestion that ch. 45 originally ended the book. But against this it should be urged that there is a logic in the present position of the oracle concerning Baruch, and 45.1 makes excellent sense as pointing out that the literary context in which it is placed is not the historical context in which it was uttered.

The language of 45.4, *What I have built, I demolish; what I have planted, I uproot*, is highly characteristic of the book of Jeremiah. We meet it first in the account of the prophet's call, and it is then echoed and re-echoed at various points, appearing as a kind of *Leitmotif* which ties the work together. (See 1.10, 12.14–17, 18.7 and 9, 24.6, 31.28 and 40 and 42.10.) In most places where this language is used it is implied that the destruction precedes and reconstruction follows. The formula is thus an implicitly optimistic one, though at one or two points we are reminded that the eventual outcome still depends on human responses. Only here, in 45.4, is it clearly and ominously stated that, after all, it is the demolishing and uprooting that are the last word.

Commentators and translators are divided about whether the destruction prophesied here is envisaged as a universal one, or as a destruction confined to Judah. The REB's *so it will be with the whole earth* presupposes the former, but the Hebrew word translated 'earth' may just as reasonably be rendered 'land'. In the context it is surely the destruction of Judah that is at issue, and that should dictate our understanding of the text.

Prophecies against Foreign Nations
46–51

The rest of the book, apart from the very last chapter, consists of a collection of oracles against foreign nations. In the Greek Jeremiah these oracles do not appear thus at the end, but in the body of the book, after 25.13a.

The pronouncing of oracles against foreign nations was a regular part of a prophet's job. In the story of Balaam in Num. 22–24 we have an illustration of the sort of context in which a prophet might be called on to exercize himself in this way. The book of Isaiah has a collection of such oracles in chs 13–23, and Ezekiel in chs 25–32. The book of Amos actually opens with such a collection. The book of Nahum consists of little else than a prophecy against Nineveh, and that of Obadiah concentrates on Edom. We may guess that the oracles of Nahum and Obadiah are actually much more typical of the output of the average Israelite prophet than are the words recorded in the major prophetic books.

The oracles against foreign nations are not the most attractive or the most widely read passages of prophetic literature, but they do have some important points to make. They show that Old Testament prophecy has no narrowly domestic focus. It is not concerned simply with Israel. In the account of Jeremiah's call God says to him (1.10): *I give you authority over nations and kingdoms, to uproot and to pull down, to destroy and to demolish, to build and to plant.* The oracles against foreign nations demonstrate that this aspect of his call was taken seriously. (This comment is not meant to imply that everything in this section is necessarily to be ascribed to Jeremiah.)

Christian preachers often think of themselves as standing within the prophetic tradition. If they are truly to stand within that tradition there must be nothing parochial about the scope of their preaching, and nothing exclusively domestic about its focus. If world affairs and world events are God's business, then they are the preacher's business. The preacher needs to read the newspaper as well as the bible. Indeed, it is at the points where these two documents interact that the word of God for today is likely to emerge.

46.1 *This came to the prophet Jeremiah* ... This verse is probably intended as an introduction to the entire section, chs 46–51.

Oracles against the Egyptians
46.2–28

Chapter 46 concerns itself almost exclusively with Egypt. The oracles that compose it have been placed together because they deal with the same topic, viz., Egypt, but they do not come from the same point in time. The first unit consists of vv.2–12.

46.2   is a prose introduction, setting the oracle in the context of Pharaoh Necho's defeat by the Babylonians at Carchemish in 605 BCE. This was the point at which the Babylonian empire was just taking over from the preceding Assyrian one. Egypt intervened to support Assyria and the Assyrians and Egyptians together were heavily defeated by Nebuchadnezzar. This was one of the most decisive battles in world history. After it, the Assyrian empire effectively disappeared, and Egypt was so seriously weakened that she took a very long time to recover. The oracle expresses all this more poetically and picturesquely. In spite of its importance, the battle of Carchemish is not mentioned in Kings or Chronicles, the historical books of the Old Testament.

The oracle proper begins with v.3. But is it an oracle? It does not, strictly speaking, prophesy anything; it simply describes, in a colourful way and in poetic form, a battle in which the Egyptians are defeated. We can, if we choose, take it as a description of a battle still to come (from the point of view of the poet), and therefore read it as a prediction, and perhaps this is what the compiler of the book of Jeremiah expects us to do. But nothing in the text, or in the tenses of the verbs, compels this interpretation. We could read it as a song celebrating a defeat which has already taken place.

46.3   *Shield and buckler.* The general view is that the *magen, shield,* was a relatively small device used by lightly armed troops, whereas the *tsinnah, buckler,* was a larger and weightier object.

The rather staccato directives in 46.3–4 may be actual military commands. The orderly and determined preparations of vv.3–4 are in sharp contrast to the chaos to which we switch abruptly in vv.5–6.

Somewhat surprisingly, in 46.7–8 we are back again with the confident Egyptian advance, the troops surging to carry all before them. But it does not happen. The Egyptians are not defeated by their enemies, who in the poem never even get a mention. They are defeated by the true adversary, *the Lord, the God of hosts*. The phrase *God of hosts* is used appropriately and advisedly here; it is a military title. The 'hosts' in question are the heavenly armies. The image of God as warrior is unfashionable in present day Christianity but it is very prominent in the Old Testament. The Old Testament writers do share with modern Christians the ideal of the 'prince of peace', but in their experience rulers who effectively established peace were generally the ones who won the wars first.

46.9 lists some of the countries from which the Egyptian mercenaries were drawn. Egypt was a rich country and could afford to keep a standing army composed largely of mercenaries. The *Cushites* are people living to the south of Egypt. The term certainly included Ethiopians and probably also Sudanese. The location *Put* is uncertain, but it was evidently in Africa. The word *Lydians* is geographically problematic. Lydia was in Asia Minor, modern Turkey, and it is extremely unlikely that there were Lydians in the Egyptian army. The text must be referring to somewhere closer to the Egyptian homeland, and perhaps the original word has been corrupted by scribes to one they were more familiar with.

In 46.10 the description of slaughter in battle turns into the imagery of bloody sacrifice. In the next verse it switches again. *Go up into Gilead and fetch balm*. (Cf. 8.22 and also Gen. 37.25.) Here we have the Egyptian quest for healing for the wounds of battle. It seems intrusive at this point because in v.12 we are back with the panic-stricken warriors fleeing in defeat.

46.13 puts the next oracle (vv.14–24) likewise into a historical context, the time of a Babylonian invasion of Egypt. But when was this invasion? There is no evidence that Nebuchadnezzar followed up his victory at Carchemish with an Egyptian invasion, so this must relate to a time some years later. We have no firm evidence of a Babylonian attack on Egypt until 568. If this is the correct setting for the oracle and if Jeremiah was still active in 568 he must have been in his seventies. His authorship of the oracle would therefore not be entirely ruled out.

46.14 *Migdol ... Noph ... Tahpanhes*. See the notes on 44.1.

The Hebrew of 46.15 is somewhat problematic. REB, in common with many translators and commentators, substantially follows the

Greek. *Why does Apis flee?* Apis is a name for the bull god. The gods of the ancient near eastern peoples were frequently portrayed in animal form and this was especially characteristic of the religion of Egypt. The bull was originally associated with the god Ptah, but later became increasingly connected with Osiris.

The beginning and end of v.16 are again problematical to understand and to translate. As to the beginning of the verse, REB's solution is probably the best that can be offered. But as to the end ...! The word rendered *oppressor's* is difficult in the context and the available suggestions as to its meaning range from the implausible to the extremely implausible.

46.17   *King Bombast, the man who missed his opportunity.* The word translated *Bombast* is in Hebrew literally 'a big noise'. Over the centuries the Egyptians in ancient times acquired a reputation for talking big and doing little; for promising what they were rarely willing to deliver. Their traditional policy was to destabilize the little western asiatic states, egging them on with offers of support to revolt against the Mesopotamian empires. But when reprisals were threatened by the imperial powers the Egyptian assistance did not usually amount to much.

46.18   ... *mighty as Tabor among the hills, as Carmel by the sea.* Tabor and Carmel are both very spectacular mountains, which is the point of the comparison. Tabor stands out in isolation, dominating the eastern end of the plain of Esdraelon. Carmel juts out as a spur from the central highlands and its extremity forms the Carmel peninsula, looking over the sea.

46.19   *Get ready your baggage for exile.* This threatened exile of the Egyptians never, to our knowledge, took place.

46.20   *Egypt was a lovely heifer.* The passage is full of bovine imagery, which the Egyptians themselves were very fond of. The goddess Hathor is frequently pictured as a cow. The *gadfly* may be thought of not only as tormenting the *lovely heifer* or provoking her to stampede but also as ruining her beautiful and healthy appearance with bites and sores.

... *from the north.* Virtually all Egypt's enemies came from the north. It was the only direction from which she was vulnerable to attack.

46.21   *The mercenaries in her land were like stall-fed calves.* See comments on 46.9. V.21 suggests that Egypt's mercenaries were well paid and well looked after, but when it came to the *time of reckoning* they did not do her much good.

V.22 is grammatically difficult and the exact sense obscure. REB's rendering is only one of several possible understandings of the text. *Egypt is hissing like a fleeing snake.* The snake is often used to represent Egypt. The simile is no doubt prompted by the winding Nile. As REB translates the verse the picture appears to be of a snake protesting as it is driven into the open by foresters destroying its habitat. But it may be that the woodcutters have nothing to do with the simile of the snake, but connect with the quite distinct image of the following verse, where the invading army with its battle axes is being compared to foresters hewing down trees.

46.25   also threatens Egypt, *her gods and her princes* with destruction. *Amon god of Thebes.* The text at this point is obscure, but REB's translation represents the best guess. Thebes was the centre for Amon worship. Each of Egypt's major sanctuary cities had its own particular deity.

46.26   does not appear in the Greek form of the book of Jeremiah and may therefore be a late addition to the text. It ascribes the threat against Egypt specifically to Nebuchadnezzar and may relate to his known campaign against Egypt in 568. If so, then its final words, *Yet after this the land will be peopled as of old* may reflect knowledge of the fact that Nebuchadnezzar established no lasting hold on Egypt.

46.27–28   appear in the Hebrew also in 30.10–11. See comments on these verses at that point. In the Greek Jeremiah they appear only here, and not in ch.30 at all. In the context of ch.46 they contrast God's promise of salvation to Israel with the preceding threats of judgment on Egypt. The language is strongly reminiscent of Deutero-Isaiah.

Oracles against the Philistines
47.1–7

Chapter 47 is a prophecy directed principally against the Philistines. 47.1 relates the content of the chapter specifically to a time *before Pharaoh's attack on Gaza.* The only such attack of which we have firm evidence took place, apparently, in 609. Herodotus, the fifth century Greek historian, tells us that after the defeat and death of Josiah at Megiddo at the hands of Pharaoh Necho in that year the pharaoh conquered 'Kadytis', which is generally taken to mean Gaza. Gaza was one of the major Philistine cities, on the coast.

However, this heading in v.1 is almost entirely missing from the

Greek Jeremiah. The Greek version says nothing at all about Pharaoh or the Egyptians, and it seems likely that the oracle originally envisaged not an attack on the Philistines by Egypt, but one by the Babylonians. 47.2 speaks of *waters rising from the north*. This is not a natural way in which to speak of an attack by Egypt, even though the Egyptian army had made a circuit by way of Megiddo. Isaiah in Isa. 8.7–8 uses the same image when speaking of an assault by the Assyrians. We know that the Babylonians did attack the Philistine cities after their victory at Carchemish in 605, and this is the most likely historical setting for the oracle.

47.4 ... *and Tyre and Sidon destroyed*. Tyre and Sidon were much further north but on the same coastal plain. They were Phoenician cities, not Philistine ones, and their inclusion here, in the middle of an oracle concerning the Philistines, is unexpected.

47.4 ... *the remnant of the isle of Caphtor*. Amos 9.7 informs us that the Philistines came from Caphtor. 'Caphtor' is widely believed to mean 'Crete'. (Another Old Testament name for the Philistines is 'Cherethi'.) They certainly came originally from somewhere in the Aegaean. They tried to settle in the Egyptian delta region but were expelled by the Egyptians after a big battle and eventually settled on the Palestinian coast. All this happened fairly shortly after the Israelites themselves, under Joshua, had settled the land from the east.

47.5 *Gaza is shorn bare, Ashkelon ruined*. Ashkelon was another sizable coastal town. We know that Nebuchadnezzar took it during his 604 campaign following Carchemish.

47.5 There are two main problems with this verse. The first relates to how it should be correctly punctuated. What REB prints as the middle line, *the remnant of the Philistine power*, may be attached to the preceding line (as REB's punctuation presupposes) or to the line that follows. REB's reading leaves line three, *How long will you gash yourselves?* entirely in the air. REB gets out of the difficulty by connecting it to v.6, but this is at the cost of inventing and inserting the words *and cry*, which are simply not there in the Hebrew text.

The second problem concerns the word which REB renders *Philistine power*. Older versions read: 'the remnant of their valley'; which is not very satisfactory. Evidence has recently emerged that the word may mean 'power', and it is this suggestion that REB is following. But a better option still is based on the observation that the Greek translators read a slightly different word, 'Anakim'. The Anakim were the legendary gigantic pre-Israelite inhabitants of the land. The remnant of the Anakim, according to Josh. 11.22, 'survived in Gath, Gaza and Ashdod'. The Greek translators may be correct in seeing a reference to these Anakim here. If both the above suggestions are accepted, the verse should be translated somewhat as follows:

> Gaza is shorn bare, Ashkelon ruined.
> O remnant of the Anakim,
> how long will you gash yourselves?

The gashing is a reference to a widespread and well known mourning rite in the ancient near east.

47.6 REB's punctuation, as we have seen above, puts this verse into the mouths of the Philistines. This is not necessary. It could still be part of the prophet's speech, arguing, as it were, with himself, and expressing his horror at the carnage he feels himself constrained to predict.

Oracles against the Moabites
48.1–47

Chapter 48 is a collection of oracles relating to Moab. It is something of a ragbag of a collection, with little discernible structure. Moab was on the eastern side of the Dead Sea. The ancient stories about Abraham and Lot (Lot being the legendary ancestor of the Moabites) suggest a consciousness that Moab and Israel had common origins, but historically relations between the two had often been strained, and sometimes violent. Gen. 13 speaks of tension even between Abraham and Lot, and the stories in Num. 22–25 record Moabite opposition to the Israelites on their journey to the promised land. II Kings 3 tells of wars between the two nations during the ninth century. But the picture is one of ambivalence rather than constant enmity. We have already heard in Jer. 27.1–11 of an attempted alliance between Israel and Moab, together with some others, apparently with the object of resisting the Babylonians. This was 'at the beginning of the reign of Zedekiah' (27.1) i.e., 594. We hear no more of this alliance and the move may therefore have been abortive, but there was, according to the Jewish historian Josephus, a Babylonian campaign in western Asia in 582, which led to the destruction of Moab and Ammon, so perhaps the alliance had in some form been revived and had provoked Babylonian retribution.

This would be around the time of Gedaliah's murder. Some of the oracular material in ch.48, threatening Moab's defeat and devastation, may relate to these events.

The chapter has many similarities to chs 15–16 of the book of Isaiah, and there are strong echoes of other biblical texts too. It may be that original oracles of Jeremiah have been filled out by incorporating Isaianic and other material. There is certainly a tendency for oracular material to 'migrate' from one prophetic book to another. A famous instance is Isa. 2.2–4 = Micah 4.1–3. But though most commentators are agreed that there are likely to be genuine oracles of Jeremiah here, there is wide disagreement about how to recognize which they are. We have very few criteria by which we can make a secure judgment on this.

We may take the first unit as being 48.1–10. The place names mentioned in vv.1–5 are in some cases known, in others not. Some of the names appear in early lists as being within the territory of the tribe of Reuben. Evidently the Reubenites were eventually squeezed out of the area by Moabite expansion. In so far as they are known, they appear mostly to be in the north of the country, which suggests that that is the direction from which the unnamed attacker comes. The likeliest attacker, if the prophecies belong in Jeremiah's lifetime, is Babylon, but in the prophet's mind that is probably irrelevant. The real enemy of Moab here is the Lord.

48.2 *Heshbon* seems to have had a particularly chequered history. In Num 21 it is said to be the capital city of Sihon, king of the Amorites. In Josh. 13.17 it is allotted at the time of the conquest to the tribe of Reuben, but in Josh. 13.26 to that of Gad. It is several times later described as a Moabite city. The fact that the plotting by Moab's enemies takes place there implies that Heshbon has already fallen into the enemies' hands.

48.2 *In Heshbon they plot … Madhmen will also perish.* The verbs here are word plays on the place names. The word play does not, of course, survive translation. This is a device that prophets were fond of. There is a striking and sustained example of such word plays in Micah 1.10–15.

The Moabite stone, an inscription prepared by King Mesha of Moab, giving an account of his victories over Israel in the ninth century (during the reign of Ahab) bears witness not only to the turbulent nature of the relationship between Moab and Israel, but to the shifting nature of the frontier between the two countries.

48.4 *Their cries are heard as far as Zoar.* Zoar was one of the 'cities of the plain', which included Sodom and Gomorrah (Gen.13.10). In Gen. 19.17–23 Zoar is spared from the destruction that engulfs the rest of the region, and Lot is allowed to take refuge there.

48.5   This verse is closely similar to Isa. 15.5. Precise translation of the verse is problematic, though its general sense is clear enough.

48.6, too, is grammatically difficult and also contains an odd word whose meaning is much disputed. Some have taken it as a place name, others as the name of a tree. NEB opted for 'sand grouse'. REB settles for *one* (who is) *destitute*.

48.7 *Because you trust in your defences and arsenals.* Another awkward verse for the translators. The Greek Jeremiah reads simply, 'Because you trusted in your strongholds', which is likely to be the original reading.

Kemosh will go into exile. Kemosh was the national god of Moab. Mesha's inscription speaks of Kemosh in exactly the same way as the Old Testament speaks of Yahweh. Israel, he says, had been allowed to conquer Moab because 'Kemosh was angry with his land.' Omri (Ahab's father) had taken territory from Moab, 'but Kemosh restored it during my days'. II Kings 3 has a report of a joint campaign by Israel and Judah against King Mesha of Moab in which the invading Israelite and Judaean armies are defeated when the king of Moab offers his son and heir as a human sacrifice on his city wall. The biblical narrator appears to assume that this sacrifice to a heathen deity was efficacious, for 'there came great wrath upon Israel' and the besiegers were obliged to withdraw.

48.9   contains another unknown word; the word which REB takes as *warning signal*, and the range of translations and interpretations the verse has given rise to is extraordinary. But that it prophesies Moab's total ruin, and perhaps exile, is manifest.

48.10   is a curious verse in that it does not seem to fit its context. Some suggest that it was originally a marginal comment by a belligerent scribe or reader, which was later incorporated into the text.

48.11–13   Verse 11 is a poetic oracle, vv.12–13 a prose interpretation and expansion. The verses centre upon a curious little piece of imagery, drawn from wine-making. There is some doubt about the details of the process, but it seems that, after the grapes were pressed, normal practice was to leave the crushed fruit in the vat in contact with the wine for several weeks while fermentation proceeded. After this time the wine was decanted off and the process of maturing continued. Moab, which was away from the trade routes and the main roads used by armies, has never been conquered or exiled by any of the major empires. It is compared to the undisturbed *wine settled upon its lees.* But the time is coming for an end to this complacency. The wine will not just be decanted, but tipped right out and the wine jars smashed. The word translated by REB as *tilt* is a rare one, and it is difficult to be sure of its precise sense, but the present context seems to demand something more violent than 'tilting'. The rest of the verse makes clear that these men are not just tilting the jars but tipping them out.

48.13 ... *as Israel was let down by Bethel, a god in whom they trusted.* The name 'Bethel' normally meets us as a place name, and some interpreters take it in that sense here, but it was also the name of a divinity, and REB is probably correct in regarding it as such in 48.13. The text then reflects knowledge of the fact that Bethel was one of the gods which Israel had once worshipped.

48.14–25 may be taken as the next convenient unit, though this is not to say that it is a tightly coherent piece of text.

48.14–15a looks at first sight like a separate little oracle, or fragment of an oracle. It suggests that the Moabites fancied themselves as warriors, but any such reputation was about to be proved false.

48.15b is best seen as the heading for the following verses. But this half verse does not appear in the Greek Jeremiah at all, and if it were omitted there would be nothing to prevent us seeing vv.14–15a, not as a detached fragment after all, but as logically connected with vv.16ff.

48.16 asserts that the catastrophe coming upon Moab is imminent. In 48.17, though it has not yet happened, her neighbours are called to mourn in anticipation.

... *commander's staff ... splendid baton.* The ceremonial staff, or sceptre, developed from the mace, which in its turn was a sophisticated form of club.

48.18 The national humiliation is focused in that of Dibon, a royal city. *Sit on the parched ground.* REB is making the best of the Hebrew text, which has, literally, 'sit down in thirst'. But this unexpected word is probably a scribe's mistake for a similar-looking one, which would give the sense: 'Sit down in the filth'.

48.19 *Aroer* is several miles from Dibon. Its inhabitants are pictured as picking up news from the Dibon refugees.

48.20 *Proclaim by the Arnon ...* The Arnon forms the natural northern boundary of Moabite territory, though there were apparently periods in history when Moab expanded beyond it.

48.21–24 These verses are in prose, and interrupt the flow of the poetry. 48.25 should probably be regarded as the climax of the poem, though some commentators prefer to see it as the beginning of the next oracle.

Moab's horn is hacked off. In the Old Testament 'horn' is a frequent metaphor for power.

48.26–28   is not an easy little passage to translate, and v.27 is especially obscure. REB represents the best that can be done with it. There is a sense in which all Bible translations are inherently misleading. A translator naturally feels obliged to produce something that makes sense, and for the reader who does not know the text in the original language this masks the fact that very frequently the original text of scripture is obscure, and sometimes incomprehensible.

48.26   *Make Moab drunk* ... See the comments on 25.15ff., and with 48.26 compare 25.27.

48.27   *Was not Israel your butt?* Zephaniah, a contemporary of Jeremiah's, confirms Moabite derision of Israel at this period (Zeph 2.8, 10).

48.28   ... *and find a home among the crags.* The whole upland area of Palestine, and especially the edges of the Jordan valley, is riddled with caves. In times of crisis, and especially when the cities could no longer hold out against an invader, people fled to the wilderness and many made their homes in caves. The remnants of such refugee encampments have been found by archaeologists in several places (Cf. Heb. 11.38). Not only refugees, but bandits and guerrilla fighters made use of the same natural facilities. The Moabites on the east of the Jordan valley evidently did the same as the Israelites of the west.

48.29–39   This unit has much in common with Isa. 15 and 16. How the similarities arise is far from certain. Did Jeremiah pick up ideas from a traditional oracle against Moab? Or did an editor of Jeremiah's oracles fill them out with material he was familiar with from elsewhere? These are just two of the possibilities.

In 48.31 it appears that the Lord himself joins in the mourning for Moab.

48.32   *The despoiler has fallen on your harvest and vintage.* To be attacked at the time of year when the harvest and vintage had not yet been gathered was the worst of scenarios, since it left the population short of supplies for the whole of the coming year

48.33   *Gladness and joy* at the bringing in of the harvest and at the time of vintage are frequently mentioned in the Old Testament. Livelihoods, and indeed life itself, depended on a good yield.

The shouts of those treading the grapes is doubtless a reference to the singing of work songs by the vintagers. All will fall silent. It is Another who will be 'trampling out the vintage'.

48.34–39 lapses into prose. The place names are mostly ones which can with reasonable certainty be identified.

48.34 *Heshbon and Elealeh utter cries of anguish.* The Hebrew here is difficult. REB has taken its cue from the parallel passage in Is 15.4.

48.36 *Therefore I wail for Moab like a reed-pipe.* The reed-pipe was used at funerals and in mourning rites, though it could also be used in celebrations. This verse is closely parallel to Isa. 16.11, but not identical. Jer. 48.36 is in a prose passage, Isa. 16.11 is part of a poem; and, curiously, the *reed-pipe* of the Jeremiah text appears in Isaiah as a harp. Clearly this is not a simple matter of straightforward borrowing.

We have had the neighbours summoned to mourning for Moab; we have had the Lord's participation in the expressions of grief; now in 48.37–38 we turn to Moab's own mourning for her fate, and her inability to cope with her shame. The customs attested in 48.37, the shaving of heads and cutting of beards, the gashing of limbs and the wearing of sackcloth, are all mourning customs mentioned elsewhere, not only in scripture but throughout the ancient near east (cf. e.g., Jer. 41.5).

Commentators have argued about how far this passage, 48.26–39, really is a prophetic oracle and how far it should be classed as a lament. The question is academic: a lament for something which has not yet happened is tantamount to a prediction.

48.40–47 This short poem ends the oracles against Moab.

48.40 *... he swoops down on Moab.* Who is the 'he' in this verse? It is probably Nebuchadnezzar. Nebuchadnezzar is compared to an eagle in Ezek. 17. Perhaps this was a conventional way of representing the Babylonians, rather like the way cartoonists at one time used to represent Russia as a bear.

48.41 The second half of the verse, comparing Moab's warriors to women in labour, is missing from the Greek Jeremiah. The point of the comparison is in any case not entirely clear.

48.43–44 appears in substantially the same form in Isa. 24.17–18a, though in Jer. 48 the words are applied to *dwellers in Moab*, in Isa. 24 to 'all you inhabitants of the earth'. With 48.44 compare Amos 5.19, where similar, though not identical imagery occurs. The situation described has something of the quality of nightmare.

48.45–47 These verses are missing from the Greek Jeremiah.

Instead of vv.45–47 the Greek has the 'vision of the cup of wine', which appears in the Hebrew at 25.15–29. With 48.45–46 compare Num. 21.28–29. It looks as if the editor of the book of Numbers and an editor of the book of Jeremiah both chose to make use of the same poem. If v.45 is correctly understood by REB then the use of this poem is apposite in the context, for it connects with the sense of v.44. The Moabites fleeing from their attackers are envisaged as running for refuge to Heshbon, only to find it already overthrown and in flames.

Flames from within Sihon ... This rendering takes Sihon as a place name. Everywhere else in scripture it is the name of a person.

An oracle against the Ammonites
49.1–6

The territory of the Ammonites was in the Transjordan, to the north of Moab. Like Judah, Ammon had been incorporated into the Babylonian empire, and like her, was rebellious. In Jer. 40.14 we are told that Baalis, king of the Ammonites, was the instigator of Gedaliah's murder. It is conceivable that this oracle against the Ammonites originated at that point in time and anticipates a punitive expedition against the Ammonites by the Babylonians, upset at the assassination of their governor. But many commentators regard the oracle as much later than Jeremiah's time.

Judah's relations with Ammon, like her relations with Moab, had historically been patchy, with frequent spells of hostility. In II Sam. 8 David is said to have conquered Ammon; and in II Sam. 10–11 he is obliged to conquer it again. It is these Ammonite wars that form the backdrop to the story of his adultery with Bathsheba.

49.1 *Why then has Milcom inherited the land of Gad?*
Milcom was the national god of the Ammonites. The tribe of Gad originally had its territory in the Transjordan. After the Assyrian attacks on Israel in the eighth century the Gaddite area was left depopulated and the Ammonites apparently moved in and took it over.

49.2 *Rabbah of the Ammonites.* The Ammonite capital, identified with modern Amman. The modern name is a scarcely altered form of the name the city bore over three thousand years ago. *And its villages will be burnt to ashes.* The Hebrew has, literally, 'and its daughters ...' This is a not uncommon way in the ancient world of referring to a city's dependent villages. The city is conceived as the mother (metro-polis) of the surrounding communities.

49.3 *Wail, Heshbon ...* Heshbon is normally regarded as a Moabite city, as in the previous chapter, so it is unexpected to find it here in an oracle against the Ammonites. The implication may be that at the time when the oracle was composed Heshbon was in Ammonite hands.

Ai is despoiled ... There was an Israelite city of Ai in the southern highlands (See Josh. 8). There was evidently a transjordanian one too, but we know nothing of it. The name 'Ai' means 'ruin'.

Score your bodies with gashes. The Hebrew is very difficult to understand and there is little unanimity about its meaning, but if the REB rendering is correct then cf. 41.5.

For Milcom will go into exile, and with him his priests and attendants. This is closely similar, though not identical, to Amos 1.15, though in Amos 1.15 REB reads 'their king' (malkam), whereas in Jer. 49.3 the same word is vocalized as the proper name 'Milkom'.

49.4 *Why do you glory in your strength?* The Hebrew at this point is extremely problematical. Literally translated the beginning of the verse appears to read: 'What do you glory in valleys? Your valley flows'. The suggestion that the word translated 'valley' has another meaning, 'strength', ameliorates the problem a little, but none of the suggestions for producing sense from the verse is totally convincing.

49.5 The picture here is of utter panic; everyone fleeing in terror, with no thought of where they are running to.

49.6 is lacking from the Greek Jeremiah. It may have been added in order to bring the oracle into line with that against Moab.

Oracles against the Edomites
49.7–22

Edom was one of Judah's nearest neighbours, occupying the rocky and barren territory to the south of Moab and the Dead Sea The ancestor of the Edomites is said to be Esau, and the story of Jacob and Esau epitomizes the love/hate relationship between the two countries, brothers but fierce rivals. When Judah was strong, as in David's time, she conquered and controlled Edom (II Sam. 8.13–14).

At the time of the exile, when Judah had been devastated by the Babylonian conquest, the Edomites took advantage of her weakness to attack her and encroach on her land. The Judaeans never forgave the Edomites for this, and several passages in post-exilic Jewish literature reflect the bitterness they felt. The present passage with its severe threats of destruction on Edom reflects something of the same bitterness. The oracle does not end with any promise of restoration. This animosity against the Edomites helps to explain why, at a much later period, Herod the Great had so much to live down in the eyes of his Jewish subjects, since he was Edomite in origin.

Jer. 49.7–22 has some material in common with the book of Obadiah, and some which occurs elsewhere in the book of Jeremiah itself. It also contains a rather messy mixture of images. So it may be that this passage is something of a pastiche, a patchwork of material put together by an editor. This does not rule out the possibility that some of it may originate with Jeremiah himself.

49.7   *Is wisdom no longer to be found in Teman?* Teman was a region of Edom. There is evidence that Edom was famous for its wisdom. One of Job's friends, Eliphaz, came from Teman.

49.8 ... *people of Dedan.* Dedan was a district on Edom's border.

49.9–10   Cf. Obad. vv.5–6. The sense, as rendered by REB, is that grape-pickers always leave some gleanings, and even thieves do not take everything, but Edom will be so thoroughly despoiled that nothing at all will remain to her. But some commentators argue that the emphasis is not on the fact that gleaners and thieves leave something, but on how little they leave.

49.11   It is not at all clear what the significance of this verse is. It puzzles most of the commentators. It could be read either as a promise or as a threat, though in the context a threat is what we expect. It could naturally be understood as a statement, but REB, by translating it as a question, comes down firmly on the side of threat.

49.12   *Those who are not doomed to drink the cup must drink it nonetheless.* A clear reference to Jer. 25.15–29. It looks like an odd statement. It amounts to saying that those who are not doomed to drink the cup nevertheless are doomed to drink it.

49.14–16   Cf. Obad. vv.1–4. Though the Jeremiah version of these oracles and the Obadiah version are too much alike for the similarities to be accidental, they are by no means identical. This suggests that the people who handed on this prophetic material felt entitled to treat it with a good deal of freedom.

49.16   The word translated by REB as *overbearing arrogance* appears nowhere else in Hebrew literature, so we can only guess at the meaning. REB's suggestion at least fits the context.

49.18   *Overthrown ... like Sodom and Gomorrah.* The site of Sodom and Gomorrah, as described in the stories in Genesis, was in the southern end of the Jordan valley, very close to the region of Edom. This verse 18 is duplicated in Jer. 50.40, in the context of an oracle against Babylon.

49.19–21 also appear in ch.50, in vv. 44–46, and with the name 'Babylon' substituted for 'Edom'.

49.19 *Like a lion coming up from Jordan's dense thickets.* The comparison of God to a beast of prey is one that would not be felt appropriate by most modern preachers. It is a comparison that did not embarass the prophets. Cf. Jer. 5.6 and Hos. 13.7–8. The fact that the prophets can so readily resort to this image, with which most of us would be very uncomfortable, suggests that their understanding of God and our own are in some respects far apart from each other. Is this because our understanding of God is more refined than theirs? Or is theological refinement a device by which we avoid facing the less congenial consequences of divine holiness?

48.21 The grammar of this verse is very difficult to sort out. On REB's understanding the earth cries out when Edom falls over. That this is what the author meant seems improbable. The cry must surely be that of the Edomites.

An oracle against Damascus
49.23–27

Damascus, then as now, is the capital of Syria, to the north-east of Israel. As with the other states on her borders, Israel's relationships with Syria had historically had their ups and downs. The Jacob/Laban stories in Genesis reflect the rivalry between the two, for Laban represents Syria. Jacob and Laban are relatives; they owe each other something; yet they are also rivals, and very mistrustful of each other. In the periods of her strength Israel's kings had ruled Syria. David certainly did so. But in the ninth century (the time of Elijah and Elisha) Syria became stronger and contested sovereignty with Israel.

In the eighth century Assyria attacked and conquered both Northern Israel and Syria. It is unlikely, therefore, that in Jeremiah's day Syria was much of a threat, although II Kings 24.2 does include Syrians among the groups that ravaged Judah during Jehoiakim's time. 49.27 is strongly reminiscent of Amos 1.4 (and cf. Amos 1.14) which may suggest that the whole oracle is in origin an eighth century one. Jer. 49.24b also reflects Isa. 13.8, another eighth-century oracle.

49.23   *Hamath and Arpad*. Damascus, Hamath and Arpad were the three principal cities of the Syrian region. The second half of v.23 is very problematical. The most one can say is that it appears to refer to the discomposure of the Syrians. In v.24 the third line, with its reference to childbirth, is missing from the Greek Jeremiah.

49.26   appears also at 50.30, where it relates to Babylon, not Damascus.

49.27   *Ben-hadad*. The name Ben-hadad was borne by more than one Syrian king. Hadad is the national god, the proper name of the deity otherwise better known by his title 'Ba'al'. His full style is 'Ba'al Hadad', 'the Lord Hadad'.

An oracle against Kedar
49.28–33

Most commentators doubt whether this oracle is by Jeremiah, but there seems to be no strong reason why it should not come from Jeremiah's period. Kedar is mentioned several times in the Old Testament. The name refers to a nomadic people of northern Arabia. Periodically they invaded the settled lands, and seem to have done this during both the seventh and the sixth centuries. The Babylonians had to fight to protect their empire against them. This is what seems to be referred to both in 49.28 and in the second half of v.30.

49.28   *Hazor* cannot be the Hazor in northern Galilee which was so important during the period of the Israelite conquest (Josh. 11). This would make no geographical sense. It presumably refers to an otherwise unknown area to the south-east of Israel. Some have suggested that it is not a place name at all but a word meaning 'tent-villages', but the implication of 49.33 is surely that a city is being referred to.

Which King Nebuchadrezzar of Babylon subdued. The perfect tense (in the Hebrew) may reflect the perspective of an editor, for whom Nebuchadrezzar's attack, prophesied in the body of the oracle, is past history.

49.29   The property said to be despoiled here is characteristic of that possessed by a nomadic people, and in 49.31 they are said to have *no barred gates*.

49.32   *To roam the fringes of the desert*. There is a long standing division of opinion about whether this phrase refers to the fringes of the desert or to a peculiarity of the hair style adopted by the nomads (cf.9.25 and 25.33).

An oracle against Elam
49.34–39

Unlike most of the oracles against foreign nations, whose date and setting we are left to guess, the oracle against Elam is dated *at the beginning of the reign of Zedekiah*, i.e. 597. Whether this dating is correct we have no way of knowing. Elam is a long way from Israel, to the east of Babylonia and in the area which today we know as Iran, and which earlier was called Persia. We know little of Elam's history and are ignorant of any circumstances that might have provoked the oracle. It may be that the author did not know much about Elam either. The oracle mentions no specific facts about Elam; does not name any of its cities, or of its deities, or its ruler. In spite of the information given in v.34 it is widely doubted whether the oracle comes from Jeremiah, or from his time. It is possible that it originated in the Persian period and that it is a disguised oracle against Persia.

49.39   *Yet in the days to come I shall restore the fortunes of Elam.* This reassuring ending brings the oracle into line with those against Egypt (46.26b), Moab (48.47) and Ammon (49.6).

Against Babylon
50.1–51.64

50.1–3 Babylon, which has destroyed Judah, will herself ultimately be destroyed. This did, of course, happen. The heyday of the Babylonian empire was less than seventy years, from Carchemish, when Nebuchadnezzar destroyed the Assyrian empire and broke Egyptian power in 605, to Cyrus the Persian's coronation as emperor of Babylon in 538.

50.2   *Declare among the nations …* It might be supposed that these words are the words of the Lord addressing the prophet, but what is not evident in English, but very plain in Hebrew, is that the imperatives are all plural. The words are not addressed to an individual.

Bel is put to shame, Marduk dismayed. Bel was the title, Marduk the name, of the Babylonian national deity. The defeat of a nation was interpreted as a defeat of its gods by the gods of the conqueror. When Judah was defeated by Babylon it was the prophets' great achievement to convince their people that this did not mean the defeat of their God, but rather his vindication.

This verse (2) is reminiscent of a prophecy of Deutero-Isaiah in Isa. 46.1, which envisages the images of the Babylonian gods, used to being carried reverently in processions, being loaded unceremoniously on the backs of pack animals as they are taken away as booty.

50.3   *A nation has come out of the north against her.* Babylon was eventually overthrown by the Persians, who can hardly be regarded as coming *out of the north*. This suggests that the oracle was composed before the Persian threat to Babylon was apparent.

50. 4–7   The previous three verses were poetry, vv.4–7 are prose. As Babylon falls, God's own people will be restored. These two themes, stated here at the outset, are elaborated throughout chapters 50–51.

50.4   *The people of Israel and the people of Judah will come together.* The re-union of the two halves of the nation, divided as long ago as the end of Solomon's reign, is a recurring dream from the seventh century onward. It became thinkable from the point at which Northern Israel's monarchy disappeared in 722, but the grip of the great powers on Israel/Judah, first of Assyria and then of Babylon, prevented it.

50.5   *Come, let us join ourselves to the Lord in an everlasting covenant.* This is very much an ideal of the Deuteronomic school, that Israel and Judah will be bound in covenant with the Lord. The exile had looked to some like the end of the covenant. The prophet here (as elsewhere) envisages its restoration.

50.6   *My people were lost sheep* ... This image, which represents the people dispersed by exile as a flock scattered and threatened in the wilderness, is a potent one, and one that is taken up powerfully in the New Testament.

50.7   When a country had been defeated in war it was vulnerable to neighbours who might take advantage of its weakness. Judah's neighbours certainly did this after 586. The prophet here tells us that such neighbours excuse themselves by saying that they are only making sure that the nation gets its deserts. There seems to be a deliberate contrast with 2.3. In the old days, when Israel enjoyed God's favour, any who devoured them were held guilty; now their devourers can claim that they are not to blame: they are only doing what Israel's own God has allowed them to do.

50.8–10   Back to the theme of Babylon's destruction, and back to poetry. There is a vindictive delight here in the prospect of Babylon's humiliation.

50.8   It is not entirely clear whether v.8 refers to Israel escaping from Babylon to return home, or whether it refers to the Babylonians themselves, fleeing from their threatened city. The REB translators are probably right that the former is the better interpretation.

50.9   ... *marshalled against her from a northern land.* In relation to Judah, Babylon was the 'foe from the north'. Now she herself is to be the victim of a 'foe from the north'.

50.11–16   The point of the metaphor in v.11 is obscure, but it may be that what the text is saying is that Babylon had made free with the property of the nations which she overran, and enjoyed the spoil her conquests produced, as a heifer employed at threshing is unmuzzled and is allowed to eat its fill. This complacent high living cannot go on.

50.12   *Your mother ... she who bore you.* It is not obvious what, or who, is being referred to here. The best suggestion is that the *mother* is the capital city of the empire, Babylon itself; cf. 49.2.

The second half of the verse is also obscure. ... *bringing up the rear of the nations* is not exactly what the text says, but it may be roughly what the author meant us to understand.

50.13   looks like a recycled version version of 19.8.

50.16   All ancient economies were agrarian economies. If there was no one to sow and no one to reap then communal life was at an end.

It is hard to see any logical connection between the first half of the verse and the second, and hard, in any case, to see what the second half means.

50.17–20   consists of two brief oracles, vv.17–19, in poetry, and v.20, in prose. The first picks up the *scattered flock* theme from 50.6f. The flock of Israel was attacked by lions; first by the Assyrians, who killed the flock, and then by the Babylonians, who scavenged on what the Assyrians left. V.17 may be the original oracle and vv.18–19 a slightly awkward expansion, for if Israel had really been devoured and had his bones gnawed in v.17 he would hardly be in a position to come *back to his own pasture, to graze,* in v.19.

... *to graze on Carmel and Bashan.* These were two of the most fertile grazing areas. Carmel is the ridge that extends from the central high-lands and juts out to the sea at the Carmel peninsula. Its very name means 'garden-land'. Bashan was east of the sea of Galilee, on Syria's southern border. It was famous for its cattle. *Ephraim's hills* are the hills of Northern Israel (the area elsewhere known as Samaria) with their broad, fertile valleys. *Gilead* was a name that covered much of the transjordan. The northern part of this territory is also very fertile.

The prose oracle of 50.20 envisages the restoration of a sinless Israel/Judah, but sinless only because forgiven.

50.21–32   The theme of these verses is again that of vengeance. In v.21 Babylon's enemies are invited to attack her.

Merathaim … Pekod were names of particular regions of Babylonia. The prophet has chosen them because he can make a word play on them in Hebrew. *Merathaim* in Hebrew suggests 'double rebellion', and *Pekod* could be read as 'punishment'.

50.23 … *the hammer of the whole world*. The word for 'hammer' here does not occur very often, but it seems to refer to a big, heavy hammer, the sort that was used for forging.

50.24 … *because you have challenged the Lord*. In what way Babylon had *challenged the Lord* is not made clear. But the idea that God could use foreign nations in order to punish his people Israel, but then at a later stage punish the punishers themselves goes back at least as far as Isaiah. Isa. 10.5–15 suggests that God is entitled to punish Assyria because, although the Assyrians were only tools of God, they did not see themselves as tools of God, and acted in arrogance. A similar thought, not spelled out in detail, may underlie the present passage.

50.25   *The Lord has opened his armoury, and brought out the weapons of his wrath*. The Lord in person has declared war on Babylon.

50.26   is difficult, but the central image seems to be a reference to the piling up of heaps of spoil at the sack of a city.

50.28 … *the vengeance of the Lord our God, the vengeance he takes for his temple*. The loss of the temple was for most Jews the bitterest blow that Babylon had inflicted on Judah. But if this oracle is by Jeremiah it is odd to see the loss of the temple featured so prominently. Jeremiah is not at all positive about the temple and seems to regard its centrality in the affections of his fellow countrymen as regrettable.

I hear the fugitives escaping from the land of Babylon. The assumption seems to be that when Babylon was attacked the Jewish exiles would take advantage of the situation to escape back to their homeland. In fact it did not happen like that. When Babylon was taken over in 538, the conquering Persians gave express permission to the Jews to leave, as the account in the book of Ezra makes clear. Again, this is evidence that if the oracles against Babylon were not produced by Jeremiah, they were nevertheless produced some time before 538.

50.29   *Let your arrows whistle …* REB has indulged in some creative translating here. Something like: 'Summon up archers against Babylon', though pedestrian, would be a more credible rendering.

50.30   is virtually identical with 49.26.

50.33–34   *The Lord of hosts has said this* (v.33), looks like a new introductory formula, beginning a fresh oracle.

50.34   *But they have a powerful advocate.* The word translated 'advocate' here is the Hebrew word *go'el*, which is traditionally translated as 'redeemer'. The 'redeemer' was an important social institution. He was the family 'strong man' who took responsibility for his poorer kinsfolk and whose duty it was to see that they were protected when in trouble and got their rights if they were threatened. It was a prominent part of his function to restore both persons and property to the family to which they properly belonged. The description of God as 'redeemer' is very common in Deutero-Isaiah but unusual in Jeremiah.

There are two possible ways of understanding the second half of v.34. REB sees it as two virtually synonymous lines, both referring to Babylon: *that he may give distress to the land and turmoil to the inhabitants of Babylon.* The verb translated *that he may give distress* is, however, ambiguous. There are two verbs in Hebrew with identical spellings but more or less opposite meanings. One means 'to disturb' (which REB has opted for here), the other 'to give rest'. Translators who take the second option see the two lines as contrasting, and referring to different objects; 'that he may give rest to the earth (i.e. to the world in general) but turmoil to the inhabitants of Babylon.'

50.35–38   is a tightly organized little poem, held together by the repeated word 'sword'. The sword signifies threat.

50.35   *The Chaldaeans* means 'the Babylonians'.

50.36   The word translated as *false prophets* is problematic. Possibly it means something like 'diviners'.

50.37   *Mixed rabble.* Ancient armies ordinarily consisted of a hard core of professional and well-armed soldiers, frequently mounted, and a larger number of occasional troops, conscripted for temporary service.

50.38   *A sword over her waters, and they will dry up.* The word *sword*, *hereb*, recalls *horeb*, 'drought' (which is actually how the Hebrew text vocalizes it at this point).

50.39–40   A prose section, which seems to be a re-using of material found in Isa. 13.19–22 and Jer. 49.18. The words rendered *marmots* and *jackals* may refer to wild animals, as the REB translators believe, or conceivably to demons. Those who interpret the words as designating wild animals do not agree as to which wild animals they refer to. *Desert-owls* is rendered by most translators as 'ostriches'.

50.41–46   This passage offers some good examples of the way in which prophetic oracles could be re-used and re-applied. 50.41–43 have been taken over from 6.22–24; but whereas in ch.6 the oracle threatens the destruction of Judah, here it is applied to Babylon.

50.44–46   In 49.19–21 this oracle is directed against Edom, though in its ch. 49 form it has an extra verse. It is conceivable that the prophet himself could have re-used his own oracles (most preachers recycle their own material quite unashamedly). Alternatively, later handlers and arrangers of the material might be responsible for similar oracles appearing in different places.

51.1–10   Vv.1–2 use the image of winnowing. The idea of the 'wind too strong for winnowing' occurs elsewhere in Jeremiah. See the comments on 4.11. Instead of *destructive wind* some translators prefer 'destructive spirit', which is a legitimate understanding of the word, but the context of winnowing imagery suggests that 'wind' is what is meant.

Leb-kamai is what the Hebrew actually says, but no such place is known, and the literal meaning, 'the heart of my opponents', makes no sense in the context. Most commentators understand it as a cryptogram for 'Chaldaea'.

51.3   is very difficult. At least one commentator writes it off as untranslatable. As REB reads it, it seems to mean either that the land will be so depleted that there will be no one to string a bow or arm himself to defend it, or that defence will be so hopeless that it will not be worthwhile bothering to string bows or strap on armour.

51.5   is also obscure. The first half seems clear enough, that Israel and Judah have not been abandoned by God; but the clause, *their land is full of guilt* does not fit here at all. The word *condemned*, which REB uses; reads rather a lot into a simple preposition. Some scholars understand the phrase *their land*, which is *full of guilt*, as referring to the land of the Chaldaeans, but this hardly solves the difficulties.

51.7–9   Babylon has been used by God as the instrument of his judgment on the nations: now she herself is the object of his judgment. The other nations may as well leave her to it; any attempt to patch her up will only be doomed to failure. *For her doom reaches to heaven* (51.9) gives the reason why Babylon's sickness is not susceptible to medical treatment. It is not an ordinary infection but a divinely inflicted punishment. For the theme of the sickness beyond healing cf. 8.22 and 46.11. The occurrence of this theme, and its connection with the image of the cup of drunkenness in 50.7 (see 25.15–29) an image to which Jeremiah reverts several times, make it very likely that we have here a genuine oracle of Jeremiah.

51.10   All this is seen as God's, and Israel's, victory. *The Lord has made our victory plain to see.* The Hebrew is literally, 'has made our righteousness plain to see.' But in the context this would be very unexpected. There is really no question of Israel being righteous. But the word can in some contexts mean 'vindication', 'victory' and such a reading makes sense here.

We need to keep reminding ourselves that these prophecies of a violent end to Babylon were not fulfilled in the way their author envisages. The Persian takeover of Babylon was a fairly peaceful affair and most of the populace seems to have welcomed the change of government.

51.11–14   once again incites Babylon's enemies to attack her, and promises them success. *The king of the Medes* (v.11) is likely to be a reference to Cyrus, the Persian king who was Babylon's eventual conqueror. Cyrus had a Medean mother and he incorporated the Medes into his empire. If it is a direct reference to Cyrus then the oracle must be dated fairly close to 538, the date of his conquest of Babylon. The oracle implies that Cyrus has already appeared on the horizon and is having some military success, but its author is anticipating a bloody battle, not a peaceful takeover, so he is presumably composing the oracle before the actual events of 538.

51.11   *Vengeance for his temple.* Cf. 50.28.

51.13   *Opulent city, standing beside great waters.* Babylon stood by the Euphrates and was surrounded by canals and moats which helped to make the city more impregnable.

51.14   *I shall fill you with enemies who will swarm like locusts.* The Hebrew is very cryptic and compressed. REB is paraphrasing here in order to bring out what it takes to be the meaning.

51.15–19   is virtually identical with 10.12–16. See the comments at that point. It is difficult to see the relevance of the verses in the context of ch.51.

51.20–24   is a poem addressed to Babylon's enemies. V.20 seems to refer to one particular enemy and it may be that by the time it was composed the author had Cyrus specifically in mind. It is curious, however, that it should begin simply with *You are my battleaxe*, without any indication of who is being addressed. Some commentators attempt to avoid the difficulty by concluding that the verses are addressed to Babylon herself. Babylon is the destroyer. But this is inconsistent with v.24, and moreover it would be odd in the context of a collection of oracles of judgment on Babylon to speak of her destruction of the nations as a series of future events, which is what the text does here. We must conclude that the *battleaxe* is an unnamed enemy.

The word translated by REB as *battleaxe* occurs nowhere else, so its precise meaning is uncertain. It comes from a root meaning 'to shatter'. Some prefer to translate as 'sledgehammer', but REB is probably right in assuming that a weapon is what the author has in mind. Battleaxes were common weapons in the ancient near east. Given the limitations of ancient metallurgy a battleaxe was a much easier weapon to fabricate than an effective sword.

51.25–26   is a prophecy of Babylon's destruction which makes use of some very curious (and rather confused) imagery. *I am against you, a destructive mountain.* Babylon is not a mountainous region; quite the reverse, and to call Babylon 'mountain of the destroyer' or 'mountain of destruction' (possible literal translations) is not, on the face of it, appropriate. And what is meant by predicting that it will become a 'mountain of burning'? One possibility is that the mountain imagery refers not to natural mountains but to the ziggurats which were such a striking feature of the city and so important in its religion and its rituals.

51.25   *And send you tumbling headlong from the rocks* makes no sense if the subject is the mountain, but the implied subject is not the mountain but the city built on it.

51.26   *No stone taken from you will be used as a corner-stone, no stone for a foundation.* Some commentators understand this as referring to stone taken from the mountain. It will not be any use as a quarry, because it will be *burnt-out*, and the limestone therefore made useless for building. All this seems most implausible. It is far easier to suppose, again, that the author has lost sight of his image, the mountain, and is thinking of the city. When a city was rebuilt the obvious way to begin was to take stone from the debris and re-use it for the new foundations. This will not happen, says the prophet, in Babylon's case, presumably because no rebuilding will take place.

51.27–32   is the next unit.

51.27   *Consecrate the nations for war.* War in the ancient near east was regarded as a sacred activity. The regular Hebrew phrase meaning 'to declare war' or 'to prepare for war' is, literally, 'to sanctify war'. Warriors were expected to be in a state of religious purity. See I Sam. 21.1–6.

The kingdoms of Ararat, Minni, and Ashkenaz were probably to the north of Mesopotamia, in the region that is now called Armenia.

Bring up horses like a dark swarm of locusts. For extended comparisons between armies and locust swarms see the book of Joel, and cf. 51.14.

51.28   *The king of the Medes*. See the note on 51.11.

51.29   The image of the earth 'quaking and writhing' when cataclysmic events take place is not uncommon in the Old Testament. In a region where earthquakes are frequent it is doubtless an obvious metaphor to use. See, e.g., Judg. 5.4, Amos 8.8.

51.31   *Runner speeds to meet runner*. On the battlefield, of course, communications are vital, and in the days before the telegraph there was no quicker alternative than runners to take messages from one part of the field to another. The prophecy envisages that runners from every section of the front will converge on battlefield headquarters, all with the same news, that the line is collapsing.

51.33–37   This little unit may not be a unit at all. It does not really hang together.

51.33   a *threshing floor* was a large, flat area of ground where threshing and winnowing could take place. Before the threshing could happen the area had to be cleared and trodden firm to make as good a surface as possible. Even so, says the prophet, is Babylon to be flattened.

Very soon harvest time will come for her. The harvest as an image of judgment is deeply embedded in the biblical tradition.

51.34   comprises words which are presumably from the mouths of the people of Judah.

Like a dragon … The *tannin*, which is the Hebrew word used here, was a legendary sea monster.

51.35   *My blood be on the Chaldeans* is a well-known Hebrew idiom asserting responsibility for an offence. Cf. Lev. 20.9, 20.11–13 and 27. Babylon is to be held responsible for crimes against Judah. The phrase appears in the New Testament in Matt.27.25.

51.36   The Lord himself will stand as Judah's avenger. *I shall dry up her river and make her waters fail*. Babylon's waters were her lifeblood. They provided the fertility of her land, a means of transport and trade, and a system of defence against military attack. To deprive her of her waters was to threaten every aspect of her being. *Dry up her river* is, in the Hebrew, literally 'dry up her sea'. The god of Babylon, Marduk, was thought to be the one who created the world by conquering and ordering the chaotic waters of *yam*, the sea. Now the Babylonians' 'sea' is to be not only subdued, but destroyed.

51.38–43   Another poem of doom on the Babylonians.

51.38   *Together they roar* ... The subject is presumably the Babylonians themselves. Like a lioness and her cubs growling over their prey, so the Babylonians have enjoyed despoiling the lands they have conquered. But no longer.

51.39   An abrupt change of image. There are obscurities in the language of this verse, but what is clear is that we have here again the image of the 'cup of wrath', the drinking of which eventually has fatal consequences (cf. 8.14, 9.15, 13.12–14, 23.9, 15, but especially 25.15–29).

Without v.39, v.40 would contrast well with v.38. The Babylonians make themselves out to be lions: God will treat them like sheep.

51.41   *Sheshak* seems to be an alternative name for Babylon. Like Leb Kamai in 51.1 it may be a cipher. 51.41b is the same as 50.23b.

51.42   Yet another abrupt change of image. *The sea has surged over Babylon*. Another allusion to the Babylonian story of creation. Marduk had defeated the sea, thus making possible all that the Babylonians understood by civilization. Now that creation story is put into reverse. The sea strikes back.

51.43   *Her towns have become waste places, a land parched and barren*. In ancient near eastern thinking, the sea was one manifestation of chaos, the desert was the other.

51.44–46   (The Greek Jeremiah leaves out everything from v.44b to v.49a.)

51.44   *I will punish Bel*. Bel was Marduk's title. The oracle describes in picturesque way the end of the Babylonian empire and the freeing of its vassals.

51.45   ... *come out from her, and let everyone save himself*. The exiled Jews, resident in Babylon, must avoid being involved in the city's destruction.

51.46   *Fear no rumours ... of violence on earth*. When a great empire loses its grip and breaks up, then violence and conflict are actually signs of hope for its subject peoples. Cf. Zech. 1.11, where the report that 'The whole world is quiet and at peace' is bad news. It means that disturbances in the empire (in this case the Persian empire) from which the Jews hoped to profit, have been quelled.

51.47–48   These verses are somewhat reminiscent of Deutero-Isaiah. Though REB prints them as poetry some editors take them as prose. As noted above, the Greek Jeremiah does not include them at all.

51.49–51   V.49 is another cryptic verse. REB represents the best that can be done with it.

51.50   is addressed most likely to Jewish exiles in Babylon who survive the anticipated destruction of the city. They are encouraged to make for their old homeland. If these words were uttered when the Persian conquest was imminent, say in the 540s BCE, we can see why they may have needed encouragement to do so. Most of these exiles would have been born and bred in Babylon.

51.51   offers us a change of perspective to a chronologically earlier point. The surrounding material suggests a context close to the Persian conquest; v.51 would seem to belong most naturally in the immediate aftermath of Jerusalem's destruction.

51.52–57   form the next unit.

51.53   *Were Babylon to reach the skies and make strong her towers in the heights* ... This is doubtless an allusion to the legend of the tower of Babylon/Babel, which in its biblical form appears in Gen. 11.

51.54   is reminiscent of 48.3, which relates not to Babylon but to Moab. In v.55 the invading armies are again compared to an incoming wave; cf. the imagery of 51.42.

51.57   is closely similar to 50.39.

51.58   has its own introduction, which gives it the status of a separate oracle.

The walls of broad Babylon ... her lofty gates ... At about the period of Jerusalem's destruction Nebuchadnezzar had extensively rebuilt and added to Babylon's already resplendent buildings.

The second half of the verse is closely similar to Hab. 2.13. It is not easy to make sense of. Some have seen it as a final comment on the entire collection of oracles against foreign nations.

51.59–63   is a short prose narrative, reporting another piece of enacted prophecy, placed here, no doubt, because it fits the subject matter of the preceding two long chapters. The story raises a number of problems. It describes how King Zedekiah went to Babylon *in the fourth year of his reign*. In the party accompanying him was a man named Seraiah (apparently Baruch's brother). The prophet deputed Seraiah, on arrival in Babylon, to *read ... aloud* the words of a scroll, given him by Jeremiah, containing prophecies against Babylon, and, having read it, to tie a stone to it and throw it into the Euphrates, uttering the words: *So will Babylon sink* ...

Did King Zedekiah really make this long journey, all the way to

Babylon? Some have considered it implausible. It may be unlikely but it is not impossible. Vassal kings who had disgraced themselves in the eyes of their overlords were sometimes summoned in person to the Great King's court to give an account of themselves. All the same, some commentators consider it more probable that Seraiah was sent to Babylon on the king's behalf, and suggest that there is a small error in the text, and that Seraiah went to Babylon not *with King Zedekiah* (v.59) but 'from King Zedekiah'. The omission of one letter from the Hebrew text would have made this difference.

Could a member of an official diplomatic mission to an imperial court really have carried out these instructions of Jeremiah's in a public manner without there being very serious consequences both for himself and for the king he represented? The answer to this question must surely be no. For this reason some suggest that the act was done in private. Crucial to this argument is the meaning of the phrase in v.61 which REB translates: *See that you read all these words aloud.* The Hebrew undeniably speaks of 'reading', but whether the word necessarily implies reading aloud or reading publicly is far from certain. But would a private performance really have satisfied the requirements of an enacted prophecy? Is it not of the essence of such an enactment that it should be publicly witnessed and make a public impact? Conceivably a performance witnessed only by members of the Jewish community could have been organized, but the more closely one considers the story the more one's credulity is strained.

A question also arises about the relation of the present account to the one in Jer. 29.1–3, which speaks of a similar embassy sent on behalf of Zedekiah. It has been suggested that 51.59 and 29.1–3 both relate to the same occasion. Both occur early in the reign of Zedekiah but there really is no evidence to support the view that the same event underlies both accounts. The embassy to Babylon referred to in 29.1–3 was the one to which Jeremiah entrusted his famous letter to the exiles. In that letter he strongly advised the exiles to settle down and make themselves at home in Babylon and to give up any hopes of an early return. The events of 29.1–3 are not precisely dated, but we get the strong impression that they occurred very shortly after the 597 deportations. That being so, can we imagine Jeremiah, as early as Zedekiah's fourth year, making prophecies of Babylon's destruction which could only stimulate exactly the sort of restlessness which his letter of ch.29 was designed to quell? It is true that the letter of ch.29 and the enacted prophecy of ch.51 are not totally irreconcilable. If any of the prophecies against Babylon are genuinely by Jeremiah then we have to conclude that in his view, though in the short, and medium, term Babylonian hegemony had to be accepted, nevertheless in the long term Babylon would fall. In spite of this, we have to conclude that the enacted prophecy of ch.51, carried out at that time, in that place, would have been a very provocative act, both from the point of view of the Babylonians and the exiled community themselves. Doubts about the historicity of the story must remain very strong.

51.59 *Seraiah son of Neriah and grandson of Mahseiah* was presumably Baruch's brother (cf. Jer. 32.12). A seal impression from this period was discovered in the late 1970s inscribed 'Belonging to Seriyahu (son of) Neriyahu'. It seems highly likely that this is the seal of the very man named in this passage. The title he is given here, *the quartermaster*, is not precisely understood. REB's suggestion is as good as any.

51.64 *Thus far are the collected sayings of Jeremiah* looks like an editorial comment. What follows is not sayings of Jeremiah but a piece of narrative, more or less duplicated in II Kings 24.18–25.30.

Appendix: The Fall of Jerusalem
52

52.1–3 offers an evaluation, very much in Deuteronomic style, of the reign of Zedekiah. This is the kind of evaluation we get regularly in the book of Kings at the end of each monarch's reign.

52.4 ... *and erected siege-towers*. Siege-towers were towers on wheels which were pushed up to the city walls, so that attackers climbing up inside the towers could emerge on a level with the battlements.

52.6–7 *While famine raged ... the city capitulated*. In spite of the siege-towers the city was not actually entered by assault; it was evidently brought down by starvation.

52.7 *When King Zedekiah of Judah saw this, he and all his armed escort left the city by night*. Oddly enough, the Hebrew of v.7 does not actually say all this. It does not mention the king, and speaks only of the troops fleeing. This omission is obviously a mistake and REB has supplied the missing information from 39.4.

The gate called Between the Two Walls. REB is almost certainly wrong here (and at 39.4). 'Between the Two Walls' can hardly be the gate's name: it is simply a description of its position.

Towards the Arabah ... i.e. in the direction of the Jordan valley.

52.9 *Riblah* ... North of Damascus.

52.11 ... *he committed him to prison*. This information is not given in the parallel passage in 39.1–10. The Greek Jeremiah says not that he was committed to prison, but to a 'house of milling'. This may be correct, since there is evidence that it was a common punishment for prisoners of war to be put to grinding grain, often after being blinded. This, it will be recalled, was the fate of Samson (Judg. 16.21).

The difference between the Babylonians' treatment of Zedekiah and that inflicted on his predecessor, Jehoiakin, is very striking (cf. 52.31–34). The Babylonians evidently held Zedekiah to blame in a way in which they did not hold Jehoiakin.

52.12 Nebuchadnezzar himself was not present at the fall of the city. He sends a representative, Nebuzaradan, to supervise its destruction, which is done very thoroughly. The temple and royal palace, all the houses of the wealthy, and the city walls, are destroyed. This left the city defenceless.

52.16 *He left behind only the poorest class of people.* Comparison with Jer. 40–43 suggests that this is a rather sweeping assertion. Chapters 40–43 bear witness to a 'court' of responsible people gathered round Gedaliah the governor. It is possible that the author of this statement has a point to make. It came to be accepted by many in the post-exilic period that the people exiled to Babylon were the faithful Israel, who preserved the true faith. One result of this evaluation was the denigration of the Palestinian community. This denigration seems to be reflected in the statement before us.

52.17–23 The looting of the temple. This elaborates a little on the less detailed passage in II Kings 25.13–17. The description presents itself as the fulfilment of Jeremiah's prophecy in 27.19–22, which uses much of the same wording.

The names of the various articles of temple equipment are in some cases imperfectly understood, but comparison with passages such as I Kings 6–7 which describes the building and furnishing of the temple by Solomon provides us with at least some useful indications of their nature and functions.

52.17 *Trolleys.* The word literally means 'stands', but the detailed description of their construction in I Kings 7.27–39 makes it clear that they had wheels. I Kings 7 also tells us that each supported a large container holding water. Notwithstanding the detailed account of their structure we have no corresponding detail about how they were used. The remains of comparable articles of temple equipment have been discovered by archaeologists, most notably in Cyprus. The point of interest about the Cypriot examples is that they were of Phoenician design, as were those of Solomon's temple.

52.18 *Pots.* The word apparently refers to a large, two-handled pot. We have to remember that in any temple not only were sacrifices burnt, but many were eaten. A temple had to have the equipment of a kitchen and of a restaurant.

Shovels were used for taking away ash from the altar.

Snuffers were for trimming the wicks of lamps and candles.

Tossing-bowls were for throwing blood against the sides of the altar.

Saucers The Hebrew word can also mean 'hand'. Here the word evidently refers to a small, shallow receptacle, most likely used for burning incense on.

52.19   The word rendered here as *cups* was some sort of small basin or goblet.

Firepans were for moving live coals to and from the altar.

Lampstands is self-explanatory. There were doubtless many lampstands in the temple, but at least in the later temple of Herod some were said to have been of imposing size. The Hebrew word here is *menorah*. The seven-branched menorah has become a characteristic symbol of judaism.

Flagons. The precise meaning of this word is uncertain, but the form of it suggests that it has something to do with expiatory rites.

52.20   *The two pillars*. Solomon's construction of these pillars is described in I Kings 7.15–22. They stood in front of the temple building. They were free standing and did not support anything.

The *sea* and its supporting *oxen* are described in I Kings 7.23–26. The 'sea' served as a reservoir of water, which would have been needed in considerable quantities for the activities of the temple. II Chron. 4.6 says that the 'sea' was specifically 'for the priests to wash in'. Ancient temples in general, i.e. pagan ones, normally had such reservoirs.

52.28–30   The numbers of the deportees.

52.28 ... *in the seventh year of his reign*. Nebuchadnezzar's seventh year was 598, so if this is a reference to the first deportation, i.e. the one that ended Jehoiakin's reign, it seems to be the wrong year. For this reason it has been suggested that there is an error in the text. But the Babylonian Chronicle dates Nebuchadnezzar's first capture of Jerusalem in his seventh year, agreeing with our present text, against other biblical accounts which place it in 597. The simplest approach is to accept the apparent discrepancy, for which there may be an explanation not available to us.

Those who postulate an error in the text suggest that we read not 'seventh' but 'seventeenth'. This would give us a date of 588. This was the year before the second fall of Jerusalem, which ended the reign of Zedekiah. Those who opt for this reading suggest that some time before Jerusalem itself fell, there was a deportation, otherwise unrecorded, of people from the rest of Judah, which had already come under Babylonian control. This seems a very laborious way out of the difficulty, to postulate an error in the text, which itself then has to be explained by inventing a deportation unknown to history.

In the eighteenth year ... i.e. 587. This clearly refers to what is normally called the second deportation, the one which involved Zedekiah. We already live with the uncertainty as to whether this was 586 or 587.

52.29 *In the eighteenth year* ... i.e. 582 BCE. This deportation may have followed Gedaliah's murder and have been a reprisal for it.

The numbers reported in vv.28–30 are not implausible. It may be that the figures refer to adult males, i.e. to heads of households. This was a common method of enumeration. What was being counted, therefore, was families. The figures reported in II Kings 24.14–16 of those deported in 597 are considerably larger than those mentioned in v.28. There is no point in agonizing over the figures. Figures given in ancient documents (and the Bible is no exception) are notoriously unreliable.

52.31–34 Jehoiachin's release from prison.

52.31 *In the thirty-seventh year of the exile of King Jehoiachin of Judah* ... i.e. in 561 BCE. King *Evil-merodach*: a hebraizing of Amel Marduk.

This change in fortunes of the exiled king marks the end of the book of Kings. It was probably understood by the compiler of Kings as a hopeful sign for the future and therefore a cheerful note on which to end. The significant thing is that he had nothing more cheerful than this to point to, which suggests that the book was completed before there were any realistic signs that the exile might come to an end. The change in Jehoiachin's fortunes, welcome as it doubtless was to the king himself, did not lead to anything further. He was never allowed to go home to Judah, and neither were his compatriots. For that, they had to wait for a change of empire.

FOR FURTHER READING

The two fullest and most detailed commentaries in recent years are:

W.L. Holladay, *Jeremiah 1 & 2* (Hermeneia), Fortress Press 1986/89
William McKane, *Jeremiah 1 & 2* (International Critical Commentary), T.&T. Clark 1985/96

but non-Hebraists may not find either of these easy to use.

Fairly brief, but designed for the non-specialist reader, are:

E.W.Nicholson, *Jeremiah 1–25, & Jeremiah 26–52* (Cambridge Bible Commentary), CUP 1973/75

and

Robert Davidson, *The Daily Study Bible, Jeremiah and Lamentations* (2 vols), Saint Andrew Press 1985

Both of these are excellent.

Somewhat longer is

John Bright, *Jeremiah* (The Anchor Bible), Doubleday 1974

Bright does quote the Hebrew, but in transliteration, and the non-Hebraist should be able to use the book profitably.

More substantial still is:

Walter Brueggemann, *To Pluck Up, To Tear Down, Jeremiah 1–25; To Build, To Plant, Jeremiah 26–52* (International Theological Commentary) Eerdmans and Handsel 1988/91

Brueggemann's is a very thorough commentary and is aimed at being accessible to non-specialists.

The work of Robert P. Carroll on Jeremiah is important. The briefest introduction to his approach is found in:

R.P. Carroll, *Jeremiah* (Old Testament Guides), JSOT Press 1989

This is a short (128 page) introduction to the book of Jeremiah. It followed his ground-breaking:

From Chaos to Covenant, SCM Press 1981, and his commentary *Jeremiah* (Old Testament Library) SCM Press 1986

Carroll's approach to Jeremiah will be found by some readers disturbingly sceptical, but the questions he raises need to be faced by those who seriously wish to understand the book.